que's®
Computer User's Dictionary
Second Edition

Bryan Pfaffenberger, Ph.D.
School of Engineering and Applied Science
University of Virginia

Que® Corporation
Carmel, Indiana

Authorized abridged version published 1992 by Thomas Nelson Publishers, Nashville, Tennessee.

Copyright © 1992, by Que Corporation

Based on *Que Computer User's Dictionary,* 2nd edition © 1991 by Que Corporation.

Library of Congress Cataloging-in-Publication Data

Que's computer user's dictionary.
    p. cm.—(21st century desk reference set)
  ISBN 0-8407-6847-8 (HB—Burgundy)
        0-8407-4231-2 (HB—Navy)
        0-8407-3480-8 (PB)
  1. Computers—Dictionaries. I. Que Corporation.
II. Series.
QA76.15.Q47 1992
004.165'03—dc20   92–12360
                                    CIP

1 2 3 4 5 6 7 8 — 98 97 96 95 94 93 92

Acknowledgments

The language of personal computing is changing as fast as the technology, and that's why Que is publishing a second edition of *Computer User's Dictionary*. In this edition, you find expanded coverage of memory management, Microsoft Windows, desktop publishing, and other exciting, new areas of personal computing hardware and applications.

In keeping with personal computing's close contact with users and Que's dedication to readers, we have responded to the many reader suggestions for new terms to include. I would like to thank all who wrote to us. Very special thanks are due to Thomas Oleszczuk, Ph.D., of the U.S. Merchant Marine Academy, who combed through the entire book, page by page, and wrote a detailed commentary; and Robert de Violini, Editor of the *Channel Islands PC Users' Group* newsletter, who also made many useful suggestions.

I would like to thank Lloyd Short once again for encouraging me to undertake this project—thanks, Lloyd, for your confidence in me. I also thank Charles Steward, the project director, for guidance that was as intelligent as it was good-humored. Special praise is due to Que's world-class editorial team for their usual superb job: Cheryl Robinson, Jo Anna Arnott, Frances Huber, and Laura Wirthlin. This book's technical editor, Brian Underdahl, subjected all that follows to his impressive breadth and depth of knowledge of personal computing.

Que gave me the freedom to attempt a totally new kind of dictionary, a user's dictionary: it's a dictionary written from the personal computer user's viewpoint. Terms are included only if they're relevant to personal computer user—and they're defined with the user's needs in mind. Academic types and lexicographers may find this approach wrong-headed or even to pose a danger to Civilization for having obfuscated nice, tidy academic distinctions, but I am the proper target for their ire, not those who aided me so much as I pursued my goal. If computer users find this dictionary of value in defining the world of computing as they see it, I will be more than satisfied.

Product Director
Charles O. Stewart III

Production Editors
Cheryl S. Robinson
Frances R. Huber

Editors
Jo Anna Arnott
Kelly Dobbs
Laura Wirthlin

Technical Editor
Brian Underdahl

Production Team
Claudia Bell
Scott Boucher
Martin Coleman
Bob LaRoche
Laurie Lee
Julie Pavey
Howard Peirce
Bruce Steed
Johnna VanHoose
Christine Young

Preface

Personal computing technology brings computing tools to ordinary people. Personal computing, however, also brings a new and daunting terminology to daily life.

These terms aren't just the unfamiliar terms of data processing and management information science—the kind of words defined in other computer dictionaries. These terms are the unfamiliar terms of personal computing, such as *page mode interleaved memory, parameter RAM,* and *zero wait states.* Personal computer users are faced with seemingly unanswerable questions every day—Do you want your new '386 to use cache memory or will a disk cache do? Do you prefer an ST506 hard disk over a SCSI-compatible drive?

The language of personal computing is distinct for reasons other than the arrival of complicated new hardware. Today's user also must learn terms derived from new applications of computing technology, such as desktop publishing and presentation graphics.

To use a page layout program effectively, for example, you should understand at least some of the terms of professional typesetting, such as the difference between *points* and *picas.* To use a presentation graphics package, you should understand the difference between the *x-axis* and the *y-axis.* In both cases, understanding these distinctions is all but essential to the productive and intelligent use of these programs.

Terms like these often are not defined in other computer dictionaries, which have two aims. First, other computer dictionaries include any and all computer terms, even if they derive from academic computer science and mainframe computing. Second, these dictionaries exclude terms not intrinsically computer-related, even if some of these terms (such as *pica* or *y-axis*) are germane to computer applications. These aims stem from the academic purpose of such dictionaries; they strive to define the scope of computer science by a comprehensive survey of its distinctive language.

Que's Computer User's Dictionary, Second Edition, is different; the purpose of this book is practical, and the focus is personal computing. Any and all terms relevant to Macintosh and IBM personal computing are included, even if some of these terms are not intrinsically computer-related. Mainframe data processing or academic computer science terms that personal computer users are not likely to encounter are excluded. This dictionary is a *user's* dictionary.

The emphasis on practicality leads to another unique feature of this dictionary: the many tips and cautions. What is the point of learning what ASCII sort order means, unless you are warned that this sort order violates standard publication guidelines and that you may have to move some sorted items if you let the computer sort text for you? This dictionary's aims are practical. The information contained should be of practical value to you, the user.

I hope that this dictionary helps you not only to understand this new language but, even more, to apply the terms you learn more productively and effectively. Every word of this book was written with this intention.

Introduction

From the user's point of view, the language of computing is a language of user appropriation—a language about those aspects of computing technology that the user can obtain, apply, and modify. The social and economic significance of personal computing lies in precisely this fact; ordinary people have appropriated the technology that, just twenty years ago, was the exclusive possession of large organizations and highly trained data processing professionals.

Appropriating a technology, however, brings with it the task of appropriating its language. You don't fly an airplane, for example, without having at least some grasp of terms such as "pitch," "yaw," and "stall."

The language of user computing is, for example, necessarily a language of adapters and expansion buses. If personal computers were closed devices which prevented the user from adding plug-in adapters, the language wouldn't involve terms such as AT bus and Extended Industry Standard Architecture (EISA). But computers are open devices, which is one of the keys to marketing a successful personal computer, as every firm in the industry has discovered.

In the same league technically are such hardware matters as memory and microprocessors. Like it or not, you need to understand the differences between 16-bit and 32-bit computers, between Intel 80286 and 80386 microprocessors, and between the real mode and the protected mode.

With the profusion of systems and system vendors, you must have a working knowledge of available systems to make intelligent choices. Other technical questions include the selection of display adapters, monitors, and printers, and the ports and interfaces by which these peripheral devices are connected. Do you want a digital monitor—or will an analog monitor do, or could it even be better for some purposes? What about keyboards, mice, and other input devices? Unlike the characters on Star Trek, we cannot simply talk to these machines and have them do complex tasks. To make meaningful comparisons among devices, you also must know the language of measurements in computing. For a given device, you apply the yardsticks of hertz (Hz) or megahertz (MHz), of bytes or megabytes (M), of characters per inch (cpi) or dots per inch (dpi).

The day-to-day business of managing the computer brings with it another large body of terms. These terms include the language of disks, disk drives, and secondary storage devices just as another set of terms exists for files and file formats and another for operating systems and utilities. The trend toward user-friendliness is well established. However, one cannot ignore the new language of user interfaces and windowing environments. Marching to a different drummer, Macintosh people have developed their own, unique terminology for many of these matters.

All the technical minutiae aside, the language of user computing is supremely a language of applications. Most users have jobs to do—professional, technical, managerial, and executive jobs. For these users, what matters most is the language of the "Big Three" applications: database management, spreadsheets, and word processing. Most users are using, or planning to use, graphics and desktop publishing applications, which means that they eventually must learn the language of fonts and typography.

The capability of sharing information with others via linked computers also introduces another set of terms. Gone are the days when personal computers were exclusively stand-alone devices, insulated from the rest of the computing world. Today's personal computers are linked via communications to other computers worldwide, and in growing numbers of organizations, local area networks are linking personal computers to each other and even with large corporate mainframes.

The language of user computing isn't simply a language of off-the-shelf devices and ready-to-run software packages. Computers are programmable, and well over half of the subscribers to a popular personal computing magazine revealed that they occasionally or frequently program their machines. The language of programming and of programming languages represents the final stage of user appropriation, in which users truly make the technology their own.

This dictionary surveys the language of computing from the user's point of view. Its principle of inclusion is simple: if the term is relevant to the user, it belongs in the dictionary. If the term is relevant to academic computer science, data processing, scientific computing, or corporate mainframe computing but is not relevant to users, it does not belong in this dictionary. (Other dictionaries cover such terms but do not do a comprehensive job of covering the language of user computing.)

Users have not merely appropriated and modified computer technology but also have appropriated and modified its language. In the language of user computing, more than a few mainframe and data processing terms have taken on a new gloss. For personal computer users, the term operating system means something very different than it does to the technicians who run mainframes. For users, an operating system is a way of maintaining and customizing a system in an orderly way that suits the applications they run. For mainframe people, an operating system is a way of running other people's work through the computer with the optimum allocation of system resources. A dictionary that is not sensitive to the distinctive semantics of user computing wouldn't be of much use to users.

Any attempt to define the language of user computing is akin to trying to change a tire on a moving truck. Hardly a week goes by without the introduction, replete with talk of "revolution," of some new computer system based on a new microprocessor, or a self-described "path-breaking" new program that will turn the entire industry on its ear. No doubt you will find the names of some chips, computers, and programs are missing from this dictionary. This dictionary is necessarily an artifact of its history, and I have not attempted to include most of today's software packages and systems; I have tried to include only the best-sellers or programs that are innovative or important in some way.

The concepts of user computing change more slowly than the changing faces of systems and software packages. One of the most widely hyped "new" applications, hypertext, was envisioned more than twenty years ago. Even if this dictionary doesn't list your favorite new application or the snazziest new microprocessor, you will find that the underlying concepts are surprisingly stable, and this dictionary should prove of lasting value to you.

Using This Dictionary To Learn Computer Concepts

If you are new to personal computing, you can use this dictionary as a way to learn the fundamental concepts of user computing. Disregarding specific brands and products, the following is a quick overview of some of the more important conceptual entries, broken down by subject category:

- **Adapters and buses**—adapter, address bus, bus, expanded memory, expansion slot, Extended Industry Standard Architecture (EISA), Micro Channel Bus, network interface card, open architecture, open bus system, and video adapter

- **Applications**—communications program, database management, database management program, desktop publishing (DTP), draw program, paint program, presentation graphics, spreadsheet program, and word processing program

- **Artificial intelligence and expert systems**—expert system, knowledge base, and knowledge representation

- **Communications**—asynchronous communication, communications program, electronic mail, modem, and terminal emulation

- **Database management**—data field, data independence, data integrity, data manipulation, data record, database, database design, database management, database management program, database management system (DBMS), database structure, relational database management, relational database management program, record-oriented database management program, and table-oriented database management program

- **Desktop publishing**—page description language (PDL), page layout program, and PostScript

- **Disks, disk drives, and secondary storage**—CD-ROM, disk drive, floppy disk, hard disk, optical disk, and secondary storage

- **Display adapters and monitors**—analog monitor, Color Graphics Adapter (CGA), color monitor, digital monitor, Enhanced Graphics Adapter (EGA), Hercules Graphics Adapter, monitor, monochrome display adapter (MDA), monochrome monitor, and Video Graphics Array (VGA)

- **Files and file formats**—binary file, file, file format, file name, graphics file format, and text file

- **Fonts and typography**—bit-mapped font, body type, display type, font, font family, outline font, printer font, screen font, and typeface

- **Graphics**—analytical graphics, animation, bit-mapped graphic, draw program, multimedia, paint program, and presentation graphics program

- **Keyboards, mice, and other input devices**—character, cursor-movement keys, extended character set, input, keyboard, keyboard layout, mouse, and trackball

- **Macintosh**—desktop, Finder, graphical user interface (GUI), icon, and System

- **Measurements**—access time, benchmark, dots per inch (dpi), kilobyte, megabyte, megahertz (MHz), pica, point, response time, and transfer rate

- **Memory**—base memory, bit, byte, cache memory, dynamic random-access memory (DRAM), expanded memory, extended memory, firmware, memory, primary storage, random access, random-access memory (RAM), read-only memory (ROM), secondary storage, sequential access, storage, virtual memory, and word

- **Microprocessors**—8-bit computer, 16-bit computer, 32-bit computer, central processing unit (CPU), chip, digital, digital computer, instruction cycle, instruction set, integrated circuit, microprocessor, numeric coprocessor, protected mode, real mode, and wait state

- **Networks**—baseband, broadband, bus network, connectivity, connectivity platform, contention, distributed processing system, electronic mail (e-mail), file server, local area network (LAN), multiplexing, network architecture, network interface card, network operating system, peer-to-peer network, platform independence, ring network, star network, token-ring network, workgroup, and workstation

- **Operating systems and utilities**—argument, argument separator, background, backup, backup utility, basic input-output system (BIOS), batch file, boot, cold boot, command processor, command-line operating system, context switching, crash, current directory, current drive, delimiter, extension, file name, graphical user interface (GUI), hard disk backup program, interactive processing, load, multitasking, system disk, system file, system prompt, system software, tree structure, warm boot, and wild card

- **Ports and interfaces**—interface, parallel port, port, RS-232, and serial port

- **Printers**—built-in font, cartridge, continuous paper, daisywheel printer, dot-matrix printer, downloadable font, friction feed, imagesetter, laser printer, letter-quality printer, nonimpact printer, page description language (PDL), parallel printer, plotter, PostScript, PostScript laser printer, print engine, printer driver, printer font, resolution, serial printer, thermal printer, toner, and tractor feed

- **Programming**—algorithm, assembly language, branch control structure, case branch, control structure, conventional programming, debugging, DO/WHILE loop, extensible, FOR/NEXT loop, high-level programming language, IF/THEN/ELSE, instruction, interpreter, loop, loop control structure, low-level programming language, machine language, macro, modular programming, nested structure, object code, object-oriented programming language, procedural language, program, sequence control structure, software command language, source code, structured programming, subroutine, and variable

- **Programming languages**—BASIC, C, Pascal, SmallTalk, bundled software, character-based program, command-driven, copy protection, default setting, documentation, freeware, graphics-based program, groupware, integrated program, menu-driven, public domain software, run-time version, shareware, software, and vaporware

- **Spreadsheets**—absolute cell reference, active cell, automatic recalculation, built-in function, cell, cell address, cell pointer, cell protection, constant, edit mode, entry line, forecasting, formula, key variable, label, macro, model, range, range expression, range name, recalculation method, relative cell reference, spreadsheet program, value, what-if analysis, worksheet, and worksheet window

- **Systems and system vendors**—clone, closed bus system, compatibility, desktop computer, hardware, hardware platform, high end, home computer, laptop computer, low end, mainframe, microcomputer, minicomputer, multiuser system, open architecture, open bus system, personal computer, portable computer, and professional workstation

- **User interface and windowing systems**—application program interface, graphical user interface (GUI), mouse, pull-down menu, scroll bar/scroll box, user interface, window, windowing environment

- **Word processing**—attribute, base font, block, block move, boilerplate, document base font, document format, embedded formatting command, emphasis, forced page break, format, hanging indent, hard space, hidden codes, indentation, initial base font, insert mode, justification, leading, mail merge, off-screen formatting, on-screen formatting, Overtype mode, proportional spacing, scroll, selection, soft carriage return, soft page break, style sheet, what-you-see-is-what-you-get (WYSIWYG), word processing, word processing program, and word wrap

286 See *Intel 80286*.

386 See *Intel 80386*.

386 enhanced mode An operating mode of Microsoft Windows that takes full advantage of the technical capabilities of Intel 80386 and later microprocessors (such as multitasking, virtual memory, and protected mode). To use the '386 enhanced mode, your computer must have an 80386 or higher microprocessor and at least 2M of RAM.

The Intel 8088 and 8086 microprocessors, employed in the earliest IBM PCs and compatibles, run DOS programs using a direct memory-addressing scheme called the *Real mode*. In the Real mode, programs have direct access to actual memory locations. This memory access technique is straightforward, but it causes problems when you try to run more than one program at a time. In Real mode, nothing prevents a poorly designed program from invading another program's memory space, resulting in a system crash and lost work. In addition, the 1M RAM limit of these chips, coupled with a DOS design decision that limits the RAM accessible to programs to 640K, has proven insufficient.

The Intel 80386 microprocessor introduced several technical improvements that directly tackled these problems. For compatibility, a '386 can run in Real mode, with the attendant 640K RAM limit and the possibility of memory conflicts. But the 80386 also offers a protected mode. In protected mode, the 80386 can address far more than 1M of memory directly—up to 4 gigabytes, in fact—far more than you can install in any PC. The chip also is capable of simulating more than one 8086 "machine" in this vast, undifferentiated ocean of RAM. These machines, called *virtual machines*, are protected from one another, preventing memory conflicts.

Running a DOS program in the protected mode of a '386 computer requires software to manage the memory. This software stands between the computer and DOS programs, which try to address memory and peripherals directly. Like a traffic policeman, this software—called *memory management* software—channels DOS programs into their own 640K virtual machines, where they execute happily without interfering with other programs. Many memory management programs are available for '386 and '486 computers, but by far the most popular is Microsoft Windows. Windows is much more than a memory management program; it's a complete application program interface for personal computing. But its memory-management capabilities have given DOS a new lease on life.

Windows doesn't automatically use the protected mode in '386 and higher machines. To run in the '386 enhanced mode, the Windows operating mode that switches on the microprocessor's protected mode, your system must have at least 2M of RAM installed; you need more RAM (at least 4M) to take full advantage of multitasking. Because each DOS program is able to run in its own virtual machine, Windows is capable of true multitasking in '386 enhanced mode (as opposed to the pseudo-multitasking characteristic of Windows' standard mode and the Mac's Multifinder, which are capable of loading several programs at once but not of running more than one at a time).

In '386 enhanced mode, Windows also takes advantage of the 80386 microprocessor's virtual memory capabilities. Virtual memory is a way of extending RAM by configuring part of the hard disk as if it were random-access memory. Most DOS applications swap program instructions and data back and forth from disk rather than keeping them in memory. For personal computing, the 80386 has pioneered the implementation of virtual memory at the system level, rather than letting each program worry about virtual memory individually. As far as the memory management software is concerned, there appears to be an unlimited amount of RAM available in which to run programs. However, disks are significantly slower than RAM. If you frequently run more than one program with Windows, you would be wise to increase the amount of extended memory in your computer. See *extended memory, Microsoft Windows, multiple program loading, multitasking, protected mode, random-access memory (RAM)*, and *real mode.*

386SX   See *Intel 80386SX*.

486   See *Intel 80486*.

8086   See *Intel 8086*.

8088   See *Intel 8088*.

68000   See *Motorola 68000*.

68020   See *Motorola 68020*.

68030   See *Motorola 68030*.

3½-inch disk   A floppy disk originally developed by Sony Corporation and used as a secondary storage medium for personal computers. The magnetic disk is enclosed in a hard plastic case.

Introduced to personal computing by the Apple Macintosh computer and later used in IBMs Personal System/2 machines, 3½-inch disks represent a significant improvement over 5¼-inch floppies, which are susceptible to fingerprint damage because of the open access hole. 3½-inch disks, unlike their larger predecessors, cover the access holes with an aluminum gate, which is opened by the disk drive only after the disk is inserted. 3½-inch disks also are easier to write-protect; instead of covering up a notch hole with a piece of tape, you move a little plastic lever on the back of the disk.

Under DOS, 3½-inch disk drives offer storage capacities of 720K (double density) or 1.44M (high density). DOS Version 3.2 began supporting the 720K disks, and DOS Version 3.3 began supporting the 1.44M disks. Macintosh computers format 3½ disks with a storage capacity of 800K (double density) or 1.4M (high density).

5¼-inch disk   A floppy disk enclosed in a flexible plastic envelope and used as a secondary storage medium for personal computers. Synonymous with *minifloppy*.

The most widely used secondary storage technology medium in personal computing, 5¼-inch disks are inexpensive and used as a distribution medium for commercial software.

8-bit computer A computer that uses a central processing unit (CPU) with an 8-bit data bus and processes one byte (eight bits) of information at a time.

8-bit computers represent the minimal configuration of computing equipment; in binary numbers, eight bits represent all letters of the alphabet and the numbers 0 through 9. The first microprocessors used in personal computers, such as the MOS Technology 6502, Intel 8080, and Zilog Z-80, found their way into 8-bit computers such as the Apple II, the MSAI 8080, and the Commodore 64.

Millions of these computers are still in use for educational and home-computing applications, but the best business and professional software is available for 16-bit and 32-bit personal computers such as the IBM Personal Computer and the Apple Macintosh. See *central processing unit (CPU)* and *microprocessor*.

8-bit video adapter A color video adapter that can display 256 colors simultaneously. See *video adapter*.

16-bit computer A computer that uses a central processing unit (CPU) with a 16-bit data bus and processes two bytes (16 bits) of information at a time.

24-bit video adapter A Macintosh color video adapter that can display more than 16 million colors simultaneously (216–16,777,216). With a 24-bit video card and monitor, a personal computer can display beautiful, photographic-quality images on-screen. A 24-bit video card and full-color monitor, however, can add as much as $7,000 to the cost of a Macintosh system.

32-bit computer A computer that uses a central processing unit (CPU) with a 32-bit data bus and processes four bytes (32 bits) of information at a time.

3-D spreadsheet program See *three-dimensional spreadsheet*.

4th Dimension   A relational database program developed by Acius, Inc., for Macintosh computers.

A sophisticated product with networking capabilities, 4th Dimension is of special interest to organizations with large mainframe databases. A special version of Oracle, a connectivity platform, enables 4th Dimension to search Oracle, DB2, and SQL databases. See *connectivity platform*.

a

abandon   To clear a document, spreadsheet, or other work from the computer's memory without saving it to disk. The work is irretrievably lost.

abort   To cancel, or terminate, a program, command, or procedure while it is in progress.

Abs key   In Lotus 1-2-3, the F4 function key that cycles a cell reference through the four possible combinations: absolute cell reference (A1), mixed cell references ($A1 and A$1), and relative cell reference (A1).

absolute cell reference   A spreadsheet cell reference that does not adjust when you copy a formula. Use an absolute cell reference to keep the reference the same when being copied.

For example, the following Lotus 1-2-3 formula contains a relative cell reference (B12) and an absolute cell reference (A6). The formula tells 1-2-3 to multiply B12 by the contents of cell A6 and place the result in the current cell:

+B12*A6

When you copy this formula to the next row down and the next column to the right, 1-2-3 changes the formula to +C13*A6.

The relative cell reference is adjusted, but the absolute cell reference stays the same.

→ **Tip:** Use absolute cell references to establish a single cell location for key variables for your worksheet. A key variable is a constant, such as a tax rate. See *key variable, low-level format,* and *relative cell reference*.

absolute value   The magnitude of a number, regardless of its algebraic sign (positive or negative), equal to the positive value of a number. The absolute value of -357, for example, is 357. In Lotus 1-2-3 and similar spreadsheet programs, the @ABS built-in function returns the absolute value of a number.

accelerator board   An adapter containing a microprocessor faster or more advanced than the one that powers your computer. If you have a Macintosh based on the Motorola 68000 chip, for example, you can purchase an accelerator board containing the faster 68030 chip. If you have an IBM PC-compatible computer based on the Intel 8088 microprocessor, you can purchase an accelerator board containing the faster 80286 or 80386 microprocessor.

accent   A mark that forms one of the accented characters of many languages other than English. The following accents are used frequently:

´	Acute	˘	Breve	ç	Cedilla
^	Circumflex	¨	Diaeresis	`	Grave
‾	Macron	~	Tilde	¨	Umlaut

You enter accents in two ways. First, you can use a dead key that enters the accent character without advancing the cursor to the next character. You then press the letter, and the two keystrokes form the accented character. Second, you can use a key code to enter the character and the accent at the same time. On a Macintosh computer, you can use both techniques. To enter the vowel *e* with an acute accent, you press Option-e (a dead key that enters an acute accent character) and then press e, and the accented character (é) appears.

▲ **Caution:** If you plan to work in foreign languages on an IBM PC-compatible computer, make sure that your printer can print the entire 254 extended character set that includes many accented characters. Not all printers can print the extended characters.

access   To retrieve data or program instructions from a secondary storage device or some other on-line computer device.

To the dismay of English teachers everywhere, the noun access is now used as a verb, as in "I cannot access that file." English usage authorities usually disparage the conversion of nouns into verbs, but this usage is sufficiently common to be included in a dictionary such as this one.

access arm   In a disk drive, the mechanical device that moves the magnetic read/write heads back and forth across the surface of the disk.

Without an access arm, the disk drive would act like a record player's arm as it moves sequentially along the grooves of an LP record and would take a long time to reach information stored away from the head's current location. See *random access* and *sequential access*.

access code   An identification number or password used to gain access to a computer system.

access hole   An opening in a floppy disk's case. The access hole enables the disk drive's read/write head to make contact with the surface of the disk. Only when this contact occurs can you perform read/write operations, in which the computer retrieves information from or stores new information on the disk.

access mechanism   In a disk drive, the mechanism used for moving the read/write head over the surface of the disk so that data can be accessed. Synonymous with *actuator*. See *disk drive* and *read/write head*.

Access System menu   In Lotus 1-2-3, the menu that appears when you type **lotus** at the DOS prompt. This menu enables you to start Lotus 1-2-3, install the program, or choose the Translate option.

→ **Tip:** You can bypass the Access System menu by typing **123** at the DOS prompt.

access time   The time that elapses between the time the operating system issues an order for data retrieval and the time the data is ready for transfer from the disk.

Typical access times for personal computer hard disks range between 9 ms (fast) and 100 ms (slow). For disk-intensive applications like database management programs or book-length word processing projects, the difference between a fast and a slow disk drive is noticeable to the user. The access time of a disk drive is determined by the following: seek time (the time the disk heads take to move to the correct track), settle time (the time the heads take to settle down after reaching the correct track), and latency (the time required for the correct sector to swing around under the head).

For hard disks, access times usually are measured in microseconds (ms).

accumulator   A temporary storage location in a central processing unit (CPU). The accumulator holds intermediary values during a computation or stores input/output information.

Many processing operations require an accumulator. Computer multiplication, for example, frequently is done by a series of additions; the accumulator holds the intermediate values until the process is completed. See *central processing unit (CPU)*.

acoustical sound enclosure   A sound insulation cabinet designed to accommodate noisy impact printers and reduce the noise such printers release into the environment. See *impact printer*.

acronym   A word formed by joining the first letters (sometimes other letters) of a series of words such as BASIC (Beginners' All-purpose Symbolic Instruction Code) and WYSIWYG (what-you-see-is-what-you-get).

active area   In a Lotus 1-2-3 worksheet, the area bounded by cell A1 and the lowest rightmost cell containing data.

active cell   In a spreadsheet, the cell in which the cursor currently is positioned. Synonymous with *current cell*.

active database   In database management, the database file that currently is in use and present in random-access memory (RAM).

active file   The worksheet currently in memory when working with Lotus 1-2-3 and other spreadsheet programs.

   ▲ **Caution:** Versions of Lotus 1-2-3 before Release 2.2 do not warn you when you leave the active file without saving your work. Lotus 1-2-3 does not update the disk file until you issue the /File Save command. If you quit 1-2-3 without saving your work, the file on disk remains unchanged.

   In some cases, leaving the file unchanged is desirable. For example, many users like to perform what-if analyses, which involves entering hypothetical values as the key variables of the worksheet. You don't want to save these changes because the data is imaginary. Early versions of Lotus and other spreadsheet programs left the decision of whether to save a session's changes to the user. Most users, however, want to be reminded when they are about to lose changes. Versions of Lotus since Release 2.2, therefore, detect changes and warn the user if they are about to be lost at the end of a session. See *what-if analysis*.

active index   In database management programs, the index file currently being used to determine the order in which data records are displayed on-screen. See *index*.

active window   In an application program or operating system that displays multiple windows, the window in which the cursor is positioned and text appears when you type.

Early windowing environments tiled the windows so that none overlapped, but too often the windows were too small for convenient use. In more recent windowing applications, the active window floats above the others. See *windowing environment*.

activity light A small red or yellow light on the computer's front panel that signals when a disk drive is reading or writing data.

actuator See *access mechanism*.

adapter A circuit board that plugs into a computer's expansion bus and gives the computer additional capabilities.

Popular adapters for personal computers include display adapters that produce video output; memory expansion adapters; input-output adapters that provide the computer with serial ports, parallel ports, and game ports; internal modems, and clock/calendar boards. Increasingly, this circuitry is being included on the motherboard of personal computer systems. The motherboard of IBM's PS/2 computer, for example, includes ports and a VGA display adapter for high-resolution video output. See *circuit board, clock/ calendar board, expansion bus, internal modem, motherboard, open bus system, parallel port,* and *serial port*.

adapter segment See *upper memory area*.

ADB See *Apple Desktop Bus (ADB)*.

add-in program An accessory or utility program designed to work with and extend the capabilities of an application program.

A popular add-in program for Lotus 1-2-3 is Allways (Funk Software) which adds desktop publishing features to 1-2-3's report capabilities. Allways prints Lotus spreadsheets with a variety of fonts, lines, shadings, and other formatting features, such as boldface and underline.

address A computer system location identified by a name, number, or code label. The address can be specified by the user or by a program. See *memory address*.

address bus   An internal electronic channel from the microprocessor to random-access memory (RAM), along which the addresses of memory storage locations are transmitted.

The address bus is necessary so that the microprocessor can locate program instructions and data stored in memory. Like a post office box, each memory location has a distinct number or address; the address bus provides the means by which every location in the memory can be activated independently.

Advanced Run-Length Limited (ARLL)   A method of storing and retrieving information on a hard disk that increases the density of Run-Length Limited (RLL) storage by more than 25 percent and offers a faster data-transfer rate (9 megabits per second). See *data-encoding scheme* and *Run-Length Limited (RLL)*.

aggregate function   In database management programs, a command that performs arithmetic operations on all of a field's values in all the records within a database or in one view of the database. dBASE, for example, performs the following aggregate functions:

Function	*Description*
Average	Computes the arithmetic mean of the values
Sum	Adds all the values
Minimum	Finds the smallest value
Maximum	Finds the largest value
Count	Counts the number of records that meet the specified criteria

aggregate operator   In a database management program, a command that instructs the program to perform an aggregate function.

Suppose that you are the owner of a video tape rental store and you want to know how many tapes are more than two weeks late. Because the date is May 19, you want to know how many rentals were due on May 5 or earlier (less than 05/06/90). The following dBASE expression finds the information:

```
COUNT FOR due_date < 05/06/90
```

You will see a response such as

2 records

See *aggregate function*.

AI See *artificial intelligence (AI)*.

AIX An IBM version of the UNIX operating system. AIX runs on PS/2 computers equipped with the Intel 80386 microprocessor, IBM workstations, minicomputers, and mainframes.

alert box In a graphical user interface, a cautionary window that appears on-screen warning you that the command you have given may result in lost work or other errors.

algorithm A specific set of well-defined, simple mathematical and logical procedures that can be followed to solve a problem in a finite number of steps.

An algorithm is a recipe for finding the right answer to a difficult problem by breaking the problem down into simple, easy steps. You already have learned many algorithms—for example, the ones you learned for grade-school arithmetic. You use algorithms every day in recipes, when mowing the lawn, placing a long-distance telephone call, and packing a grocery bag.

Not every list of instructions constitutes an algorithm, however. An algorithm must satisfy the following three basic criteria:

- The list of instructions must be finite and short enough that they can be carried out.
- Each instruction must be executable; you must be able to perform the actions or operations named.
- The algorithm must enable execution to end at some point.

alias A secondary or symbolic name for a file or computer device. In a spreadsheet, for example, a range name, such as *Income,* is an alias for a range, such as A3..K3.

aliasing In computer graphics, the undesirable jagged or stair-stepped appearance of diagonal lines in computer-generated graphic images. Synonymous with the *jaggies*. See *antialiasing*.

alignment 1. The adjustment of tolerances within a disk drive's mechanism so that read/write operations occur without error. 2. In word processing, the horizontal arrangement of lines on the page with respect to the left and right margins (flush left, centered, flush right, or justified).

all points addressable (APA) graphics See *bit-mapped graphic*.

alpha test The first stage in the testing of computer software before commercial release. Alpha tests usually are conducted within a company. See *beta test*.

alphanumeric characters Any character you can type, including upper- and lowercase letters A through Z, numbers 0 through 9, punctuation marks, and special keyboard symbols. See *data type*.

Alt key On IBM PC-compatible keyboards, a key that programs frequently use in combination with other keys to generate commands. In Microsoft Word, for example, pressing Alt-B boldfaces the selected text.

ALU See *arithmetic logic unit (ALU)*.

American National Standards Institute (ANSI) An organization devoted to the development of voluntary standards that will enhance the productivity and international competitiveness of American industrial enterprises. ANSI committees have developed standard versions of computer languages such as COBOL and FORTRAN.

American Standard Code for Information Interchange (ASCII) Pronounced "ask'-ee." A standard computer character set devised in 1968 to enable efficient data communication and achieve compatibility among different computer devices.

The standard ASCII code consists of 96 displayed upper- and

lowercase letters, plus 32 non-displayed control characters. An individual character code is composed of seven bits plus one parity bit for error checking. The code enables the expression of English-language textual data but is inadequate for many foreign languages and technical applications. Because ASCII code includes no graphics characters, most modern computers use an extended character set containing needed characters. See *extended character set*.

Amiga   Pronounced "uh-mee'-ga." A personal computer developed by Commodore International and based on the Motorola 68000 microprocessor. The Amiga is used for home computing applications.

With outstanding color graphics and multichannel stereo sound, the Amiga is considered by some to be the computer of choice for playing computer games and composing music. The machine has found little acceptance as a business computer, however, because of the lack of business software for the machine.

The Amiga is not compatible with the Macintosh computer, which uses the same microprocessor but a different operating system. See *Musical Instrument Digital Interface (MIDI)*.

ampersand   A character (&) sometimes used in place of the English *and;* originally a ligature of *et,* the Latin for *and*.

analog   A form of measurement or representation in which an indicator is varied continuously, often to reflect ongoing changes in the phenomenon being measured or represented.

Analog representation is used, for example, in a thermometer: the hotter the patient, the longer the mercury. Analog techniques also are used for the reproduction of music in standard LP records and audio cassettes. See *digital*.

analog computer   A computer that draws a comparison, or analogy, between the computer representation and the object being represented, making the object easy to measure. Analog computation is used widely in laboratory settings to monitor on-going, continuous changes and to record these changes in charts or graphs. See *digital computer*.

analog device   A computer peripheral that handles information in
continuously variable quantities rather than digitizing the information into discrete, digital representations. An analog monitor, for
example, can display thousands of colors with smooth, continuous
gradations.

analog/digital converter   An adapter that enables a digital computer
(such as an IBM Personal Computer) to accept analog input from
laboratory instruments. Analog/digital converters are frequently
used for the real-time monitoring of temperature, movement, and
other continuously varied conditions. See *analog, digital,* and *real
time.*

analog monitor   A monitor that accepts a continuously varied video
input signal and consequently is capable of displaying continuously
varied colors. See *digital monitor* and *Video Graphics Array (VGA).*

analog transmission   A communications scheme that uses a continuous signal varied by amplification. See *broadband* and *digital
transmission.*

analytical graphics   The preparation of charts and graphs to aid a
professional in the interpretation of data.
     Many spreadsheet programs' graphs fall into this category: they
are useful for clarifying trends in worksheet numbers, but you don't
want to show them to the company's stockholders. Presentation
graphics packages can accept and enhance graphs created by
spreadsheet programs. See *presentation graphics.*

anchor cell   In Lotus 1-2-3, the cell in which the pointer is anchored
as you press the cursor-movement keys to define a range.

anchored graphic   A graph or picture that is fixed in an absolute position on the page so that text flows around it. See *floating graphic.*

animation   The creation of the illusion of movement in a computer
program by recording a series of images that show slight incremental changes in one of the displayed objects and playing these images

back fast enough that the eye perceives smooth movement. See *cell animation* and *MacroMind Director*.

annotation   Synonymous with *remark*.

ANSI   See *American National Standards Institute (ANSI)*.

ANSI screen control   A set of standards developed by the American National Standards Institute (ANSI) to control the display of information on computer screens. See *ANSI.SYS*.

ANSI.SYS   In DOS and OS/2, a configuration file containing instructions needed to display information, following the recommendations of the American National Standards Institute.

→ **Tip:** Some programs require that you include the instruction DEVICE = ANSI.SYS in a CONFIG.SYS file, which must be present on the disk you use to start your computer. See *CONFIG.SYS*.

answer mode   See *auto-dial/auto-answer modem*.

answer/originate   In data communications, the property of a communications device such that the device can receive (answer) and send (originate) messages.

antialiasing   The automatic removal or reduction of stair-step distortions in a computer-generated graphic image. See *aliasing*.

antistatic mat   A mat or pad placed on or near a computer device. This pad absorbs static electricity, which can damage semiconductor devices if the devices are not properly grounded.

antivirus program   See *vaccine*.

APA graphics   See *bit-mapped graphic*.

API   See *application program interface (API)*.

append   To add data at the end of a file or a database. In database management, for example, to append a record is to add a new record, which is placed after all existing records (preserving the chronological order of data entry).

Apple Desktop Bus (ADB) An interface standard for connecting keyboards, mice, trackballs, and other input devices to Apple's Macintosh SE, Macintosh II, and IIGS computers. These computers come with an ADB port capable of a maximum data transfer rate of 4.5 kilobits per second. Up to 16 devices can be connected to one ADB port.

Apple Desktop Interface A set of user interface guidelines developed by Apple Computer (published by Addison-Wesley) and intended to ensure that all Macintosh applications appear and work in similar ways.

Apple File Exchange A utility program provided with each Macintosh computer that enables Macs equipped with suitable disk drives to exchange data with IBM PC-compatible computers.

Apple Macintosh See *Macintosh*.

AppleShare A network operating system developed by Apple Computer, Inc. AppleShare transforms a Macintosh computer into a file server for an AppleTalk network. The Macintosh used as the server cannot be used for other applications; that computer becomes a "slave" of the network.

After AppleShare is installed, users see a virtual device—an additional hard disk icon on the desktop—which they can access just as if the drive were present in their systems. See *AppleTalk, local area network (LAN), LocalTalk*, and *virtual device*.

AppleTalk A local area network standard developed by Apple Computer, Inc. AppleTalk is capable of linking as many as 32 Macintosh computers, IBM PC-compatible computers, and peripherals like laser printers. Every Macintosh computer has an AppleTalk port, through which the machine can be connected to an AppleTalk network using a bus topology. Most AppleTalk networks are simple;

they link a few Macintosh computers with a LaserWriter printer.

A significant advantage of AppleTalk is that the network also can accommodate IBM PC-compatible computers; several companies manufacture adapters that provide AppleTalk ports for IBM PC-compatible computers. Microsoft Mail, an application developed by Microsoft Corporation, enables electronic mail to be sent among all users of an AppleTalk network, including users of IBM PC compatibles.

Another advantage of AppleTalk is that almost anyone can quickly set up an AppleTalk network. In many offices, AppleTalk networks are used for sharing access to a laser printer.

AppleTalk also is priced right. Because every Macintosh includes an AppleTalk network port, the only hardware required for an AppleTalk network is connectors and cable. The physical connections among the computers and peripherals are made by Apple's LocalTalk hardware. Each device has a LocalTalk connector, a small box containing a transformer that insulates the computer or peripheral from electrical interference and provides plugs for the network interface. The LocalTalk boxes are connected by ordinary telephone wire (called twisted-pair cable) with standard modular connectors.

AppleTalk networks are slow compared to high-speed systems like EtherNet. AppleTalk is capable of transmitting up to 320 bits per second, but EtherNet and other networks using network interface cards that connect directly to the computer's high-speed internal bus are capable of speeds of up to 20M bits per second. However, AppleTalk's simplicity and low cost make it an attractive option for networks of modest size and use.

→ **Tip:** If you are considering an AppleTalk installation, you can save money and extend an AppleTalk network's capabilities by using PhoneNet hardware (Farallon Computing, Inc.). After equipping each node with a PhoneNet connector (instead of the LocalTalk connector), you can wire the network using ordinary telephone cabling, considerably cheaper than LocalTalk cable. In some circumstances, you can use existing telephone wiring to create the network. A PhoneNet network can transmit data 3,000 feet, three times the extent of a LocalTalk network; Farallon also offers repeaters and other devices that make even larger networks possible. See *AppleShare, bus network, local area network (LAN), LocalTalk, node, repeater,* and *twisted-pair cable*.

application   The use of a computer for a specific purpose, such as writing a novel, printing payroll checks, or laying out the text and graphics of a newsletter. This term also is used to refer to a software program that accomplishes a specific task.

application control menu   In Microsoft Windows and Windows applications, a menu that appears on the extreme left of the menu bar. This menu is used to copy and paste information among Windows applications, to minimize and maximize the application window, to move the application window or icon, and to switch to other active Windows applications.

application development system   A coordinated set of program development tools, typically including a full-screen editor, a programming language with a compiler, and an extensive library of ready-to-use program modules. The use of an application development system substantially lowers the effort required to develop a standalone application program, especially compared to the more primitive tools typically provided as part of an operating system's programming environment.

application heap   In a Macintosh computer, the area set aside for user programs. Synonymous with *base memory*.

application icon   In Microsoft Windows, an on-screen, graphic representation of a program that has been minimized. The icon appears on the desktop.

In Windows, you can work with more than one application program at a time. After you click the Minimize button to shrink the active window, the application remains in your computer's memory, even though it is no longer visible in an on-screen window. To remind you that the application is still present in memory, Windows places an application icon on the desktop. See *icon* and *Microsoft Windows*.

application program interface (API)   System software that provides resources on which programmers can draw to create user interface features, such as pull-down menus and windows, and to route programs or data to local area networks (LANs).

An application program interface greatly benefits the user. With an API, all programs written for a computer can draw from a common repertoire of command names, menus, windows, dialog boxes, keyboard commands, and other interface features. Such standards substantially lower the cost of learning a new program and lead to measurable increases in the number of programs a typical user is likely to use. For example, Macintosh users typically use more programs and use their computers for longer portions of the workday than do users of DOS systems. The Macintosh was the first personal computer to use the API concept. See *Presentation Manager*.

application shortcut key   In Microsoft Windows' 386 enhanced mode, a shortcut key you assign to bring an application to the foreground. If you assign the shortcut key Ctrl-Alt-W to Word for Windows, for example, pressing this key combination brings Word to the foreground if the program is running. You assign the keyboard shortcut using the Advanced Options in the PIF Editor dialog box. You also can use application shortcut keys with the MS-DOS 5 task switcher. See *386 enhanced mode* and *Microsoft Windows*.

application software   Programs that perform specific tasks, such as word processing or database management; unlike system software that maintains and organizes the computer system and utilities that assist you in maintaining and organizing the system. Synonymous with *read-only memory (ROM)*. See *database management program, page layout program, spreadsheet program, system software, utility program,* and *word processing program*.

application window   In Microsoft Windows, an on-screen window that contains a running application. The name of the application and its associated document, as well as the applications menu bar, appear at the top of the window. See *Microsoft Windows*.

architecture   The overall design by which the individual hardware components of a computer system are interrelated.

This term frequently is used to describe the internal data-handling capacity of a computer. The 8-bit architecture of the Intel 8088 microprocessor, for example, is determined by the 8-bit data bus that transmits only one byte of data at a time. See *microprocessor*.

archival backup   A backup procedure in which a hard disk backup program backs up all files on the hard disk by copying them to floppy disks or some other backup medium. See *hard disk backup program* and *incremental backup*.

archive   A compressed file that is designed for space-efficient backup storage and contains one or more files.

A program for compressing and decompressing PC-compatible files is ARC, a shareware program created by Systems Enhancement Associates. The program is available from many bulletin board systems; look for files named ARC*xxx*, where *xxx* is the version number. A recent version is ARC500. The Macintosh file compression utility of choice is Stuffit, a shareware program created by Raymond Lau.

Almost all bulletin board systems store files in archives, because archived files take up considerably less space. You must use the file compression program to extract archived files. See *file compression utility*.

archive attribute   In DOS and OS/2, a hidden code, stored with a file's directory entry, that indicates whether the file has been changed since the last backup operation.

When you archive a file by using the BACKUP command, DOS turns off the archive attribute. When the archive attribute is off, these commands may be instructed to ignore the file. However, when you use an application program to modify the file after the archive attribute has been turned off, DOS turns on the archive attribute. The next time you use the BACKUP command, therefore, you can instruct the command to back up only the modified file. A file's archive attribute enables you to back up or copy only the files you have changed since the last backup procedure.

ARCnet   See *Attached Resource Computer Network (ARCnet)*.

area graph   In presentation graphics, a line graph in which the area below the line is filled in to emphasize the change in volume from one time period to the next. The x-axis (categories axis) is the horizontal axis, and the y-axis (values axis) is the vertical axis.

When more than one data series is displayed, each series is shown in a distinctive cross-hatching pattern. See *column graph, line graph, presentation graphics, x-axis,* and *y-axis*.

argument   Words, phrases, or numbers you enter on the same line as a command or a statement to expand or modify the command or statement. The command acts on the argument.

In the dBASE expression, USE customer, *USE* is the command and *customer* is the argument. In Lotus 1-2-3, the arguments of built-in functions are enclosed in parentheses, as in @SUM(B1..B3).

→ **Tip:** Think of the command as a verb and the argument as an object of the verb.

See *argument separator* and *parameter*.

argument separator   In spreadsheet programs and programming languages, a comma or other punctuation mark that sets off one argument from another in a command or statement.

Many commands, such as the built-in functions of spreadsheet programs, require you to provide information, called an argument, that the program needs to execute the command. For example, the @CTERM function in Lotus 1-2-3 requires three arguments: interest, future value, and present value. You must specify all three arguments, separated by commas:

@CTERM(.012,14000,9000)

The argument separator is essential in commands that take more than one argument. Without the separator, the program cannot tell one argument from another.

→ **Tip:** If you are having trouble getting a command or function to work, make sure that you know exactly how many arguments the command or function requires and that you have separated the arguments with the correct separator. Some programs don't allow spaces after the separator. If you are used to pressing the space bar after typing a comma, you may have to delete unnecessary spaces.

arithmetic operator   A symbol that tells the program how to perform an arithmetic operation, such as addition, subtraction, multiplication, and division.

In almost all computer programs, addition is represented by a plus sign (+), subtraction by a hyphen (-), multiplication by an asterisk (*), and division by a slash (/). See *comparison operator* and *logical operator*.

arithmetic/logic unit (ALU)   The portion of the central processing unit (CPU) devoted to the execution of fundamental arithmetic and logical operations on data.

array   One of the fundamental data structures in computer programming; a single- or multidimensional table that the program treats as one data item.

arrow keys   See *cursor-movement keys*.

artificial intelligence (AI)   A computer science field that attempts to improve computers by endowing them with some of the characteristics associated with human intelligence, such as the capability to understand natural language and to reason under conditions of uncertainty.

ascending order   A sort in which items are arranged from smallest to largest (1, 2, 3) or from first to last (a, b, c). Ascending order is the default sort order for virtually all applications that perform sorting operations. See *descending sort*.

ASCII   Pronounced "ask´-kee." See *American Standard Code for Information Interchange (ASCII)*.

ASCII character set   Pronounced "ask´-kee." A character set consisting only of the characters included in the original 128-character ASCII standard. See *extended character set*.

ASCII file   Pronounced "ask´-kee." A file that contains only characters drawn from the ASCII character set. See *binary file*.

ASCII sort order   Pronounced "ask´-kee." A sort order determined by the sequence used to number the standard ASCII character set.

When you use the greater than (>) or less than (<) logical operators, the strings are compared character-by-character to determine which string has the greater or lesser value. A character with a high-order designation is greater than a character with a low-order designation. The order of alphanumeric characters is as follows:

> *Lower Order*
> (space)!"#$%&'(apostrophe)( )*+,(comma)-.(period)
> /0…9:;<=>?@ABC…XYZ[\]^abc…xyz
>
> > *Higher Order*

▲ **Caution:** Programs that sort data in ASCII sort order may violate publication guidelines—all capitalized words, for instance, come before words beginning with lowercase letters—so you may have to perform some manual rearrangement of the data. In addition, ASCII sorts may not handle foreign language characters properly. See *dictionary sort*.

aspect ratio   In computer graphics, the ratio of the horizontal dimension of an image to the vertical dimension. In sizing a graphic, maintaining the height-to-width ratio is important to avoid distortions.

assign To give a value to a named variable.

assignment statement In computer programming, a program statement that places a value into a variable. In BASIC, for example, the statement LET A = 10 places the value 10 into the variable A. See *BASIC*.

associate In Microsoft Windows and MS-DOS 5.0, to create a link between a data file's extension (such as .DOC) and a specific application program. After you create the link, Windows automatically places the associated files in the application's workspace. In addition, if you select an associated file, Windows automatically opens the linked application program.

→ **Tip:** Windows automatically associates Windows applications with their data files. You need to associate files manually only when you use non-Windows applications.

associated document A file that is linked at the system level with the application that created it. You can start an application by choosing one of its associated documents.

DOS doesn't have any facilities for associated documents; you can't start Lotus 1-2-3, for example, by choosing FALLQTR.WK1. In Microsoft Windows, Windows applications automatically establish associations with their documents, but you must manually associate non-Windows applications and documents. In the Macintosh Finder and Multifinder, all documents are associated with the applications that created them. The association is controlled by the creator type code, a four-letter code that identifies the application used to create the file. See *creator type, Finder, Microsoft Windows,* and *Multifinder*.

asterisk In DOS and OS/2, a wild-card symbol that stands for one or more characters, unlike the question mark wildcard, which stands for only one character.

asynchronous communication   Method of data communication in which the transmission of bits of data is not synchronized by a clock signal but is accomplished by sending the bits one after another, with a start bit and a stop bit to mark the beginning and end of the data unit.

The two communicating devices must be set to the same speed. This speed is called the baud rate. Parity also may be used to check each byte transferred for accuracy. Each device must be set to the same parity. Asynchronous communication normally is used for transmission speeds of less than 19,200 baud.

Asynchronous communication is popular among personal computer developers. Because of the lower communication speeds, normal telephone lines can be used for asynchronous communication. See *baud rate, bus, modem, synchronous communication*, and *Universal Asynchronous Receiver/Transmitter (UART)*.

AT   See *IBM Personal Computer AT*.

AT bus   The 16-bit expansion bus used in the IBM Personal Computer AT, as distinguished from the 8-bit bus of the original IBM Personal Computer and the 32-bit bus of computers using the Intel 80386 and 80486 micro-processors. Most 80386 and 80486 machines contain AT-compatible slots. See *expansion bus, IBM Personal Computer, IBM Personal Computer AT, Intel 80386, Intel 80486*, and *Micro Channel Bus*.

Attached Resource Computer Network (ARCnet)   A popular local area network for IBM Personal Computers and compatibles originally developed by Datapoint Corporation and now available from several vendors. ARCnet interface cards are inexpensive and easily installed. ARCnet networks employ a star topology, a token-passing protocol, and coaxial or twisted-pair cable. The network is capable of transmitting data at speeds of 2.5M per second. See *coaxial cable, local area network (LAN), network interface card, network protocol, network topology*, and *twisted-pair cable*.

attenuation   In local area networks, the loss of signal strength when the system's cables exceed the maximum range stated in the network's specifications. The attenuation of a signal prevents successful data communications. The maximum length of a network's cable can be extended by using a device called a repeater. See *local area network (LAN)* and *repeater.*

attribute   In many word processing and graphics programs, a character emphasis, such as boldface and italic, and other characteristics of character formatting, such as typeface and type size. In WordPerfect, for example, attributes include appearance attributes (boldface, underline, double underline, italic, outline, shadow, small caps, strikeout, and redline) and size attributes. See *archive attribute* and *file attribute.*

audit trail   In an accounting program, an automatic program feature that keeps a record of transactions so that you can locate the origin of specific figures that appear on reports.

authoring language   A computer-assisted instruction (CAI) application that provides tools for creating instructional or presentation software.
   A popular authoring language for Macintosh computers is Hyper-Card, provided free with every Macintosh computer. Using Hyper-Card, educators can develop instructional programs quickly and easily. HyperCard applications can control video disk players and CD-ROM drives, making the application useful as a front end for large text or video databases.

AutoCAD   Pronounced "auto*'*-cad." A computer-aided design (CAD) program developed by AutoDesk and widely used for professional CAD applications. See *computer-aided design (CAD).*

auto-dial/auto-answer modem   A modem capable of generating tones to dial the receiving computer and of answering a ringing telephone to establish a connection when a call is received. See *modem.*

AUTOEXEC.BAT   In DOS, a batch file consulted by DOS when the system is started or restarted.

AUTOEXEC.BAT is not mandatory for IBM PC-compatible computers, but when you are running a hard disk loaded with several applications and a computer to which you have attached several peripherals, the file is all but essential for efficient operation. Ingredients in an AUTOEXEC.BAT file are PATH command statements that tell DOS where to find application programs and the names of system-configuration programs, such as MODE, that set up your computer for the use of peripherals, such as a serial printer and mouse. Such commands and programs do not remain in your computer's memory when you shut off the power. You must enter all this information manually at the start of every operating session. AUTOEXEC.BAT does the task for you.

automatic backup   An application program feature that saves a document automatically at a period the user specifies, such as every five or ten minutes. After a power outage or system crash, you see your work on-screen (up to the last time it was backed up) when you restart the application. This feature can help you avoid catastrophic work losses.

automatic font downloading   The transmission of disk-based, downloadable printer fonts to the printer, done by an application program as the fonts are needed to complete a printing job. See *downloading utility* and *printer font*.

automatic hyphenation   See *hyphenation*.

automatic mode switching   The automatic detection and adjustment of a display adapter's internal circuitry to adjust the video output of a program on an IBM PC-compatible computer. Most Video Graphics Array (VGA) adapters, for example, switch to adjust to CGA, MDA, EGA, or VGA output from applications.

automatic recalculation   In a spreadsheet, a mode in which cell values are recalculated every time any cell is changed in the worksheet.

autorepeat key   A key that repeatedly enters a character as long as you press and hold down the key.

autosave   See *timed backup*.

autotrace   In a graphics program, such as Adobe Illustrator, a command that transforms an imported bit-mapped image into its object-oriented counterpart.

   The bit-mapped images created by a paint program, such as Mac-Paint, can print at the maximum resolution of the Macintosh screen (72 dots per inch). Object-oriented graphics, however, print at the printer's maximum resolution (up to 300 dots per inch for laser printers). Using the autotrace tool, you can transform low-resolution graphics into art that prints at substantially higher resolution. See *bit-mapped graphic, object-oriented graphic,* and *paint program*.

auxiliary storage   See *secondary storage*.

axis   See *x-axis, y-axis,* and *z-axis*.

b

back end   The portion of a program that does not interact with the user and that accomplishes the processing job that the program is designed to perform. In a local area network, the back-end application may be stored on the file server; front-end programs handle the user interface on each workstation. See *client/server architecture* and *front end*.

back up   To copy a data or program file to a removable secondary storage device so that it can be kept in a safe off-site location.

background In computers that can do more than one task at a time, the environment in which low-priority operations (such as printing a document or downloading a file) are carried out while the user works with an application in the foreground.

In a computer system that lacks multitasking capabilities, the background task is carried out during brief pauses in the execution of the system's primary (foreground) task(s). Many word processing programs use this technique to provide background printing. See *multitasking*.

background communication Data communication, such as downloading a file, accomplished in the background while the user concentrates on another application in the foreground. See *multitasking*.

background noise The random or extraneous signals that infiltrate a communications channel, unlike the signals that convey information.

background printing The printing of a document in the background while a program is active in the foreground.

→ **Tip:** Background printing can bring major productivity benefits if you frequently print long documents or use a slow printer. Without background printing, you cannot use your computer system while the document is printing. With background printing, you can continue to work while the document prints.

Background printing can work four ways. First, some word processing programs, such as Microsoft Word, provide a background printing command that enables the user to print one document while editing another. Second, commercially available print spooling programs extend background printing to all or most of your applications. Third, some operating systems, such as OS/2, provide background printing (bringing another application to the foreground while printing in the background). Fourth, you can add a print buffer to your system. A print buffer is a hardware device that connects your computer and the printer. The buffer contains memory chips that store the computer's output until the printer is ready. The computer thinks that it is hooked up to a super-fast printer and sends the output at maximum speed. You return to your work, and the buffer feeds the output to the printer. See *multitasking, print queue,* and *print spooling program.*

background processes   In a multitasking operating system, the operations occurring in the background (such as printing or downloading a program from a bulletin board) while you work with an application program in the foreground.

background recalculation   In spreadsheet programs, such as Lotus 1-2-3, an option that enables you to make changes to a large spreadsheet while the program performs recalculations in the background.

backlit display   See *liquid crystal display* (LCD).

backplane   The rear panel of a computing device where you find receptacles for peripheral devices and power cords.

backspace   A key that deletes the character to the left of the cursor's position or the act of moving one space to the left by using the cursor-movement keys.

backup   A copy of a program or document file made for archival purposes. See *global backup* and *incremental backup.*

backup utility   A utility program that makes it easier to back up program and data files from a hard disk to a backup medium, such as floppy disks.

　　A good backup utility can back up an entire hard disk on a series of floppies; the program prompts you when one disk is full and the next one is needed.

　　DOS and the Macintosh operating system include backup utilities, but the DOS BACKUP command is not particularly easy to use, and the Mac's HD Backup program does not perform incremental backups. (An incremental backup is a copying operation that backs up only the files that have been modified since the last backup procedure.) Backup utilities are popular options in both environments. See *incremental backup*.

backward search In database management or word processing, a search that begins at the cursor's location and proceeds backward toward the beginning of a database or document (rather than the default forward search).

bad break An improperly hyphenated line break. See *automatic hyphenation*.

bad page break In word processing and desktop publishing, an inappropriate or unattractive soft page break that has been inserted by the word processing or page layout program.

A common flaw in documents produced on computers, bad page breaks should be caught by a final careful proofreading before a document goes out the door. Headings can be widowed at the bottom of pages; units of text that should be kept together (such as tables) are split; and single lines of text (orphans) can be left at the top of a page.

The best policy is to use block protection features that prevent bad page breaks from occurring. These features are found in high-quality word processing programs, such as WordPerfect and Microsoft Word.

bad sector An area of a floppy or hard disk that will not reliably record data.

Almost all hard disks have some bad sectors as a result of manufacturing defects. If you run a disk diagnostic program such as CHKDSK and the diagnostic program reports a few bad sectors, don't worry. The operating system locks these sectors out of reading and writing operations. Aside from the loss of a few bytes of storage, you can use the disk as if the bad sectors did not exist.

▲ **Caution:** Bad sectors on floppy disks present serious problems. Most operating systems reject new disks containing bad sectors. If an attempt to format a floppy disk fails, discard the disk. See *bad track table*.

bad track table　A list attached to or packaged with a hard disk. The bad track table lists the bad sectors or the defective areas of the disk.

Almost every hard disk comes off the assembly line with some defects. During the low-level format, these defective areas of the disk are locked out so that system software cannot access them. See *low-level format*.

bandwidth　A measurement, expressed in cycles per second (hertz) or bits per second (bps), of the amount of information that can flow through a channel. The higher the frequency, the higher the bandwidth.

bank switching　A way of expanding memory beyond an operating system's or microprocessor's limitations by switching rapidly between two banks of memory chips. See *expanded memory*.

bar code　A printed pattern of wide and narrow vertical bars used to represent numerical codes in machine-readable form.

Bar codes are printed on almost every product sold in supermarkets. These bar codes conform to the Universal Product Code (UPC), a standard bar code format that lists the product maker's identification number and a product number. When the bar code is dragged past an optical scanner at the check-out counter, the point-of-sale computer matches the product number with its database of price lists and rings up the correct amount.

bar code reader　An input device equipped with a stylus that scans bar codes; the device then converts the bar code into a number displayed on-screen. See *bar code*.

bar graph　In presentation graphics, a graph with horizontal bars, commonly used to show the values of independent items. The x-axis (categories axis) is the vertical axis, and the y-axis (values axis) is the horizontal axis.

Properly, the term bar graph is used only for graphs with horizontal bars. If the bars are vertical, the graph is a column graph. In practice, however, the term bar graph is used for both. In professional presentation graphics, bar graphs are used to display the values of discrete items (apples, oranges, grapefruit, and papaya), and column graphs are used to show the changes in one or more items over time (for example, apples vs. oranges in January, February, March, and so on). See *column graph, line graph, paired bar graph, x-axis,* and *y-axis.*

base memory   See *conventional memory.*

baseband   In local area networks, a communications method in which the information-bearing signal is placed directly on the cable in digital form without modulation.

A computer's signals can be conveyed over cables in two ways: by analog signals or by digital signals. Analog signals, such as the signals that travel from a high-fidelity amplifier to its speakers, are continuous signals that vary in a wave-like pattern. The number of variations or cycles per second is the signal's frequency, measured in hertz (Hz). Digital signals are discrete signals that alternate between high current or low current.

Because a computer's signals are digital signals, they must be transformed by a process called *modulation* before they can be conveyed over an analog-signal network. A modem performs this task. An analog communication network is called a *broadband network.*

Digital communication networks are called *baseband networks.* The advantage of a baseband network is that considerably less circuitry is required to convey the signal to and from the computer. In addition, because many baseband networks can use twisted-pair (ordinary telephone) cables, baseband networks are cheaper to install than broadband networks that require coaxial cable. However, a baseband system is limited in its geographic extent and provides only one channel of communication at a time. Most personal computer local area networks are baseband networks. See *broadband.*

baseline In typography, the lowest point characters reach (excluding descenders). For example, the baseline of a line of text is the lowermost point of letters like a and x, excluding the lowest points of p and q.

BASIC An easy-to-use (but widely criticized) high-level programming language available on personal computers.

Developed in 1964 by John G. Kemeny and Thomas E. Kurtz, two Dartmouth College professors, BASIC (Beginner's All-Purpose Symbolic Instruction Code) was designed to make computer programming accessible to people who are not computer scientists. Like predecessors FORTRAN and ALGOL (the forerunner of Pascal), BASIC is a procedural language that tells the computer what to do step-by-step. A program consists of lines of text, with each line containing one or more statements. Unlike its predecessors, BASIC programs run in an interactive environment, complete with a text editor, debugger, and interpreter that translates and executes the BASIC source code line-by-line. You develop a program interactively, trying alternatives and testing program integrity each step of the way. The result is a process of program construction highly conducive to learning. More recently created compilers transform BASIC code into stand-alone executable programs.

Examples of modernized BASIC include Microsoft's QuickBASIC and Borland's TurboBASIC. Both versions include compilers that make the production of professional executable object code programs possible. Although these modern versions of BASIC are hardly the language of choice for professional program development, some commercially viable software (and a great many shareware programs) are written in a compiled BASIC. C is far more popular for professional program development. See *C, compiler, control structure, debugger, interpreter, procedural language, QuickBASIC,* and *structured programming.*

basic input-output system (BIOS) Pronounced "buy'-ose." A set of programs encoded in read-only memory (ROM) on IBM PC-compatible computers. These programs facilitate the transfer of data and control instructions between the computer and peripherals, such as disk drives.

The BIOS programs of IBM Personal Computers, XTs, ATs, and PS/2s are copyrighted. PC-compatible manufacturers, such as Compaq Corporation, must create a BIOS that emulates the IBM BIOS without actually using IBM's code. Companies that manufacture IBM PC-compatible computers can choose to create the BIOS emulation themselves or purchase an emulation from other companies, such as Phoenix Technologies.

batch file   A file containing a series of DOS commands executed one after the other, as if you typed them. Batch files are useful when you repeatedly need to type the same series of DOS commands. Almost all hard disk users have an AUTOEXEC.BAT file, a batch file that DOS loads at the start of every operating session. See *AUTOEXEC-.BAT.*

batch processing   A mode of computer operation in which program instructions are executed one after the other without user intervention.

Batch processing efficiently uses computer resources in a multi-user system, but batch processing is not convenient for users. Often, you discover a programming or data input error only after the computer has run the job and spewed out reams of useless printout. In interactive processing, you see the results of your commands on-screen so that you can correct errors and make necessary adjustments before completing the operation. See *interactive processing* and *multiuser system*.

baud   Pronounced "bawd." A measure of the number of times per second that switching can occur in a communications channel. See *baud rate*.

baud rate   The transmission speed of an asynchronous communications channel.

Technically, baud rate refers to the maximum number of changes that can occur per second in the electrical state of a communications circuit. Under RS-232C communications protocols, 300 baud is likely to equal 300 bits per second (bps), but at higher baud rates, the number of bits per second transmitted is actually higher than the baud rate because one change can represent more than one bit of data. For example, 1200 bps is usually sent at 600 baud by sending two bits of information with each change in the electrical state of the circuit.

In personal computing, baud rates are frequently cited to measure the speed of modems. Although 1200-baud modems are standard, most frequent users of telecommunications prefer 2400-baud modems. With serial printers, you must set up your computer's serial port so that the computer sends the printer signals at the correct speed. The Apple LaserWriter, for example, requires serial transmissions at 9600 baud. Under DOS, you set the serial transmission speed by using the MODE command. See *asynchronous communication, LaserWriter, modem, serial port, serial printer,* and *telecommunications*.

BBS   See *bulletin board system (BBS)*.

BCD   See *binary coded decimal (BCD)*.

bells and whistles   An application program's or computer system's advanced features.

Many people say bells and whistles, such as mail-merging capabilities in a word processing program, aren't desirable for novices and recommend programs that lack such features. If advanced features do not clutter up the user interface, however, you should buy full-featured software you can grow into. A feature that seems hopelessly advanced right now may turn out to be vital.

Microsoft Word 4.0 for the Macintosh offers the best of both worlds. You can choose a user interface that hides the program's complexity by including only a few features on the program's menus. You also can choose a standard interface that includes the advanced features. See *mail merge*.

benchmark   A standard measurement used to test the performance of different brands of equipment.

In computing, standard benchmark tests (such as Dhrystones and Whetstones) do not provide accurate measures of a system's actual performance in an end-user computing environment. Most of these tests are CPU-intensive; they put the central processing unit through a mix of instructions, such as floating-point calculations, but do not test the performance of system components such as disk drives and internal communications.

The speed of these components greatly affects the performance of end-user application programs. Benchmarks developed for personal computers, such as the Norton SI, include the performance of peripherals. See *Norton SI* and *throughput*.

benchmark program   A utility program used to measure a computer's processing speed so that its performance can be compared to that of other computers running the same program.

Benchmark programs provide some indication of the number-crunching prowess of a central processing unit (CPU), but the results they generate may be close to meaningless. What counts for users is a system's throughput, its capability to push data not only through the CPU but also through all the system's peripheral components, including its disk drives. A computer with a fast processor (and a numeric coprocessor) performs well on benchmarks, but if the computer is equipped with a sluggish hard disk and lacks cache memory, the performance may disappoint the user. See *cache memory, central processing unit (CPU), throughput,* and *utility program*.

Bernoulli box   Pronounced "ber-noo'-lee." An innovative removable mass storage system developed by Iomega Corporation for IBM PC-compatible and Macintosh computers.

Bernoulli boxes have removable cartridges containing flexible disks capable of holding up to 44M of programs and data. Unlike floppy disk drives, however, these disks spin at high speeds; the latest Bernoulli boxes are capable of up to 22 ms access time. The Bernoulli box is named for the Swiss scientist who predicted the dynamics of a rapidly spinning, flexible disk around a fixed object. Bernoulli said that owing to the force of air pressure, the disk would bend around the object (read/write head) just enough to maintain a slight space between the object and the disk. Unlike hard disks, which use a massive, fixed platter, this design is resistant to head crashes, in which the read/write head collides with and ruins the disk. Crashes often are caused by shock, but you can drop a Bernoulli cartridge to the floor without damaging the disk or data. Bernoulli cartridges also are removable and relatively inexpensive. Therefore, you can use Bernoulli boxes to create a virtually unlimited mass storage system. See *hard disk* and *secondary storage*.

beta site   The place where a beta test occurs. When developing a program or a version of an existing program, a company chooses beta sites where the program is subjected to demanding, heavy-duty usage. This process reveals the program's remaining bugs and shortcomings.

beta software   In computer software testing, a preliminary version of a program that is widely distributed to users who attempt to operate the program under realistic conditions. See *alpha test, beta site,* and *beta test*.

beta test   The second stage in the testing of computer software before the commercial release. Beta tests usually are conducted outside the company manufacturing the software. See *alpha test*.

Bézier curve   A mathematically generated line that can display non-uniform curves.

Bézier curves are named after the French mathematician Pierre Bézier, who first described their properties. In a Bézier curve, the location of two midpoints—called control handles—is sufficient to describe the overall shape of an irregular curve. In computer graphics applications, you manipulate the control handles usually shown as small boxes on-screen. By clicking on these points and dragging with the mouse, you manipulate the complexity and shape of the curve.

bibliographic retrieval service   An on-line information service that specializes in maintaining huge computerized indexes to scholarly, scientific, medical, and technical literature.

The databases offered by these services are almost identical to the indexes available in the reference section of major university libraries. Most databases do not contain the text of the works cited—only the bibliographic citation and an abstract that may not contain useful information. To get the full benefit of the literature, you have to retrieve the original document. These service firms offer the original documents, but the price is stiff.

The two leading information firms are BRS Information Technologies (Latham, NY) and DIALOG Information Services (Menlo Park, CA). Serving mainly corporate and institutional customers, these companies' fees are steep—well over an average of $1 per minute. Personal computer users can access, at substantially lower rates, special menu-driven night and weekend versions of these services, BRS/After Dark and Knowledge Index.

→ **Tip:** Before signing on, find out whether your local library makes databases available on CD-ROM disks. If so, you can search these databases for free. Because no clock is ticking away, you can make full use of the interactive searching potential of this information. See *on-line information service*.

Big Blue   Slang for International Business Machines Corp., which uses blue as its corporate color.

binary coded decimal (BCD)   A method of coding long decimal numbers so that they can be processed with precision in a computer using an 8-bit data word.

Most personal computers process data in 8-bit chunks called bytes, but that size causes problems for number crunching. When working with binary numbers, the biggest number that can be represented with 8 bits is 256. The data word length must be increased to about 60 bits to work effectively with binary numbers. That increase is exactly what numeric coprocessors are for.

Some programs get around the 8-bit limitation by using BCD notation, a way of coding decimal numbers in binary form without really translating them into binary. You cannot fit 260 into 8 bits, but you can fit the codes for 2, 6, and 0 into 3 adjacent bytes. A 3-digit decimal number takes up 3 bytes of storage; larger numbers can be accommodated by increasing the number of bytes set aside in memory to store the number. Therefore, you have no limit to the precision that can be achieved in coding and processing numbers.

binary file   A file containing data or program instructions in a computer-readable format. You cannot display the contents of a binary file using the DOS Type command or a word processing program.

→ **Tip:** Don't panic if you open a strangely named file only to see an appalling collection of happy faces, spades, clubs, and other odd symbols: chances are that you have opened a binary file by accident. Just close the file and try again.

binary numbers   A number system with a base (or radix) of 2, unlike the number systems most people use, which have bases of 10 (decimal numbers), 12 (measurement in feet and inches), and 60 (time).

Binary numbers are preferred for computers for precision and economy. Constructing an electronic circuit that can detect the difference between 2 states (high current and low current) is easy and inexpensive; building a circuit that detects the difference among 10 states is much more difficult and expensive.

binary search   A search algorithm that avoids a slow sequential search by starting in the middle of the sorted database and determining whether the desired record is above or below the midpoint. Having reduced the number of records to be searched by 50 percent, the search proceeds to the middle of the remaining records, and so on, until the desired record is found.

binding offset   An extra-wide margin that shifts text away from the edge of the page when the document is bound.

You use binding offsets only for documents printed or reproduced on both sides of the page (duplex printing); the margin is increased on the right side of verso (left, even-numbered) pages and the left side of recto (right, odd-numbered) pages. See *gutter*.

→ **Tip:** If you are planning to bind a document printed or reproduced on only one side of the page, don't use a binding offset. Just increase the left margin to make room for the binding.

BIOS   See *basic input-output system (BIOS)*.

bit   The basic unit of information in a binary numbering system (BInary digiT).

Computers work with binary numbers, and the internal circuit can represent one of the two numbers in a binary system: 1 or 0. These basic either/or, yes/no units of information are called bits. Because building a reliable circuit that tells the difference between a 1 (represented by high current) and a 0 (represented by low current) is easy and inexpensive, computers are accurate in their internal processing capabilities. Computers typically make fewer than one internal error in every 100 billion processing operations. Note, however, that such internal errors have nothing to do with programming errors, which are much more common and account for almost all computer glitches. See *byte*.

bit map   The representation of a video image stored in a computer's memory. Each picture element (pixel) is represented by bits stored in the memory.

Bit-mapped graphics are notorious consumers of memory. Up to 1M of video memory may be required to store a bit map for a high-resolution screen display. See *block graphics* and *pixel*.

bit-mapped font   A screen or printer font in which each character is composed of a pattern of dots. Bit-mapped fonts represent characters with a matrix of dots. To display or print bit-mapped fonts, the computer or printer must keep a full representation of each character in memory.

"Font" should be taken literally as a complete set of characters of a given typeface, weight, posture, and size. For example, if you want to use Palatino (Roman) 12 and Palatino Italic 14, you must load two complete sets of characters into memory. Bit-mapped fonts cannot be scaled up or down without introducing grotesque staircase distortions, called aliasing. Distortions are clearly visible when you attempt to scale Macintosh bit-mapped screen fonts to a size not represented by a corresponding font in the System Folder.

Because the computer's or printer's memory must contain a complete set of characters for each font you use, bit-mapped fonts consume enormous amounts of disk and memory space. Outline fonts, however, are constructed from mathematical formulas and can be scaled up or down without distortion. Outline fonts are considered technically superior. Printers that can print outline fonts, therefore, are more expensive. These fonts require processing circuitry to decode the formulas and memory to store the bit map constructed from the formulas. See *aliasing, LaserJet, LaserWriter, outline font, printer font,* and *screen font.*

bit-mapped graphic   A graphic image formed by a pattern of pixels (screen dots) and limited in resolution to the maximum screen resolution of the device being used. Bit-mapped graphics are produced by paint programs, such as MacPaint, SuperPaint, GEM Paint, PC Paintbrush, and some scanners.

Considered inferior to object-oriented graphics for most applications, bit-mapped graphics tie the printed resolution to the resolution of the video display currently in use, even if the printer is capable of higher resolution. Macintosh Systems, for example, display bit-mapped graphics with a resolution of 72 dpi, even though LaserWriter printers can print at 300 dpi. Such graphics may be afflicted with aliasing, rough diagonal lines attributable to the square shape of the pixels. The irregular patterns are visible when the image includes a straight diagonal line. However, a skillful illustrator can create beautiful air-brush effects with paint packages.

Bit-mapped graphics have other drawbacks. Unlike object-oriented and Encapsulated PostScript (EPS) graphics, bit-mapped graphics consume considerable memory and disk space. Resizing a bit-mapped graphic image without introducing distortions is almost impossible. Scaling up the graphic produces a chunky effect because the lines thicken proportionately; scaling down causes the bits to run together, resulting in an inky effect. Unlike object-oriented graphics, in which each object, such as a line, can be edited or moved independently, bit-mapped graphic images are difficult to edit or modify. See *aliasing, encapsulated PostScript (EPS) file, object-oriented graphic, paint program, pixel, resolution,* and *scanner.*

bits per second (bps) In asynchronous communications, a measurement of data transmission speed.

In personal computing, bps rates frequently are used to measure the performance of modems and other serial communications devices, such as serial ports. The bps rates are enumerated incrementally using a doubling scheme: 110 bps; 150 bps; 300 bps; 600 bps; 1,200 bps; 2,400 bps; 4,800 bps; 9,600 bps; 19,200 bps; 38,400 bps; 57,600 bps, and 115,200 bps. See *asynchronous communication, baud,* and *modem.*

blank cell In a spreadsheet program, a cell that contains no values, labels, or formatting different from the worksheet's global formats.

blessed folder Macintosh's System Folder, equivalent to a DOS subdirectory and containing files loaded at the beginning of an operating session.

The Macintosh operating system, the System, consults this folder when the computer cannot locate a program file. The blessed folder is like a DOS directory named in the PATH command. A major limitation of the Macintosh operating system, however, is that the System Folder is the only folder the System consults when it cannot find a file. Macintosh users, therefore, are obliged to place all the configuration files required by their application programs in this folder, which can quickly grow so large that keeping track of its contents is difficult. See *System* and *System Folder*.

board See *adapter* and *circuit board*.

block 1. A unit of information processed or transferred. The unit may vary in size. In communications, a unit of information passed from one computer to another is a block. For example, using XMODEM, a communications protocol for transferring files, 128 bytes is considered a block. Under DOS, a block transferred from a disk drive is 512 bytes. 2. In word processing, a unit of text highlighted to be moved, copied, or otherwise affected by a block operation. See *block operation*.

In word processing, techniques for marking blocks vary. The earliest word processing programs required the user to enter a keyboard command at the beginning and end of the block. More recent programs enable the user to mark the block by using a process called selection, in which the cursor-movement keys are used to highlight the marked text in reverse video. When the block is marked, block operations are possible, such as copying, moving, deleting, formatting, or saving the block to a named file.

block definition See *selection*.

block move A fundamental editing technique in word processing in which a marked block of text is cut from one location and inserted in another.

Writing experts agree that the major determinant of a written work's quality is its logical coherence: the ideas and facts must be presented in a logical progression. To achieve coherence, restructuring larges amounts of text often is necessary.

Because word processing software enables a writer to restructure large text domains with ease, some writing teachers thought the technology would lead to improved writing.

block operation The act of transferring a chunk or block of information from one area to another. In word processing, an editing or formatting operation performed on a marked block of text, such as copying, deleting, moving, or underlining. See *block move*.

block protection   In word processing and page layout programs, the prevention of soft page breaks within a block of text. See *bad page break* and *soft page break*.

body type   The font (usually 8- to 12-point) used to set the paragraphs of the text (distinguished from the typefaces used to set headings, subheadings, captions, and other typographical elements).

→ **Tip:** Serif typefaces, such as Century, Garamond, and Times Roman, are preferred over sans serif typefaces for body type because they are more legible. See *sans serif* and *serif.*

boilerplate   A standard passage of text used over and over in letters, memos, or reports.

→ **Tip:** Use boilerplate to achieve big gains in your writing productivity. If your job involves answering routine inquiry letters, develop boilerplate responses to questions on such matters as warranty, sales terms, and the like, and attach these passages to glossaries (named storage areas for boilerplate text and other frequently used items, such as logos). Then you can write a letter just by inserting two or three glossaries and adding a few personalized touches. See *glossary.*

boldface   A character emphasis visibly darker and heavier in weight than normal type. See *emphasis* and *weight*.

bomb   Synonymous with *crash*.

Boolean operator   See *logical operator*.

boot   To initiate an automatic routine that clears the memory, loads the operating system, and prepares the computer for use.

The term boot is derived from the saying "pulling yourself up by your own bootstraps." Personal computers must do just that because random-access memory (RAM) does not retain program instructions when the power is shut off.

Buried within the computers read-only memory (ROM) circuits is an autostart program that comes into play when the power is switched on (a cold boot). Unlike RAM, ROM circuits retain data and program instructions without requiring power. The autostart program instructs the computer's disk drives to search for the disk containing the computer's operating system.

After a system crash occurs, you usually must reboot the computer. With most systems, you can perform a warm boot that restarts the system without the stress on electronic components caused by switching the power off and on again. See *cold boot* and *warm boot*.

boot record   The first track on an IBM PC-compatible disk (track 0). After you turn on the power, the boot-up software in ROM instructs the computer to read this track to begin loading DOS. See *boot*.

bps   See *bits per second (bps)*.

branch control structure   A control structure in which program control branches in two or more directions, depending on the results of a conditional test. Synonymous with *selection*. See *case branch, control structure*.

break   A user-initiated signal that interrupts processing or the reception of data. See *Ctrl-Break*.

bridge   In local area networks, a device that enables two networks (even ones dissimilar in topology, wiring, or communications protocols) to exchange data.

broadband   In local area networks, an analog communications method characterized by high bandwidth. The signal usually is split, or multiplexed, to provide multiple communications channels.

A broadband system uses analog transmissions. Because the microcomputer is a digital device, a device similar to a modem is required at either end of the transmission cable to convert the digital signal to analog and back again.

Broadband communications can extend over great distances and operate at extremely high speeds. A broadband network can, like a cable TV network, convey two or more communication channels at a time (the channels are separated by frequency). Therefore, a broadband network can handle voice and data communications. See *analog, analog transmission, bandwidth, baseband,* and *digital*.

browse mode   In a database management program, a program mode in which data records are displayed in a columnar format for quick on-screen review. Synonymous with list view or table view in some programs. See *Edit mode*.

buffer   A unit of memory given the task of holding information temporarily, especially when such temporary storage is needed to compensate for differences in speed between computer components.

bug   A programming error that causes a program or a computer system to perform erratically, produce incorrect results, or crash.

The term bug was coined when a real insect was discovered to have fouled up one of the circuits of the first electronic digital computer, the ENIAC.

built-in font   A printer font encoded permanently in the printer's read-only memory (ROM).

All laser printers offer at least one built-in font family. You should purchase a printer with a range of built-in fonts, including (at the minimum) a Roman-style serif font (such as Times Roman or Dutch) and an attractive, clean sans serif font (such as Helvetica or Swiss). PostScript-compatible laser printers have a nice range of built-in fonts from Adobe Systems, Inc. These fonts include Avant Garde, Bookman, New Century Schoolbook, Palatino, and Zapf Chancery. See *cartridge font, downloadable font,* and *screen font*.

built-in function In a spreadsheet program, a ready-to-use formula that performs mathematical, statistical, trigonometric, financial, calendrical, logical, and other calculations.

A built-in function is prefaced by a special symbol (usually @) and followed by a keyword (such as AVG or SUM) that describes the formula's purpose. Most built-in functions require one or more arguments. In Lotus 1-2-3, for example, the @ROUND function requires you to provide the number to be rounded (or a cell reference) and the number of decimal places to which the number should be rounded. The following built-in function rounds the value in cell C5 to two decimal places: @ROUND(C5,2).

When a built-in function has more than one argument, you must use argument separators, the comma in the preceding example, so that the program can tell one part of the expression from the others. See *argument, argument separator,* and *keyword*.

bulk storage A secondary storage device (usually using magnetic tape) that can store one terabyte of data or more. Synonymous with *mass storage*.

bullet An open or closed circle (•), about the height of a lowercase letter, used to set off items in a list.

Often combined with a hanging indent, bullets are effective for listing items whose content is roughly equal in emphasis or significance. If you want to list items that vary in their significance or are arranged chronologically, choose a numbered list. See *hanging indent*.

bulletin board system (BBS) A private telecommunications utility, usually set up by a personal computer hobbyist for the enjoyment of other hobbyists.

bundled software Software included with a computer system as part of the system's total price.

burn-in A power-on test of a computer system performed on behalf of the customer.

Semiconductor components such as memory chips and microprocessors tend to fail at two times: early or late in their lives but seldom during the middle. Responsible computer retailers, therefore, burn in systems for 24 to 48 hours before releasing the systems to customers. Defective chips are likely to fail during the burn-in period.

bus An internal pathway along which signals are sent from one part of the computer to another.

Personal computers have a bus design with three pathways:

- The data bus sends data back and forth between the memory and the microprocessor.
- The address bus identifies which memory location will come into play.
- The control bus carries the control unit's signals.

The data bus and address bus are wired in parallel so that all the bits in a binary number can travel simultaneously, like 8 cars side-by-side on a 16-lane freeway. See *expansion bus*.

bus mouse A mouse connected to the computer by an adapter inserted into an available expansion slot. See *serial mouse*.

bus network In local area networks, a decentralized network in which a single connecting line, the bus, is shared by a number of nodes, including workstations, shared peripherals, and file servers.

In a bus network, a workstation sends a message to all other workstations. Each node in the network, however, has a unique address, and its reception circuitry constantly monitors the bus to determine whether a message is being sent to the node. A message sent to the Laser Printer node, for example, is ignored by the other nodes in the network.

→ **Tip:** Bus networks have a significant advantage over competing network topologies (star networks and ring networks); the failure of a single node does not disrupt the rest of the network. Most commercial local area networks, such as AppleTalk and EtherNet, use a bus topology. Extending a bus network also is a simple matter. You lengthen the bus and add nodes, up to the system's maximum. The signal, however, cannot travel more than about 1,000 feet without an added device called a repeater. See *node* and *repeater*.

button   In the industry-standard and graphical user interfaces, a dialog box option that the user can choose to determine how a command will function. See *cancel button*, *OK button*, *pushbutton*, and *radio button*.

byte   Pronounced "bite." Eight contiguous bits, the fundamental data word of personal computers.

Storing the equivalent of one character, the byte provides a basic comprehensible unit of measurement for computer storage. Because a single page of double-spaced text contains about 1,375 characters, about 1,500 bytes are required to store the page (allowing for spaces, control characters, and other needed information). Because many bytes of memory are required to store information in a computer, byte counts tend to involve very large numbers—many personal computers have millions of bytes of memory. Because computer architecture is based (for the most part) on binary numbers, bytes are counted in powers of two. The most frequently used units are kilobyte (K), or $2^{10} = 1,024$ bytes, and megabyte (M) ($2^{20} = 1,048,576$).

The terms kilo (in kilobyte) and mega (in megabyte) are misleading: they derive from decimal (base 10) numbers. Kilo suggests 1,000, and mega suggests 1,000,000. Many computer scientsts criticize these terms for their inherent inaccuracy and irrelevance to computer architecture. However, 2^{10} and 2^{20} are logical places to establish benchmarks for measurement, and the fact that they are close to 1,000 and 1,000,000 (respectively) gives those who think in decimal numbers a nice handle on the measurement of memory. See *bit* and *kilobyte (K)*.

C

C A high-level programming language widely used for professional programming. C is highly portable and produces efficient, fast-running programs.

Developed by Dennis Ritchie of Bell Laboratories in 1972, C is a descendant of an earlier language called B. Most major professional software companies prefer C over other programming languages. A general-purpose procedural language like FORTRAN, BASIC, and Pascal, C combines the virtues of high-level programming languages with the efficiency of an assembly language.

The program's syntax encourages the creation of well-structured programs using modern control structures. At the same time, the programmer can embed instructions that directly address the processor's internal management of individual data bits. Because these instructions perform computations at the processing unit's highest speed, compiled C programs run significantly faster than programs written in other high-level programming languages. You can think of C, in fact, as a modular and structured framework for the expression of assembly language instructions. The framework of the program expresses the algorithm for the application; the assembly language instructions reach the bit-by-bit representation of data inside the processing unit to enhance the speed and efficiency of the program's operations.

Assembly language programs usually are not portable to other processing environments because assembly language programs are tied to a specific processing unit's design. A C program is rewritten easily and quickly so that the program runs on a new computer, if the target environment has a C compiler. The language's portability is an important factor in its widespread adoption by professional programmers, who hope to find the widest possible market for their products. The portability of C is evident in UNIX. This operating system (also developed at Bell Laboratories) was written in C and is portable across all processor architectures. Most UNIX systems include C compilers. See *algorithm, assembly language, control structure, high-level programming language, portable computer, procedural language, syntax,* and *UNIX.*

C++ A high-level programming language developed by AT&T's Bell Laboratories. Based on its predecessor, C, C++ is an object-oriented programming language that combines the benefits of C with the modularity of object-oriented programming. The language has been chosen by several large software publishers for major development projects. See *C* and *object-oriented programming language.*

cache controller Pronounced "cash." A hard disk controller that includes its own disk cache memory. The cache memory stores frequently accessed program instructions and data in random-access memory (RAM) chips, which your computer can access much faster than it can access the disk. See *disk cache* and *disk drive controller.*

cache memory Pronounced "cash." A special fast section of random-access memory (RAM) set aside to store the most frequently accessed information stored in RAM.

A cache memory is a special section of ultra-fast RAM chips (such as static RAM chips). This section is controlled by a cache controller chip, such as the Intel 82385. Cache memory dramatically improves the speed of a computer because the microprocessor need not wait for the slower dynamic random-access memory chips (DRAM) to catch up. With a cache memory and cache controller, even a fast 80386 microprocessor can operate without wait states. Cache memory is distinguished from a disk cache, an area of ordinary RAM set aside to store information frequently accessed from disk drives. See *disk cache, static random-access memory (RAM),* and *wait state.*

CAD See *computer-aided design (CAD).*

CADD See *computer-aided design and drafting (CADD).*

CAI See *computer-aided instruction (CAI)*.

calculated field In a database management program, a data field that contains the results of calculations performed on other fields. Synonymous with *derived field*. See *data field* and *field*.

call In programming, a statement that directs the flow of program control to a subroutine, procedure, or function.

camera-ready copy A printed and finished manuscript or illustration ready to be photographed by the printer for reproduction.

cancel button In the industry-standard and graphical user interfaces, a pushbutton in a dialog box that the user can activate to cancel a command and return to the active document.

→ **Tip:** With most programs, you can activate the cancel button by pressing Esc. See *pushbutton*.

Caps Lock key A toggle key that locks the keyboard so that uppercase letters are entered without you pressing the Shift key.

Some keyboards have a light that shows when you toggle the keyboard into the uppercase mode. If the keyboard has no light, you must look at what you are typing before you know which mode you have selected. Some programs display a message when you are in uppercase mode.

▲ **Caution:** Unlike the Caps Lock key of a typewriter, the keyboard's Caps Lock key has no effect on the number and punctuation keys. To use the punctuation marks on the row of number keys, you must press Shift whether or not you have pressed Caps Lock.

card An electronic circuit board designed to fit into the slots of a computer's expansion bus. Synonymous with *adapter*. See *expansion bus*.

caret A symbol (^) commonly found over the 6 key on computer keyboards. The caret sometimes is used to stand for the Ctrl key in computer documentation, as in "Press ^C."

carpal tunnel syndrome   See *repetitive strain injury (RSI)*.

carriage return   See *Enter/Return*.

carrier sense multiple access with collision detect (CSMA/CD)
In local area networks, a widely used method for controlling a computer's access to the communication channel. With CSMA/CD,
each component of the network (called a node) has an equal right
to access the communication channel. If two computers try to access
the network at the same time (an unlikely occurrence), the network
uses a random number to decide which computer gets on to the network.

 This channel access method works well with relatively small- to
medium-sized networks (two or three dozen nodes). This method
is used by the two most popular network architectures: EtherNet
and AppleTalk. When you have many workstations, and network
traffic volume is high, however, many data collisions occur. The entire system can become overloaded and lock up, with each station
behaving as if it is trying to access the system and failing because
the system is in use. Large networks, therefore, use alternative
channel access methods, such as polling and token passing. See *AppleTalk, EtherNet, local area network (LAN), node, polling,* and *token passing*.

cartridge   In secondary storage, a removable module containing secondary storage media such as magnetic tape and magnetic disks. In
computer printers, a removable module that expands the printer's
memory or font capabilities.

cartridge font   A printer font supplied in the form of a read-only
memory (ROM) cartridge that plugs into a receptacle on Hewlett-
Packard LaserJet printers and clones.

 Hewlett-Packard LaserJet printers rely heavily on cartridge fonts
that have some merits over their chief competition, downloadable
fonts. Unlike downloadable fonts, the ROM-based cartridge font is
immediately available to the printer and does not consume space in
the printer's random-access memory (RAM), which can be used up

quickly when printing documents loaded with graphics. See *font* and *typeface*.

cascading windows   In applications capable of displaying more than one on-screen window, a method of arranging windows so that they overlap with only the title bars of the hidden windows showing.

case-sensitive   Responsive to the difference between upper- and lowercase letters. DOS is not case-sensitive; you can type DOS commands in upper- or lowercase letters.

case-sensitive search   A search in which the program attempts to match the exact pattern of upper- and lowercase letters in the search string. A case-sensitive search for Porter, for example, matches Porter but not PORTER, porter, or pOrter.

catalog   In dBASE, a list of related database files you have grouped together so that they are distinguished easily from others.

Like all relational database management programs, dBASE can work with more than one file at a time. Frequently, the results of relational operations (such as a join) produce a new file. In addition, you create several indexes and other files that support the application. The Catalog menu helps you track all these related files in a unit. See *dBASE, join*, and *relational database management system (RDBMS)*.

cathode ray tube (CRT)   A computer monitor that uses an electron gun (cathode) to emit a beam of electrons that paint the phosphors on the screen as the beam sweeps across.

CBT   See *computer-based training (CBT)*.

CDEV   See *control panel device (CDEV)*.

CD-ROM   Pronounced "see dee rahm'." A read-only optical storage technology that uses compact discs.

CD-ROM disks can store up to 650M of data, all of which can be made available interactively on the computer's display. CD-ROM currently is used to produce encyclopedias, dictionaries, and software libraries available to personal computer users. New compression techniques enable you to pack up to 250,000 text pages on one CD-ROM disk. See *compact disc (CD)* and *optical disk*.

CD-ROM disk drive A read-only disk drive designed to access and read the data encoded on compact discs and to transfer this data to a computer.

With audio compact disc players selling for as little as $99, personal computer users often are appalled at the high price of CD-ROM drives. The two devices, however, are dissimilar. A CD-ROM disk drive contains circuitry optimized to locate data at high speeds; CD players need to locate only the beginning of audio tracks, which they play sequentially. As the number of these drives increases, the prices of CD-ROM drives will drop to more reasonable levels. See *compact disc (CD)*.

cell In a spreadsheet, the rectangle formed by the intersection of a row and column. You can place constants, labels, or formulas in cells. See *constant, label,* and *formula*.

cell address In a spreadsheet, a code that identifies a cell's location on the worksheet by specifying the cell's row and column (A3, B9, C2, and so on). When used in a formula, the cell address becomes a cell reference. See *cell reference* and *formula*.

cell definition The actual contents of a cell in a spreadsheet, as displayed on the entry line.

The cell definition may differ from what is displayed in the worksheet. If you place a formula in the cell, the program displays the value generated by the formula rather than the formula itself. See *cell protection, entry line, formula,* and *value*.

cell format In a spreadsheet, the way the program displays values and labels on-screen.

You can format labels and values two ways: first, by choosing a global format that affects all the cells of a worksheet; second, by choosing a range format that affects one or more cells in a rectangular block. Label formats for character-based programs like Lotus 1-2-3 are limited to label alignment; graphics spreadsheets can use multiple typefaces and type sizes. Numeric formats include currency (dollar signs, commas, and two decimal places), fixed (user-specified number of decimal places), and general (all significant digits displayed). See *character-based program, current cell, global format, graphics spreadsheet, label, label alignment, numeric format, range format,* and *value.*

cell pointer   In Lotus 1-2-3, the rectangular highlight that indicates the location on-screen of the current cell, where values and labels appear after you type them and press Enter. Synonymous with *cursor.*

cell protection   In a spreadsheet program, a format applied to a cell, a range of cells, or an entire file. The format prevents you from altering the contents of protected cells.

cell reference   In a spreadsheet formula, a cell address that specifies the location of a value to be used to solve the formula. Cell references are the keys to a spreadsheet program's power and usefulness. A spreadsheet program would not be very useful if you had to write formulas with constants, such as $2+2$. Because formulas are not visible on the worksheet, you would have to edit the formula to perform the exploratory what-if recalculations that make spreadsheets useful. Using cell references instead of values, you write the formula as $B1+B2$. B1 and B2 are cell addresses. When used in a formula, they instruct the program to go to the named cell (such as B1) and to use the value appearing in that cell. If you want to change the constants, you don't have to edit the formula; you type a new constant in cell B1 or cell B2.

Cell references enable the user to create an intricate pattern of links among the cells in a worksheet. A cell reference also can refer to a cell containing a formula. The value produced by the formula is referenced. Because the formula may contain its own cell references to other cells, which can themselves contain formulas, the worksheet can contain an unbroken chain of mathematical links. A change made to any constant in such a worksheet affects intermediate values and, ultimately, the bottom line. See *cell address, constant, formula, recalculation, value,* and *what-if analysis.*

central mass storage   See *file server.*

central processing unit (CPU)   The computer's internal storage, processing, and control circuitry, including the arithmetic-logic unit (ALU), the control unit, and the primary storage.

   Only the ALU and control unit are wholly contained on the microprocessor chip; the primary storage is elsewhere on the motherboard or an adapter on the expansion bus. See *adapter, arithmetic/logic unit (ALU), control unit, expansion bus, microprocessor, motherboard,* and *primary storage.*

CGA   See *Color Graphics Adapter (CGA).*

CGM   See *Computer Graphics Metafile (CGM).*

channel access   In local area networks, the method used to gain access to the data communication channel that links the computers. Three common methods are contention, polling, and token ring. See *contention, local area network (LAN), polling,* and *token-ring network.*

character   Any letter, number, punctuation mark, or symbol that can be produced on-screen by pressing a key.

character-based program   In IBM PC-compatible computing, a program that relies on the IBM PC's built-in character set and block graphics rather than taking advantage of a windowing environment to display on-screen fonts and bit-mapped graphics. See *Lotus 1-2-3, Microsoft Windows,* and *windowing environment.*

character-mapped display   A method of displaying characters in which a special section of memory is set aside to represent the display; programs generate a display by inserting characters into the memory-based representation of the screen. The whole screen, therefore, remains active, not just one line, and the user or the program can modify characters anywhere on-screen. See *teletype (TTY) display*.

character mode   In IBM and IBM-compatible computers, a display adapter mode in which the computer displays only those characters contained in its built-in character set. Synonymous with text mode. See *character set, character view,* and *graphics mode*.

character set   The fixed set of keyboard codes that a particular computer system uses. See *American Standard Code for Information Interchange (ASCII), code page,* and *extended character set*.

characters per inch (cpi)   The number of characters that fit within a linear inch in a given font. Standard units drawn from typewriting are pica (10 cpi) and elite (12 cpi).

characters per second (cps)   A measurement of the speed of a communications or printing device.

character view   In some non-Windows DOS applications, a mode in which the program switches the display adapter circuitry to its character mode. In the character mode, the computer is capable of displaying only those characters that are contained in the computer's built-in character set. See *character mode* and *graphics view*.

check box   In the industry-standard or graphical user interfaces, a square box that appears in a dialog box and that you choose to toggle an option on or off. When the option is turned on, an "X" appears in the check box. A check box may appear alone or with other check boxes in a list of items. Unlike radio buttons, you can choose more than one check box.

     → **Tip:** In IBM applications that employ dialog boxes, you usually can toggle a check box on or off in three ways. If the option has a boldfaced letter, such as **R**eplace without Confirmation, you can

hold down the Alt key and press the option's boldfaced letter
(Alt-C). You also can position the cursor in the check box and press
the space bar. If you have a mouse, you place the pointer in the
check box and click the button. See *industry-standard user interface, graphical user interface (GUI), dialog box,* and *radio button.*

checksum   In data communications, an error-checking technique in
which the number of bits in a unit of data is summed and transmitted
along with the data. The receiving computer then checks the sum.

   If the sum differs, an error probably occurred in transmission. A
commonly used personal computer communications protocol called
XMODEM uses the checksum technique. See *XMODEM.*

chip   A miniaturized electronic circuit mass-produced on a tiny chip
or wafer of silicon.

   The electronic age began in earnest with the 1947 invention of the
transistor, a switching and amplifying device that replaces huge,
power-hungry, and unreliable vacuum tubes. As important as the
transistor was, it did not solve the biggest problem facing any firm
that wanted to manufacture complex electronic components: the ne-
cessity of wiring all those components together.

   Various automated procedures were devised, but in the end, at
least some of the wiring and soldering had to be done manually.
Complex electronic devices, therefore, were very expensive.

   In the late 1950s, Jack Kilby (an engineer at Texas Instruments)
and Robert Noyce (an engineer at Fairchild Semiconductor) discovered that they could create an integrated circuit, a chip made out of
semiconducting materials that could duplicate the function of several transistors and other electronic components.

   Semiconductors, materials such as silicon, can be chemically altered in a process called doping so that their conductive properties
are improved or reduced. By doping a chip of silicon in a series of
layers, each with differing conductive properties, the equivalent of
one or more transistors can be created.

   The first integrated circuits contained only a few components, but
an impressive and sustained drive of technological development cre-

ated chips containing thousands, tens of thousands, and more components on one tiny chip. The same techniques now can generate 16 million components on a chip so tiny that it can be placed on the tip of your finger.

Of even greater economic and social significance than the chip's miniaturization is the fact that it can be mass-produced. After a chip is designed, the circuit pattern is transferred to a series of lithographic plates called photomasks. The photomasks then are used to coat the chip with materials that, when exposed to light, lay down a pattern of hardened and unhardened areas. Acid is applied to etch out the unhardened areas, and then chemicals are forced into these areas to alter the silicon's conductive properties.

Through multiple applications of the photomask, a chip with several layers of silicon with varying conductive properties is created, and the result is the equivalent of a complex electronic circuit. The process is largely automated, and chips can be produced at low prices.

Today's Intel 80486 microprocessor, for example, sells for a few hundred dollars, but this microprocessor is the electronic equivalent of a mainframe computer priced at several million dollars just 20 years ago. The achievement of chip-manufacturing technology has made possible the diffusion of computer technology throughout society.

Memory chips and microprocessors are the two chips most applicable to user's needs, but many kinds of special-purpose chips are manufactured for a variety of applications. These chips include microprocessor support chips, chips for the control of disk drives, and chips for generating video displays. See *integrated circuit* and *microprocessor*.

choose In a program that uses menus and dialog boxes, to pick an option that begins an action.

Highlighting an option is often different from *choosing* it. In many programs, you can use the arrow keys to highlight a menu option without choosing it. To choose the highlighted option, you press Enter.

> **→ Tip:** If you use a mouse, investigate the ways you can save time by double-clicking an option. In many applications, double-clicking an option highlights and chooses it in one quick action. To double-click the mouse, you press the button twice in rapid succession.

circular reference   In a spreadsheet, an error condition caused by two or more formulas referencing each other. For example, a circular reference occurs when the formula +B5 is placed in cell A1 and the formula +A1 is placed in cell B5.

Circular references do not always result in errors. They can be used deliberately, for example, to create an iterative function in a spreadsheet: each recalculation increases the values of the two formulas. However, circular references frequently arise from unintentional typing errors. Unintended circular references may produce erroneous results.

> **→ Tip:** If you see an error message informing you that a circular reference exists in your worksheet, track down the circular reference. Eliminate any unwanted circular references before placing confidence in the spreadsheet's accuracy.

circuit board   A flat plastic board on which electrically conductive circuits have been laminated. Synonymous with *printed circuit board*. See *adapter* and *motherboard*.

CISC   See *complex instruction set computer (CISC)*.

clear   To remove a document or other work from the computer's random-access memory (RAM) so that you can start with a fresh, blank workspace. Synonymous with *abandon*.

click   To press and quickly release a mouse button.

client   In a local area network, a workstation with processing capabilities, such as a personal computer, that can request information or applications from the network's file server. See *client-server network, file server,* and *local area network (LAN)*.

client-based application   In a local area network, an application that resides on a personal computer workstation and is not available for use by others on the network.

    Client-based applications do not make sharing common data easy, but they are resistant to the system-wide failure that occurs when a server-based application becomes unavailable after the file server crashes. See *client-server network, file server, local area network (LAN),* and *server-based application*.

client/server architecture   A design model for applications running on a local area network, in which the bulk of the back-end processing, such as performing a physical search of a database, takes place on the file server. The front-end processing, which involves communicating with the user, is handled by smaller programs distributed to the client workstations. See *local area network (LAN)*.

client-server network   A method of allocating resources in a local area network so that computing power is distributed among the personal computers in the network, but some shared resources are centralized in a file server. See *file server* and *peer-to-peer network*.

clip art   A collection of graphics images, stored on disk and available for use in a page layout or presentation graphics program.

    The term clip art is derived from graphics design tradition; portfolios of printed clip art are sold and actually clipped out by layout artists to enhance newsletters, brochures, and presentation graphics. Now available on disk, clip art collections can be read by most page layout or presentation graphics programs.

clipboard   In a windowing environment such as Microsoft Windows or the Macintosh Finder, a temporary storage area in memory where text and/or graphics are stored as you copy or move them.

clock   An electronic circuit that generates evenly spaced pulses at speeds of millions of cycles per second; the pulses are used to synchronize the flow of information through the computer's internal communication channels.

Some computers also contain a circuit that tracks hours, minutes, and seconds. See *clock speed* and *clock/calendar board*.

clock/calendar board   An adapter that includes a battery-powered clock for tracking the system time and date and is used in computers that lack such facilities on their motherboards. See *adapter* and *motherboard*.

clock speed   The speed of the internal clock of a microprocessor that sets the pace (measured in megahertz [MHz]) at which operations proceed within the computer's internal processing circuitry.

Each successive model of microprocessor has produced a faster clock speed. The original microprocessor of IBM Personal Computers, the Intel 8088, operated at a speed of 4.77 MHz. The chip powering the original IBM Personal Computer AT, the Intel 80286, operated at 6 MHz, with more recent versions operating at up to 25 MHz. The Intel 80386 microprocessor operates at speeds ranging from 16 to 33 MHz.

Clock speed affects performance but is not the only determinant. Faster clock speeds bring noticeable gains in CPU-intensive tasks, such as recalculating a spreadsheet. Disk-intensive application programs perform slowly, however, if the disk drives are sluggish. See *Intel 8088, Intel 80286,* and *Intel 80386*.

clone   A functional copy of a hardware device, such as a non-IBM PC-compatible computer that runs software and uses peripherals intended for an IBM PC-compatible computer, or of a program, such as a spreadsheet program that reads Lotus 1-2-3 files and recognizes most or all of the commands.

close   In a program that can display more than one document window, to remove a window from the display.

▲ **Caution:** In many applications, you must save your work before you close a window. If you haven't saved your work, the program probably will display an alert box warning you to save. To abandon your work, confirm that you don't want to save the document. See *document window*.

closed bus system A computer design in which the computer's internal data bus does not contain receptacles and is not easily upgraded by users. See *open bus system*.

cluster In a floppy disk or hard disk, a unit of storage that includes one or more sectors.

When DOS stores a file on disk, DOS breaks down the file's contents and distributes them among dozens or even hundreds of clusters drawn from hither and thither all over the disk. The file allocation table (FAT) tracks how all the sectors on a disk are connected. See *file allocation table (FAT)*, *file fragmentation*, and *sector*.

CMOS See *Complementary Metal-Oxide Semiconductor (CMOS)*.

coaxial cable In local area networks, a high-bandwidth connecting cable in which an insulated wire runs through the middle of the cable. Surrounding the insulated wire is a second wire made of solid or mesh metal.

Coaxial cable is much more expensive than twisted-pair cable (ordinary telephone wire), but coaxial cable can carry more data. Coaxial cables are required for high-bandwidth broadband systems and for fast baseband systems such as EtherNet. See *bandwidth*, *broadband*, *local area network (LAN)*, and *twisted pair cable*.

COBOL Pronounced "co'-ball." A high-level programming language specially designed for business applications.

Short for COmmon Business Oriented Language, COBOL is a compiled language that originated in a 1959 committee representing business, government, defense, and academic organizations. Released in 1964, the language was the first to introduce the data record as a principal data structure. Because COBOL is designed to store, retrieve, and process corporate accounting information and to automate such functions as inventory control, billing, and payroll, the language quickly became the language of choice in businesses. COBOL programs are verbose but easy to read because most commands resemble English. The programmer, therefore, hardly can help documenting the program, and program maintenance and enhancement are easy even if personnel change frequently. COBOL is the most widely used programming language in corporate mainframe environments.

Versions of COBOL are available for personal computers, but the language's strengths for corporate computing are of little relevance to stand-alone workstations. Business applications for personal computers far more frequently are created and maintained in the dBASE command language that taps the flexible data record capabilities of this popular database management system. See *dBASE* and *high-level programming language*.

code   To express a problem-solving algorithm in a programming language. See *algorithm*.

code page   In DOS and OS/2, a table of 256 codes for an IBM PC-compatible computer's character set.

Code pages are classed as two kinds:

- Hardware code page, the character set built into the computer's ROM
- Prepared code page, a disk-based character set you can use to override the hardware code page

Prepared code pages contain character sets appropriate for foreign languages. (Supported by DOS 4.0, for example, are Canadian French, Danish, Finnish, French, German, Italian, Latin American Spanish, Dutch, Norwegian, Portuguese, Peninsular Spanish, U.K. English, and U.S. English.) To override the hardware code page, use the CHANGE CODE PAGE (CHCP) command. See *character set*.

cold boot   A system start-up initiated by turning on the system's power switch. See *boot* and *warm boot*.

cold link   A method of copying information from one document (the source document) to another (the target document) so that the link can be updated. To update the link, you choose a command that opens the source document, reads the information, and recopies the information if it has changed. See *hot link, dynamic data exchange (DDE), inter-application communication (IAC),* and *System 7.*

collate   Pronounced "co'-late." Synonymous with *sort.*

collating sequence   See *sort order.*

collision   In local area networks, a garbled transmission that results from simultaneous transmissions by two or more workstations to the same network cable. See *local area network (LAN).*

Color Graphics Adapter (CGA)   A bit-mapped graphics display adapter for IBM PC-compatible computers. This adapter displays four colors simultaneously with a resolution of 200 pixels horizontally and 320 pixels vertically or displays one color with a resolution of 640 pixels horizontally and 200 vertically.

   CGAs can drive composite color monitors and RGB monitors, but screen resolution produced by CGA adapters is inferior to that of EGA and VGA adapters. See *bit-mapped graphic, composite color monitor, Enhanced Graphics Adapter (EGA), RGB monitor,* and *Video Graphics Array (VGA).*

color monitor   A computer display device that can display an image in multiple colors, unlike a monochrome monitor that displays one color on a black or white background.

color separation   The creation of a multicolor graphic by creating several layers, with each layer corresponding to one of the colors that will be printed when the graphic is reproduced by a professional printer.

column   In character-based video displays, a vertical one-character-wide line down the screen. In a spreadsheet, a vertical block of cells, identified (in most programs) by a unique alphabetical letter.

In a database management program, *column* is sometimes used synonymously with *field*.

column graph   In presentation and analytical graphics, a graph with vertical columns. Column graphs commonly are used to show the values of items as they vary at precise intervals over a period of time. The x-axis (categories axis) is the horizontal axis, and the y-axis (values axis) is the vertical axis.

Technically, bar graph refers only to graphs with horizontal bars; if the bars are vertical, the graph is a column graph. In practice, however, bar graph is used to name both types. In presentation graphics, bar graphs are used to display the values of discrete items (apples, oranges, grapefruit, and papaya), and column graphs are used to show the change in one or more items over time (for example, apples vs. oranges in January, February, March, and so on).

Column graphs also should be differentiated from line graphs, which suggest a continuous change over time. Column graphs suggest that the information was obtained at intervals. In this sense, column graphs are more honest than line graphs in some cases, because a line graph suggests that you are making data observations all along instead of once a month or once every two weeks.

When displaying more than one data series, clustering the columns or overlapping them is helpful. With caution, you also can create a three-dimensional effect to differentiate the columns, if it really helps clarify the data. See *bar graph, line graph, histogram, stacked column graph, x-axis,* and *y-axis.*

column indicator   In word processing programs, an on-screen status message that shows the current number of horizontal spaces, or columns, the cursor has moved across the screen.

column text chart   In presentation graphics, a text chart used to show related text items side-by-side in two or three columns.

column-wise recalculation   In spreadsheet programs, a recalculation order that calculates all the values in column A before moving to column B, and so on.

▲ **Caution:** If your spreadsheet program does not offer natural recalculation, use column-wise recalculation for worksheets in which columns are summed and the totals are forwarded. Row-wise recalculation may produce an erroneous result. See *natural recalculation, optimal recalculation,* and *row-wise recalculation.*

COM In DOS and OS/2, a code that refers to a serial port. You use this code in commands like MODE, which configures the communications parameters of a serial port. The code COM1:, for example, refers to the system's first serial port. See *communications parameters* and *serial port.*

COM file In DOS and OS/2, an executable program file designed to operate in a specific part of the base memory.

comma-delimited file A data file, usually in ASCII file format, in which the data items have been separated by commas. See *American Standard Code for Information Interchange (ASCII), file format,* and *tab-delimited file.*

command A user-initiated signal given to a computer program that initiates, terminates, or otherwise controls the execution of a specific operation.

In command-driven programs, the user must memorize the command statement and its associated syntax and type the command. In a menu-driven program, the user chooses a command from an on-screen menu. See *command-driven program, graphical user interface (GUI),* and *menu-driven program.*

COMMAND.COM In DOS, an essential system disk file that contains the command processor. This file must be present on the start-up disk for DOS to run.

command-driven program A system, utility, or application program that requires you to memorize keyboard commands and to rely on your memory to type command statements with the correct syntax and nomenclature. See *graphical user interface (GUI)* and *menu-driven program*.

command language   See *software command language*.

command-line operating system   A command-driven operating system, such as DOS, that requires you to type commands at the keyboard.

command processor   The portion of a command-line operating system that handles user input and displays messages, such as prompts, confirmation messages, and error messages. See *command-line operating system*.

comment   See *remark*.

communications parameters   In telecommunications and serial printing, the settings (parameters) that customize serial communications for the hardware you are contacting. See *baud rate, communications protocol, full duplex, half duplex, parameter, parity bit*, and *stop bit*.

communications program   An application program that turns your computer into a terminal for transmitting data to and receiving data from distant computers through the telephone system.

A good communications program includes a software command language that you can use to automate cumbersome log-on procedures, the support of two or more file-transfer protocols (such as Xmodem and Kermit), terminal emulation of two or more popular mainframe terminals (such as the DEC VT100), and on-screen timing so that you can keep track of time charges and facilities for storing and retrieving telephone numbers.

communications protocol   A list of communications parameters (settings) and standards that govern the transfer of information among computers using telecommunications. Both computers must have the same settings and follow the same standards to avoid errors.

When you use a modem to access a bulletin board or information service, such as CompuServe, you must choose the correct communications protocol—the one established by the host computer system. Your communications program enables you to choose the necessary parameters, including baud rate, data bits, duplex, parity, and stop bits. The baud rate usually is determined by your modem's capabilities. Most communications services use eight data bits and one stop bit; full duplex is also common. Before you attempt to establish communication with an on-line service, read the documentation to find out which communications parameters to use. The settings are displayed prominently at the beginning of the documentation.

You may have to specify an additional parameter called handshaking. This parameter establishes the way one computer tells the other device when to wait. Almost all computers and many peripheral devices use XON/XOFF handshaking, the default for most communications programs. See *asynchronous communication, baud rate, communications parameters, communications program, file transfer protocol, handshaking, mode, modem, parity, stop bit,* and *terminal emulation*.

communications settings   See *communications parameters* and *communications protocol*.

compact disc (CD)   A plastic disk, 4.75 inches in diameter, that uses optical storage techniques to store up to 72 minutes of music or 650M of digitally encoded computer data.

In an optical storage medium, digital data is stored as microscopic pits and smooth areas with different reflective properties. A precisely controlled beam of laser light shines on the disk so that the reflections can be detected and translated into digital data.

Compact discs provide read-only secondary storage. The computer can read information from the disk, but you cannot change this information or write new information to the disk. Therefore, this storage medium accurately is termed CD-ROM (read-only memory). Erasable optical disk drives are now available and are expected to have a major impact on secondary storage techniques in the 1990s. In the meantime, however, compact discs are expected to become popular for the distribution of huge databases to personal computer users who have systems equipped with CD-ROM disk drives. Currently, the disks tend to be very expensive because the market is small, but as CD-ROM disk drives become available at lower prices, the price of the disks also should drop. The average computer user eventually may work with a system capable of displaying, in an on-screen window, the contents of huge databases, such as the complete works of William Shakespeare or the *Encyclopedia of Science and Technology.* See *CD-ROM disk drive, erasable optical disk drive, optical disk,* and *secondary storage.*

company network   A wide-area computer network, such as DEC ENET (the internal engineering network of Digital Equipment Corporation), that often has automatic gateways to cooperative networks such as ARPANET or BITNET for functions such as electronic mail and file transfer.

comparison operator   See *relational operator.*

compatibility   The capability of a peripheral, a program, or an adapter to function with or substitute for a given make and model of computer. Also, the capability of one computer to run the software of another company's computer.

▲ **Caution:** To be truly compatible, a program or device should operate on a given system without modification; all features should operate as intended, and a computer claiming to be compatible with another should run all the other computer's software without modification.

→ **Tip:** In IBM PC-compatible computing, a frequently used index of 100-percent IBM compatibility is a computer's capability to run Microsoft Flight Simulator. See *clone.*

compiler   A program that reads the statements written in a human-readable programming language, such as Pascal or Modula-2, and translates the statements into a machine-readable executable program.

Compiled programs run significantly faster than interpreted ones because the entire program has been translated into machine language and need not share memory space with the interpreter. See *interpreter* and *machine language*.

Complementary Metal-Oxide Semiconductor (CMOS)   A chip fabricated to duplicate the functions of other chips, such as memory chips or microprocessors. A CMOS chip draws less power.

CMOS chips are used in battery-powered portable computers. See *chip*.

complex instruction set computer (CISC)   A central processing unit (CPU) that can recognize as many as 100 or more instructions, enough to carry out most computations directly.

Most microprocessors are CISC chips. The use of RISC technology is becoming increasingly common, however, in professional workstations and is expected to migrate to personal computers in the early 1990s. See *central processing unit (CPU)* and *reduced instruction set computer (RISC)*.

composite color monitor   A monitor that accepts a standard analog video signal that mixes red, green, and blue signals to produce the color image.

The composite video standard of the National Television Standards Committee uses a standard RCA-type connector, found on the Color Graphics Adapter (CGA). Display quality is inferior to that of RGB monitors. See *RGB monitor*.

composite video   A standard for video signals in which the red, green, and blue signals are mixed together.

The standard, regulated by the U.S. National Television Standards Committee (NTSC), is used for television. Some computers have composite video outputs that use a standard RCA phono plug and cable such as on the backplane of a high-fidelity system. See *composite color monitor* and *RGB monitor*.

compressed file A file that a file compression utility has written to a special disk format that minimizes the storage space required. See *file compression utility.*

CompuServe The largest and most successful personal computer information service.

Essentially a for-profit version of a bulletin board system (BBS) coupled with the resources of an on-line information service, CompuServe offers file downloading, electronic mail, current news, up-to-the-minute stock quotes, an on-line encyclopedia, and conferences on a variety of topics. However, the character-based command-line user interface is technically antiquated and challenging to novice users. If you are interested in using CompuServe, consider using a front-end program like CompuServe Navigator. See *bulletin board system (BBS), on-line information service,* and *Prodigy.*

computation The successful execution of an algorithm whose steps are finite, executable, and capable of termination. A computation is not only a numerical operation; a successfully completed textual search or sort also is a computation. See *algorithm.*

computer A machine capable of following instructions to alter data in a desirable way and to perform at least some of these operations without human intervention.

Do not think that computers are devices for performing only calculations, although that function is one of many computer tasks. Computers represent and manipulate text, graphics, symbols, and music, as well as numbers. See *analog computer* and *digital computer.*

computer-aided design (CAD) The use of the computer and a computer-aided design program as the environment for the design of a wide range of industrial artifacts, ranging from machine parts to modern homes.

CAD has become a mainstay in a variety of design-related fields, such as architecture, civil engineering, electrical engineering, mechanical engineering, and interior design. But, computer-aided design has been dominated until recently by expensive dedicated minicomputer systems. CAD applications are graphics and calculation-intensive, requiring fast processors and high-resolution video displays. CAD programs often include sophisticated statistical analysis routines that help designers optimize their applications, as well as extensive symbol libraries. All these features require huge amounts of processing power, and that requirement kept CAD off early personal computers.

Like many other professional computer applications based on expensive mainframe or minicomputer systems, however, CAD is migrating to powerful personal computers, such as those based on the Intel 80386 and Motorola 68030 microprocessors. CAD software for personal computers blends the object-oriented graphics found in draw programs with precision scaling in two and three dimensions. Drawings can be produced with an intricate level of detail. See *draw program, Intel 80386, Motorola 68030*, and *object-oriented graphic*.

computer-aided design and drafting (CADD)   Pronounced "cad." The use of a computer system for industrial design and technical drawing.

CADD software closely resembles computer-aided design (CAD) software but has additional features that enable the artist to produce drawings conforming to engineering conventions.

computer-assisted instruction (CAI)   The use of instructional programs to perform instructional tasks, such as drill and practice, tutorials, and tests.

computer-based training (CBT)   The use of computer-aided instruction (CAI) techniques to train adults for specific skills, such as operating a numerically controlled lathe.

Computer Graphics Metafile (CGM)   An international graphics file format that stores object-oriented graphics in device-independent form so that you can exchange CGM files among users of different systems (and different programs).

Personal computer programs that can read and write to CGM file formats include Harvard Graphics and Ventura Publisher. See *object-oriented graphic* and *Windows Metafile file format (WMF)*.

computer system   A complete computer installation—including peripherals, such as disk drives, a monitor, and a printer—in which all the components are designed to work with each other.

concatenation   Pronounced "con-cat′-uh-nay′-shun." The combination of two or more units of information, such as text or files, so that they form one unit.

concordance file   A file containing the words you want a word processing program to include in the index the program constructs.

concurrency control   In a LAN-aware, network version of an application program, the features built into the program that govern what happens when two or more people try to access the same program feature or data file.

Many application programs that are not designed for networks can run on a network and enable more than one person to access a document, but the results may be catastrophic: nothing prevents one person from inadvertently destroying another person's work. Concurrency control addresses this problem by enabling multiple access where such access can occur without loss of data and by restricting multiple access where such access could result in destroyed work. See *file locking, LAN-aware program,* and *LAN-ignorant program*.

concurrency management   The capability of an application written for use on a local area network (LAN) to ensure that data files are not corrupted by simultaneous modification or multiple input.

concurrent processing   See *multitasking*.

condensed type   Type narrowed in width so that more characters will fit into a linear inch. In dot-matrix printers, condensed type usually is set to print 17 characters per inch (cpi). See *characters per inch (cpi)*.

CONFIG.SYS   In DOS and OS/2, an ASCII text file that contains configuration commands.

DOS consults this file at system start-up. If no CONFIG.SYS file is on the start-up disk, DOS uses the default configuration values. Most programs work well with the default configuration settings. Nonstandard peripherals and some application programs, however, may require that a CONFIG.SYS file be present in the root directory so that these configurations are modified.

The following list is an overview of the configuration commands:

- DEVICE. Specifies the driver DOS requires to use a peripheral device. If you are using a mouse, for example, you need to create a CONFIG.SYS file with a statement such as DEVICE = MOUSE.SYS. The root directory must contain a file called MOUSE.SYS. If your mouse doesn't work, check to see whether you have erased CONFIG.SYS. If you recently installed another program, you may have erased your old CONFIG.SYS; you will have to put the DEVICE statement back into the file by using your word processing program.

  Some programs require you to place the following command in your configuration file: DEVICE = ANSI.SYS. ANSI is an acronym for American National Standards Institute, and the file ANSI.SYS (on every DOS disk) contains procedures for controlling the display of information. The file called ANSI.SYS must be present in the root directory.

- BUFFERS. Determines the number of areas DOS sets aside in memory to store disk data temporarily. The default setting varies with the version of DOS. Some application programs require you to specify more buffers than the DOS default number. You may need to

add a statement such as $BUFFERS = 15$ before these
programs will work.
- FILES. Determines the number of files that can be
open at the same time. The default setting is 8 files.

If the preceding material seems too technical, do not worry: the
peripherals and programs that require CONFIG.SYS statements
usually create them automatically when you follow the standard installation procedure. Knowing about these commands is worth-
while, however, especially if you accidentally erase CONFIG.SYS
or—as sometimes happens—if an installation program erases the
existing CONFIG.SYS and substitutes its own.

▲ **Caution:** If an application program you are using has written
a CONFIG.SYS file to your start-up disk, do not erase the CON-
FIG.SYS file. If you do, the program may not run, or some features
may be disabled. If you erase CONFIG.SYS accidentally, repeat the
program's installation procedure. See *American National Standards Institute (ANSI), ANSI.SYS, American Standard Code for Information Interchange (ASCII), buffer, driver, mouse, peripheral,*
and *root directory.*

configuration   The choices made in setting up a computer system or
an application program so that it meets the user's needs.

Getting one's system or program configured properly is one of
the more onerous tasks of personal computing and, sad to say, it has
not been eliminated by the arrival of windowing environments.
Microsoft Windows 3.0, for example, is equipped with sophisticated installation software that analyzes your system's capabilities
and chooses an appropriate configuration, but often you must perform some manual configuration to obtain maximum performance
from Windows and to take full advantage of the memory available
on your system. Along the way, you are obliged to distinguish among
upper memory, high memory, extended memory, and expanded
memory, in addition to the usual kinds of memory: memory, more
memory, and not enough memory.

Once established, the configuration is saved to a configuration file, where it is vulnerable to accidental erasure. Windows, for example, stores the user's configuration choices in a file called WIN.INI, which you should be very careful not to erase. In addition to creating configuration files, programs also frequently perform surreptitious modifications to AUTOEXEC.BAT and CONFIG.SYS, the two files that DOS consults when you start your system. If you delete these files, your system may not perform as you expect, and applications—if they run at all—may revert to their preconfigured states or prevent you from choosing certain commands.

configuration file A file, created by an application program, that stores the choices you make when you install the program so that they are available the next time you start the program. In Microsoft Word, for example, the file MW.INI stores the choices you make from the Options menu.

confirmation message An on-screen message asking you to confirm a potentially destructive action, such as closing a window without saving your work. See *alert box*.

connectivity The extent to which a given computer or program can function in a network setting.

connectivity platform A program or utility designed to enhance another program's capability to exchange data with other programs through a local area network. Oracle for the Macintosh, for example, provides HyperCard with the connectivity required to search for and retrieve information from large corporate databases. See *HyperCard* and *local area network (LAN)*.

console A display terminal, consisting of a monitor and keyboard.
   In multiuser systems, console is synonymous with terminal, but console also is used in personal computer operating systems to refer to the keyboard and display.

constant In a spreadsheet program, a number you type directly into a cell or place in a formula.

You see two kinds of numbers in a worksheet's cells. Constants are numbers you type on the entry line. These numbers do not change unless you edit the cell contents or type a new value in the cell. The second kind of number is the value produced by a hidden formula. You cannot tell the difference between a constant and a value produced by a formula just by looking at the worksheet. If you place the pointer on the cell, however, the actual cell definition—including a formula if present—appears on the entry line.

▲ **Caution:** If you type a constant in a cell with a value produced by a formula, you erase the formula in the cell. This mistake is a common cause of major errors in spreadsheet calculations.

→ **Tip:** You should avoid entering constants in formulas. Suppose that you have created a worksheet in which each column computes a commission of 5 percent. You enter this constant into 15 formulas. If you decide to compute the commission at 6 percent, you must change all 15 formulas.

A better solution is to place the constant in one cell, called a key, and place this cell at the top of the worksheet. You then reference this cell in the formulas. This way, you make only one change instead of 15 if you change the constant. See *cell definition* and *key variable*.

contention In local area networks, a channel access method in which access to the communication channel is based on a first-come, first-served policy. See *carrier sense multiple access with collision detect (CSMA/CD)*.

context switching The immediate activation of a program loaded into random-access memory (RAM) along with one or more other programs in a multiple loading operating system.

Unlike true multitasking, a multiple loading operating system, such as the Macintosh system equipped with MultiFinder, enables you to load more than one program at a time, but while you are using the foreground program, the background program stops executing.

For a stand-alone computer, multiple loading operating systems provide a high level of functionality because you can switch rapidly from one program to another. When combined with a graphical user interface and cut-and-paste facilities provided by a clipboard, context switching enables you to move data rapidly and easily from one application to another. See *multiple program loading* and *multitasking*.

context-sensitive help In an application package, a user-assistance mode that displays on-screen documentation relevant to the command, mode, or action the user currently is performing.

Context-sensitive help is a desirable program feature because it reduces the time and keystrokes needed to get on-screen help. In WordPerfect, for example, if you press Help (F3) after pressing Format (Shift-F8), you see a help screen explaining the options available on the Format menu. Without context-sensitive help, you have to locate the desired information manually from an index or menu.

continuous paper Paper manufactured in one long strip, with perforations separating the pages, so that the paper can be fed into printer with a tractor-feed mechanism.

continuous tone An illustration, whether black-and-white or color, in which tones change smoothly and continuously from the darkest to the lightest, without noticeable gradations.

Control-Break In DOS and OS/2, a keyboard command that suspends the execution of a program at the next available break point.

control code In the American Standard Code for Information Interchange (ASCII), a code reserved for hardware-control purposes, such as advancing a page on the printer. There are 32 ASCII control codes.

Control (Ctrl) key In IBM PC-compatible computing, a key frequently pressed with other keys for program commands. In WordStar, for example, pressing Ctrl-Y deletes a line.

control menu   In Microsoft Windows, a pull-down menu found in most windows and dialog boxes that contains options for managing the active window. The control menu icon, shaped like a hyphen, is always on the left edge of the title bar. The contents of this menu vary, but usually include commands to move, size, maximize, and minimize windows, as well as to close the current window or switch to another application window or the next document window.

→ **Tip:** To display the control menu of an application window or a dialog box quickly, press Alt-spacebar. To open a document window's control menu, press Alt-hyphen.

control panel   1. In Lotus 1-2-3, the top three lines of the display screen. The top line contains the current cell indicator, the mode indicator, and the entry line. The second and third lines contain menus and prompts. 2. In the Macintosh, Windows, and OS/2 Presentation Manager, a utility menu that lists user options for hardware devices, such as the mouse, monitor, and keyboard.

control panel device (CDEV)   Pronounced "see-dev." A Macintosh utility program placed in the System Folder that appears as an option in the Control Panel.

control unit   A component of the central processing unit (CPU) that obtains program instructions and emits signals to carry them out. See *arithmetic/logic unit (ALU)* and *central processing unit (CPU)*.

controller   See *disk drive controller*.

controller card   An adapter that connects disk drives to the computer. Most personal computer controller cards contain circuitry to connect one or more floppy disks and hard disks. See *adapter*.

conventional memory   In any personal computer employing an Intel 8086, 8088, 80286, 80386, or 80486 microprocessor, the first 640K of the computer's random-access memory (RAM) that is accessible to programs running under DOS.

The Intel 8086 and 8088 microprocessors, which were available when the IBM Personal Computer (PC) was designed, can directly use one megabyte of random-access memory (RAM). The PC's designers decided to make 640K of RAM accessible to programs, leaving the rest of the 1 megabyte memory space available for internal system functions.

640K seemed like a lot of memory in the early 1980s—in fact, the figure was chosen because it was exactly 10 times the amount of memory available for the leading microcomputers of the time! 640K has since proved insufficient, however, because users frequently want to run more than one program at a time. For this reason, many users equip their systems with extended or expanded memory and with the programs (called extended memory managers or expanded memory managers) that are required to access this memory. See *expanded memory, expanded memory manager, extended memory, extended memory manager, high memory, Microsoft Windows, protected mode,* and *real mode.*

conventional programming   The use of a procedural programming language, such as BASIC, FORTRAN, or assembly language, to code an algorithm in machine-readable form.

In conventional programming, the programmer must be concerned with the sequence in which events occur within the computer. Nonprocedural programming languages enable the programmer to focus on the problem, without worrying about the precise procedure the computer must follow to solve the problem. See *declarative language* and *procedural language.*

coprocessor   A microprocessor support chip optimized for a specific processing operation, such as handling mathematical computations or displaying images on the video display. See *microprocessor* and *numeric coprocessor.*

copy   The text of a publication, exclusive of all graphics, before the text is formatted and laid out for publication.

copy editing   A rigorous and exact critique of copy to make sure that it conforms to the publisher's standards for facts, grammar, spelling, clarity, coherence, usage, and punctuation.

copy fitting   In desktop publishing, a method used to determine the amount of copy (text) that, using a specified font, will fit into a given area on a page or in a publication.

copy protection   The inclusion in a program of hidden instructions intended to prevent you from making unauthorized copies of software. Because most copy-protection schemes impose penalties on legitimate owners of programs, such as forcing them to insert a specially encoded key disk before using a program, most business software publishers have given up using these schemes. Copy protection is still common, however, in recreational and educational software.

corrupted file   A file that contains scrambled and unrecoverable data.

cost-benefit analysis   A projection of the costs and benefits of installing a computer system. The analysis compares the costs of operating an enterprise with and without the computer system and calculates the return (if any) on the original investment.

▲ **Caution:** Cost-benefit analyses often involve overly optimistic assumptions about the tangible cost savings of installing a computer system. A word processing program may enable you to revise a document faster, but the technology invites the user to keep working on the document until it is close to perfect, and the user may spend more time than he or she would have originally.

Computerization also may prove more costly than standard methods if the enterprise must carry out its business in an inefficient or unprofitable way. More than a few businesses have failed after installing expensive accounting and inventory systems that proved to be inflexible as the businesses' needs changed.

counter   In typography, the space enclosed by the fully or partially enclosed bowl of a letter. See *bowl*.

Courier   A monospace typeface, commonly included as a built-in font in laser printers, that simulates the output of office typewriters. For example: This is Courier type.

courseware   Software developed for computer-assisted instruction (CAI) or computer-based training (CBT) applications.

cpi   See *characters per inch (cpi)*.

CPM   See *critical-path method (CPM)*.

cps   See *characters per second (cps)*.

CPU   See *central processing unit (CPU)*.

crash   An abnormal termination of program execution, usually (but not always) resulting in a frozen keyboard or an unstable state. In most cases, you must reboot the computer to recover from a crash.

creator type   In the Macintosh, a four-letter code that identifies the application program used to create a document. The code associates the document with the application so that you can start the application by opening the document. Apple Computer maintains a registry of creator type codes so that no two applications use the same code. See *associated document*.

criteria range   In spreadsheet programs that include data management functions, the range that tells the program which records to retrieve from a database. The range contains the conditions you specify to govern how a search is conducted.

critical-path method (CPM)   In project management, a technique for planning and timing the execution of tasks that relies on the identification of a critical path—a series of tasks that must be completed in a timely fashion if the entire project is to be completed on time. Project management software helps the project manager identify the critical path.

cropping   A graphics editing operation in which edges are trimmed from a graphic to make it fit into a given space or to remove unnecessary parts of the image.

cross-hatching   The black-and-white patterns added to areas within a pie, bar, or column graph to distinguish one data range from another.

   ▲ **Caution:** The overuse of cross-hatching may negatively affect computer-generated graphics: Moiré vibrations, which result from visual interference between cross-hatching patterns. If your graph seems to flicker, reduce the cross-hatching. See *Moiré distortion*.

cross-linked files   In DOS, a file-storage error that occurs when two files claim the same disk cluster.

   Like lost clusters, cross-linked files occur when the computer is interrupted (by a system crash or a power outage) while it is writing a file. See *lost cluster*.

   → **Tip:** To repair cross-linked files, run CHKDSK frequently with the /F switch.

cross-reference   In word processing programs, a code name referring to material previously discussed in a document. When printed, the reference is changed so that the correct page number of this material appears in its place.

   Cross-references, such as "See the discussion of burnishing methods on page 19," are helpful to the reader, but they can become a nightmare if you add or delete text. Therefore, the best word processing programs (such as WordPerfect and Microsoft Word) contain cross-reference features. Instead of typing the cross-reference, you mark the original text and assign a code name to the marked text, such as BURNISH. Then you type the code name (not the page number) when you want to cross-reference the original text. When you print your document, the program substitutes the correct page number for the code name. If you discover after printing that you need to add or delete text, the code names are still there, and you can perform the edit and print again without worrying about the cross-references.

crosstalk The interference generated by cables that are too close to one another.

You sometimes hear crosstalk on the telephone. When speaking long-distance, hearing other voices or entire conversations in the background of your conversation is not uncommon.

Crosstalk A popular communications program developed by DCA/Crosstalk Communications for IBM PC-compatible computers.

CRT See *cathode ray tube (CRT)*.

CSMA/CD See *carrier sense multiple access with collision detection (CSMA/CD)*.

Ctrl See *Control (Ctrl) key*.

Ctrl-Break In DOS, a keyboard command that cancels the last command you gave.

cumulative trauma disorder See *repetitive strain injury (RSI)*.

current cell In a spreadsheet program such as Lotus 1-2-3, the cell in which the pointer is positioned. Synonymous with *active cell*.

current cell indicator In Lotus 1-2-3, a message that displays the address of the cell in which the pointer is positioned. If the cell has contents, the program also displays the cell format, its protection status, the column width, and the cell definition.

current directory The directory that DOS or an application uses to store and retrieve files.

Within an application, the current directory is usually the one from which you start that application program. Some programs, however, enable you to change the current directory so that you can save data files in a directory other than the one in which the program's files are stored. Synonymous with *default directory*.

current drive   The drive the operating system uses for an operation unless you specifically instruct otherwise. Synonymous with *default drive*.

current graph   In Lotus 1-2-3, the graph that the program creates when you choose /Graph View and retains in memory until you save the graph or quit the worksheet.

cursor   An on-screen blinking character that shows where the next character will appear. See *pointer*.

cursor-movement keys   The keys that move the on-screen cursor.

With most programs, the arrow keys on the numeric keypad move the cursor in the directions of the arrows. You can move the cursor one character left or right or one line up or down. Like the keys in the typing area, these keys are autorepeat keys. If you hold down the key, the cursor keeps moving in the direction indicated.

The newest keyboards often include a separate cursor keypad with keys that perform the same function as the arrow keys on the numeric keypad.

Some programs configure additional keys so that they move the cursor. These keys include Home, End, Tab, Shift-Tab, PgUp, and PgDn.

Cursor movement is distinguished from scrolling by some programs. The Macintosh version of Microsoft Word, for example, has scrolling commands that display a different portion of the document without moving the cursor. More commonly, however, scrolling commands move the cursor as well as display a different portion of the document. See *cursor-movement keys* and *scroll*.

cut and paste   See *block move*.

cut-sheet feeder   A paper-feed mechanism that feeds separate sheets of paper into the printer, where a friction-feed mechanism draws the paper through the printer.

You can purchase cut-sheet feeding mechanisms as optional accessories for dot-matrix and letter-quality printers, but they are standard equipment with laser printers and high-quality inkjet printers. See *friction feed* and *tractor feed mechanism*.

cyclic redundancy check (CRC)   In DOS, an automatic error-checking method in which the operating system performs a computation on the data stored in a disk sector and writes the result of the computation at the end of the sector. When the system reads the data from the file, the computation is performed again, and the result is compared to the value stored at the end of the sector. If the two values disagree, the operating system attempts to read the data again, which usually solves the problem. If you see an error such as "CRC ERROR READING DRIVE C," however, it signals serious problems with the disk. CRC checks are more commonly used by the file compression utilities (such as PKZIP) and for data communications error detection.

→ **Tip:** If DOS can't read a file due to a CRC error, don't give up hope. A disaster recovery program such as Diskfix (included with PC Tools) may be able to recover the file.

cylinder   In disk drives, a unit of storage consisting of the set of tracks that occupy the same position.

On a double-sided disk, a cylinder includes track 1 of the top and the bottom sides. On hard disks in which several disks are stacked on top of one another, a cylinder consists of the tracks in a specific location on all the disks.

d

daisy chain See *chain printing*.

daisywheel printer An impact printer that simulates the typescript produced by an office typewriter.

"Daisywheel" refers to the mechanism used to produce the printout; the characters are mounted in a circular pattern and connected to a hub with spokes, resembling a daisy. To produce a character, the printer spins the wheel until the desired character is in place. Then the printer strikes the inked ribbon with the character, transferring the image to paper. Because the daisywheels can be removed and replaced, these printers can print multiple typefaces.

However, changing fonts within a document is tedious because the daisywheel must be changed manually.

Once the ultimate in printing technology, daisywheel printers have all but disappeared from the market, due to the development of inexpensive laser printers. A laser printer can change fonts and typefaces within a document. See *impact printer*.

DASD Acronym for Direct Access Storage Device. A storage device such as a magnetic disk that can write anywhere on its surface.

data Factual information stored on magnetic media that can be used to generate calculations or to make decisions.

data communication The transfer of information from one computer to another.

The transfer can occur via direct cable connections, as in local area networks or via telecommunications links involving the telephone system and modems. See *local area network (LAN)* and *telecommunications*.

data deletion In a database management program, an operation that deletes records according to specified criteria.

Some database programs do not actually delete the records in such operations; they merely mark the records so that they are not included in data retrieval operations. Therefore, you usually can restore the deleted records if you make a mistake.

data dictionary   In a database management program, an on-screen listing of all the database files, indexes, views, and other files relevant to a database application.

data-encoding scheme   The technique a disk controller users to record bits of data on the magnetic surface of a floppy disk or hard disk. See *Advanced Run-Length Limited (ARLL)*, *Modified Frequency Modulation (MFM)*, and *Run-Length Limited (RLL)*.

data-entry form   In a database management program, an on-screen form that makes entering and editing data easier by displaying only one data record on-screen at a time. The data fields are listed vertically as in the following example:

TITLE	Barney, the Loyal Puppy
CATEGORY	Children
RATING	G
RENTED TO	325-1234
DUE DATE	12/31/90

dBASE, for example, displays a standard data-entry form when you add records. You also can create a custom data-entry form.

data field   In a database management program, a space for a specified piece of information in a data record. In a table-oriented database management program, in which all retrieval operations produce a table with rows and columns, data fields are displayed as vertical columns.

In the following example, the headings in all capital letters are the data field titles. The information typed into these fields is to the right of the headings.

TITLE	Harold, the Friendly Dinosaur
CATEGORY	Children
RATING	PG
RENTED TO	325-9178
DUE DATE	12/31/90

See *field definition,* and *table-oriented database management program.*

data file   A disk file containing the work you create with a program, unlike a program file that contains instructions for the computer.

data independence   In database management, the storage of data so that users can gain access to the data without knowing where the data is located.

Ideally, you should be able to say to the computer, "Give me information on Acme International." You should not have to say, "Go to record #1142 and match the text string Acme International." Many recent database management programs include command languages, called query languages, that enable you to phrase questions without worrying about the data's physical location. Even the best query languages require you to know some procedures, such as which database to search, but databases are evolving toward complete data independence. In the future, anyone using a corporate computer will be able to send a query out on a network, searching the company's shared databases and the small, personal ones on some of the computers connected to the network. See *query language* and *Structured Query Language (SQL).*

data insertion   In a database management program, an operation that appends new records to the database. See *append.*

data integrity   The accuracy, completeness, and internal consistency of the information stored in a database.

A good database management program ensures data integrity by making it difficult (or impossible) to accidentally erase or alter data.

Relational database management programs help to ensure data integrity by eliminating data redundancy. See *data redundancy*.

data interchange format (DIF) file   In spreadsheet programs and some database programs, a standard file format that enables the exchange of data among different brands or versions of spreadsheet programs.

Originally developed by Software Arts, the creators of VisiCalc, DIF is supported by Lotus 1-2-3 and other spreadsheet programs that can read spreadsheets saved in the DIF format.

data manipulation   In database management, the four fundamental database manipulation operations are *data deletion*, *data insertion*, *data modification*, and *data retrieval*.

data mask   See *field template*.

data modification   In database management, an operation that updates one or more records according to specified criteria.

You specify the criteria for the update using a query language. For example, the following statement, written in a simplified form of Structured Query Language (SQL), instructs the program to update the inventory database by finding records in which the supplier field contains "CC" and incrementing the value in the price data field by 15 percent.

```
UPDATE inventory
    SET price = price * 1.15
    WHERE supplier = "CC"
```

See *query language* and *Structured Query Language (SQL)*.

data privacy   In local area networks, the limiting of access to a file so that other participants in the network cannot display its contents. See *encryption*, *field privilege*, *file privilege*, and *password protection*.

data processing   Preparing, storing, or manipulating information with a computer. See *word processing program*.

data record In a database management program, a complete unit of related data items expressed in named data fields. In a relational database, data record is synonymous with row.

A data record contains all the information related to a unit of related information in the database. In a video store's database, for example, the data record lists the following information for each tape the store stocks: title, category (horror, adventure, and so on), rating (G, PG, PG–13, and so on), the telephone number of the customer, and the due date. Most programs display data records in two ways: as data-entry forms and as data tables.

In a table-oriented relational database-management program, which displays the results of all retrieval operations as a table with rows and columns, the data records are displayed as horizontal rows.

data redundancy In database management, the repetition of the same data in two or more data records.

Generally, you should not enter the same data in two different places within a database—someone may mistype just one character, destroying accurate retrieval. To the computer, Acme is not Acmee. Suppose that one data record contains the supplier name Meg Smith, and another has Megan Smith. The program fails to retrieve both data records if you search for all the records with Megan Smith in the Supplier Name field. Integrity is a serious issue for any database management system. Relational database management programs can reduce the data redundancy problem.

data retrieval In database management programs, an operation that retrieves information from the database according to the criteria specified in a query.

A database management program is useless if the program displays all the information at once. You must be able to access only needed information. The following query, written in simplified Structured Query Language (SQL), instructs a program to choose data from the first_name, last_name, phone_no, and due_date fields of the Rentals database, when the due date field contains a date equal to or earlier than May 5, 1990. The query then instructs the program to sort the displayed data by the due date, so that those customers with the most overdue tapes are at the top of the list.

SELECT first_name, last_name, phone_no, due_date
FROM rentals
WHERE due_date = < 05/05/90
ORDER BY due_date

The result of this query is a data table:

first_name	last_name	phone_no	due_date
ANGELINA	BAKER	499-1234	03/19/90
TERRENCE	TARDY	499-9876	04/30/90
BERMUDA	JAKE	499-5432	05/05/90

A program that displays data tables as the result of retrieval operations is a table-oriented database-management program. Record-oriented database management programs are less useful because they display all the information on all the data records retrieved.

data table In a database management program, an on-screen view of information in a columnar (two-dimensional) format, with the field names at the top.

Data tables provide a good way to summarize the data contained in a database for convenient viewing. Most database management programs display data tables as the result of sorting or querying operations. See *data-entry form.*

data type In a database management program, a definition that governs the kind of data that you can enter in a data field.

In dBASE, for example, you can choose among the following data types:

- Character (or text) field. You can place any character you can type at the keyboard into a character field, including numbers. But numbers are treated as strings (text), and the program cannot perform computations on strings. A character field can contain approximately one line of text.

- Memo field. A memo field can contain more text than a character field. Memo fields are used to store extensive notes about the information contained in a record.
- Numeric field. Stores numbers in such a way that the program can perform calculations on them.
- Logical field. Stores information in a true/false, yes/no format.
- Date field. Stores dates so that the program can recognize and compare them.

See *field template*.

database   A collection of related information about a subject organized in a useful manner that provides a base or foundation for procedures such as retrieving information, drawing conclusions, and making decisions.

Any collection of information that serves these purposes qualifies as a database, even if the information is not stored on a computer. In fact, important predecessors of today's sophisticated business database systems were files kept on index cards and stored in file cabinets.

Information usually is divided into distinct data records, each with one or more data fields. For example, a video store's record about a children's film may include the following information:

TITLE	The Blue Fountain
CATEGORY	Children
RATING	G
RETAIL PRICE	$24.95
RENTED TO	325-1234
DUE DATE	12/31/90

A data record is a form that includes headings that prompt the user to fill in specific information. You can create a database without dividing the record into distinct fields, but headings make accidental omissions more obvious and make retrieval operations function more quickly. See *data field* and *data record*.

database design The choice and arrangement of data fields in a database so that fundamental errors (such as data redundancy and repeating fields) are avoided or minimized. See *data redundancy* and *repeating field*.

database driver In Lotus 1-2-3 Release 3.0, a program that enables 1-2-3 to exchange data with database programs such as dBASE.

database management Tasks related to creating, maintaining, organizing, and retrieving information from a database. See *data manipulation*.

database management program An application program that provides the tools for data retrieval, modification, deletion, and insertion. Such programs also can create a database and produce meaningful output on the printer or on-screen. In personal computing, three kinds of database management programs exist: flat-file, relational, and text-oriented.

   Using computers for database management is easier than traditional methods. A computer can sort the records in a few seconds and in several different ways. For example, in a video store's database, you can sort the records by title, category, rating, availability, and so on. Furthermore, a database management program can select just those records that meet the criteria you specify in a query. The results of sorts or selections can be displayed on-screen or printed in a report. See *flat-file database management program, relational database management* and *text-oriented database management program*.

database management system (DBMS) 1. In mainframe computing, a computer system organized for the systematic management of a large collection of information. 2. In personal computing, a program such as dBASE with similar information storage, organization, and retrieval capacities, sometimes including simultaneous access to multiple databases through a shared field (relational database management). See *flat-file database management program*.

database structure   In database management, a definition of the data records in which information is stored, including: the number of data fields; a set of field definitions that for each field specify the type of information, the length, and other characteristics; and a list of field names.

In the following example, the database structure includes six fields:

TITLE	The Blue Fountain
CATEGORY	Children
RATING	G
RETAIL PRICE	$24.95
RENTED TO	325-1234
DUE DATE	12/31/90

The first field is a text field that can accommodate up to 60 characters. The last field is a date field that accepts only eight characters entered in the date format (mm/dd/yy).

DBMS   See *database management system (DBMS)*.

DDE   See *dynamic data exchange (DDE)*.

decimal tab   In a word processing or page layout program, a tab stop configured so that values align at the decimal point.

decryption   The process of deciphering data from an encrypted form so that the data can be read. See *encryption*.

dedicated file server   In a local area network, a file server dedicated to providing services to the users of the network and running the network operating system.

Not all file servers are dedicated so that they cannot be used for other purposes. In peer-to-peer networks, for example, all the networked computers are potential file servers, although they are being used for stand-alone applications.

default button   See *pushbutton*.

default directory   See *current directory*.

default extension   The three-letter extension an application program uses to save and retrieve files, unless you override the default by specifying another file name.

   → Tip: If the program you are using supplies a default extension, use the default instead of your own extension. Many programs, such as Lotus 1-2-3 and Microsoft Word, assign extensions if you do not provide one. When saving a file with Microsoft Word, for example, the program assigns the extension DOC. During retrieval operations, such programs display a list of the files with the default extension, making retrieving a file easier. If you give the file an extension that differs from the default extension, however, the file does not appear on the list. You still can retrieve the file, but you must remember the file's name without any help from the program. See *extension* and *file name*.

default numeric format   In a spreadsheet program, the numeric format that the program uses for all cells unless you choose a different one. See *numeric format*.

default printer   In Microsoft Windows, the printer that Windows applications uses automatically when you choose Print. Non-Windows programs, such as 1-2-3, also enable you to install several printers. See *Microsoft Windows*.

default setting   A command option a program uses unless you specify another setting. In Lotus 1-2-3, for example, the default column width is 9 characters.

   → Tip: An important step toward the mastery of an application program is learning the program defaults. You should learn how to change defaults so that the program works the way you want. Most programs save the changes you make so that they are in effect for the next working session, but some options may not be saved under any circumstances. Microsoft Word, for example, saves the printer driver you select, but it does not save settings like the number of copies to be printed (the default is always one). If the program saved the number of copies, you may inadvertently print unwanted copies of a document the next time you choose the Print command.

default value   A value an application program chooses when you do not specify one.

defragmentation   A procedure in which all the files on a hard disk are rewritten so that all parts of each file are written to contiguous sectors. The result is a significant improvement—up to 75 percent or more—in the disk's speed in retrieval operations. During normal operations, the files on a hard disk become fragmented so that parts of a file are written all over the disk, slowing down retrieval operations. The defragmentation process is accomplished by a commercial utility program.

Delete key   A key that erases the character at the cursor.

→ **Tip:** Use the Backspace and Delete keys to correct mistakes as you type. If you discover you have made a typing error, press Backspace to erase the error and retype. Use the Delete key to erase a character at the cursor.

delimiter   A symbol that marks the end of one section of a command and the beginning of another section.

demo   A program designed to emulate some of the functions of an application program for marketing purposes.

demodulation   In telecommunications, the process of receiving and transforming an analog signal into its digital equivalent that can be used by a computer. See *modulation* and *telecommunications*.

demount   To remove a disk from a disk drive. See *mount*.

density   A measurement of the amount of information (in bits) that can be packed reliably into a square inch of a magnetic secondary storage device, such as a floppy disk. See *double density, high density,* and *single density*.

derived field See *calculated field*.

descending sort A sort that reverses the normal ascending sort order. Instead of sorting A, B, C, D and 1, 2, 3, 4; a descending sort lists D, C, B, A and 4, 3, 2, 1.

descriptor In database management, a term used to classify a data record so that all records sharing a common subject can be retrieved as a group.

In a video store's database, for example, the descriptor Adventure appears in the data records of all action-oriented films. See *identifier*.

desk accessory (DA) In a graphical user interface, a set of utility programs that assist with day-to-day tasks such as jotting down notes, performing calculations on an on-screen calculator, maintaining a list of names and phone numbers, and displaying an on-screen calendar.

desktop In a graphical user interface, a computer representation of your day-to-day work, as if you are looking at an actual desk littered with folders full of work to do. See *graphical user interface (GUI)*.

desktop computer A personal computer or professional workstation designed to fit on a standard-sized office desk and equipped with sufficient memory and secondary storage to perform business computing tasks. See *laptop computer*.

desktop presentation The use of a presentation graphics program's slide show module to create a presentation which can be run on a desktop computer. The presentation can run automatically, or the viewer of the presentation can be given a menu of options. See *presentation graphics program* and *slide show*.

desktop publishing (DTP) The use of a personal computer as an inexpensive production system for generating typeset-quality text and graphics. Desktop publishers often merge text and graphics on the same page and print pages on a high-resolution laser printer or type-setting machine.

One of the fastest-growing applications in personal computing, desktop publishing offers cost-saving, productivity, and time-saving advantages that have helped speed the proliferation of desktop computers.

desktop video A multimedia application in which a personal computer, in tandem with a videocassette recorder or laser disc player, is used to control the display of still or motion images.

destination file In many DOS commands, the file that data or program instructions are copied into. See *source file*.

device Any hardware component or peripheral, such as a printer, modem, monitor, or mouse, that can receive and/or send data.

device driver A program that extends the operating system's capabilities by enabling the operating system to work with a specific hardware device (such as a printer).

In DOS and OS/2, device drivers are files with the extension SYS. To use a device driver, you must enter a configuration command that identifies the file containing the driver. You place the command in the CONFIG.SYS file. The following command, for example, tells DOS to use a mouse driver:

DEVICE = MOUSE.SYS

DOS does not need DEVICE commands to work with most keyboards, monitors, and printers. You use DEVICE commands, however, to install a mouse and files that set up RAM disks.

▲ **Caution:** After you install a mouse on your system, beware of accidentally erasing the CONFIG.SYS file. If you do, the mouse will not work.

device independence The capability of a computer program, operating system, or programming language to work on a variety of computers or computer peripherals, despite their electronic variation.

Examples of device independence include UNIX and PostScript. UNIX, an operating system for multiuser computer systems, is designed to run on a wide variety of computers, from PCs to mainframes. The portability of UNIX (its capability to run on a variety of hardware platforms) stems from the C language in which it is written. In C, a programmer may embed assembly language instructions that take advantage of a specific computer's electronic capabilities, without sacrificing the overall structure of the program, which can remain the same in its various incarnations. PostScript, a page description language for high-quality printing, relies on a different method: a PostScript-compatible printer must include its own processing circuitry, which includes an interpreter for the PostScript language, in order to print PostScript-encoded files. See *C, portable, PostScript, UNIX.*

device name In DOS and OS/2, the abbreviation that refers to a peripheral device. See *CON, LPT,* and *PRN.*

diacritical marks Marks added to characters to represent their phonetic value in a foreign language, such as accents. See *accent.*

diagnostic program A utility program that tests computer hardware and software to determine whether they are operating properly.

➜ **Tip:** Most computers initiate a diagnostic check at the start of every operating session. A particular focus of attention is the memory. If any errors are found, you see an error message, and the computer does not proceed. If you run into this problem, try starting the computer again. If you see the error message again, you may have to replace a memory chip. Because the error message specifies the location of the faulty chip, be sure to write down the number you see on-screen.

dialog box In a graphical user interface, an on-screen message box that conveys or requests information from the user. See *graphical user interface (GUI).*

dictionary sort   A sort operation that ignores the case of characters as data is rearranged. See *sort* and *sort order*.

DIF   See *data interchange format (DIF) file*.

digital   A form of representation in which discrete (separate) objects (digits) are used to stand for something so that counting and other operations can be performed precisely.

Information represented digitally can be manipulated to produce a calculation, a sort, or some other computation. In an abacus, for example, quantities are represented by positioning beads on a wire. A trained abacus operator can perform calculations at high rates of speed by following an algorithm, a recipe for solving the problem. In digital electronic computers, two electrical states correspond to the 1s and 0s of binary numbers, and the algorithm is embodied in a computer program. See *algorithm, analog, binary numbers, computation*, and *program*.

digital computer   A computer that represents information using digits, or objects clearly separate and different from each other, and performs computations on this information using at least partly automatic procedures. See *analog computer* and *computer*.

digital monitor   A cathode-ray-tube (CRT) display that accepts digital output from the display adapter and converts the digital signal to an analog signal.

Digital monitors cannot accept input unless the input conforms to a prearranged standard, such as the IBM Monochrome Display Adapter (MDA), Color Graphics Adapter (CGA), or Enhanced Graphics adapter (EGA). All these adapters produce digital output.

Digital monitors are fast and produce sharp, clear images. However, they have a major disadvantage: unlike analog monitors, they cannot display continuously variable colors. Simple digital color monitors can display colors in two modes, on and off; more complex color digital monitors recognize more intensity modes. For the Video Graphics Array (VGA) standard, IBM chose to use analog monitors so that continuously variable images can be displayed on-screen. See *analog monitor, Color Graphics Adapter (CGA), digital, Enhanced Graphics Adapter (EGA), monochrome display adapter (MDA),* and *Video Graphics Array (VGA).*

digital transmission A data communications technique that passes information encoded as discrete, on-off pulses. Unlike analog transmission, which uses a continuous wave form to transmit data, digital transmission does not require the use of digital-to-analog converters at each end of the transmission. However, analog transmission is faster and can carry more than one channel at a time. See *analog transmission.*

digitize To transform a continuous-tone image into computer-readable data using a device called a scanner. See *scanner.*

dimmed command In a command menu, an option that is not currently available.

dimmed icon In the graphical user interface, a disk, program, or document that cannot be accessed at the present time.

dingbats Ornamental characters such as bullets, stars, and flowers used to decorate a page.

DIP (Dual In-line Package) switch A switch, usually hidden on an internal circuit board, used to choose operating parameters, such as the amount of memory that should be recognized by the operating system or the printer file format the printer should expect.

"Dual in-line package" refers to the switch's plastic housing designed to be attached directly to a circuit board. The trend in computer and peripheral design is to make such switches more accessible by placing them on the exterior of the component's case or to eliminate them entirely in favor of more easily manipulated controls.

direct-connect modem A modem that makes a direct connection to the telephone line via modular connectors, unlike an acoustic coupler modem designed to cradle a telephone headset. See *acoustic coupler*.

directory   An index to the files stored on a disk or a portion of a disk that can be displayed on-screen.

The contents of a disk are not obvious to the eye. A good operating system keeps an up-to-date record of the files stored on a disk, with ample information about the file's content, time of creation, and size.

In DOS and OS/2, the DIR command displays a disk directory. A typical directory display appears as follows:

```
Volume in Drive A has no label
Directory of A:\
ANSI       SYS      1651    3-21-86     0:01a
DRIVER     SYS      1102    3-21-86     7:47a
RAMDRIVE   SYS      6462    7-07-86    12:00p
CONFIG     SYS        15    1-17-89     3:37p
COMMAND    COM     23612    9-30-86    12:00p
APPEND     COM      1725    3-21-86    11:00p
ASSIGN     COM      1523    3-21-86     4:50p
CLOCK      COM       505    2-10-87    12:00p
FORMAT     COM     11597    9-30-86     9:00a
SYS        COM      4607    8-01-87    12:00p
ATTRIB     EXE      8234    3-21-86    12:00p
CHKDSK     EXE      9680    3-21-86    12:00p
DEBUG      EXE      5647    3-21-86     8:19p
13 File(s) 12876 bytes free
```

This disk directory contains the following information:

- Volume label. When formatting a disk, you can name it; the name is called a volume label. You also can name the disk later using the VOL command. If you give the disk a volume label, you see the name at the top of the directory when you use the DIR command.

- File name. DOS file names have two parts, the file name and the extension. The first two columns of the directory table show the file name and the extension of each file on the disk.
- File size. The third column of the disk directory table shows the size of each file (in bytes).
- Date last modified. The fourth column of the disk directory shows the date on which the file was last modified.
- Time last modified. The fifth column of the disk directory shows the time when the file was last modified.
- Space remaining. The number of bytes of storage space left on the disk is shown at the bottom of the directory. This information is important because you cannot write a file to a disk with insufficient room.

→ **Tip:** If your computer is not equipped with a clock/calendar board, be sure to set the system time and system date manually when you start the computer. DOS and OS/2 use this information to create the date and time listings in disk directories. If the date and time are not set, the dates listed for files are incorrect. See *clock/calendar board* and *subdirectory*.

directory markers   In DOS and OS/2, symbols displayed in a subdirectory's on-screen directory that represent the current directory (.) and the parent directory (..). See *current directory*, *directory*, *parent directory*, and *subdirectory*.

directory sorting   The organized display of the files in a disk directory sorted by name, extension, or date and time of creation. DOS 5.0 introduced directory sorting at the system level; previously, directory sorting was possible only with add-on utility programs.

disk See *floppy disk* and *hard disk*.

disk buffer See *disk cache*.

disk cache Pronounced "cash." An area of random-access memory (RAM) set aside by the operating system to store frequently accessed data and program instructions. A disk cache can improve the speed of disk-intensive applications such as database management programs. If the central processing unit (CPU) must wait for this information from disk, processing speed slows noticeably.

When the CPU repeatedly accesses the same information, you can obtain modest speed gains by placing the frequently accessed information in a buffer (a temporary storage place in memory). Although using a disk cache does not eliminate disk accesses, the number of accesses is reduced. See *cache controller, central processing unit (CPU), RAM cache* and *random-access memory (RAM)*.

disk capacity The storage capacity of a floppy disk or hard disk, measured in kilobytes (K) or megabytes (M).

The capacity of a floppy disk depends on the size of the disk, the density of the magnetic particles on its surface, and the capabilities of the drive used to format the disk. The two most popular disk sizes are 5.25-inch floppy disks and 3.5-inch micro floppy disks. Single-sided disks were once common, but are all but obsolete now; double-sided disks are the norm. Also now standard is the double-density disk; available at a higher cost is the high-density disk. The third variable is the operating system used to format the disk and the capabilities of the disk drive you are using. The following table shows the relationship of the variables.

Size	Density	System	Drive	Capacity
3.5"	DD	DOS	standard	720K
3.5"	DD	Mac	standard	800K
3.5"	HD	Mac	SuperDrive	1.4M
3.5"	HD	DOS	high density	1.44M
3.5"	HD	DOS 5	high density	2.88M

Size	Density	System	Drive	Capacity
5.25"	DD	DOS	standard	360K
5.25"	HD	DOS	high density	1.2M

disk drive   A secondary storage medium such as a floppy disk drive or a hard disk. This term usually refers to floppy disk drives.

A floppy disk drive is an economical secondary storage medium that uses a removable magnetic disk. Like all magnetic media, a floppy disk can be recorded, erased, and re-used over and over. The recording and erasing operations are performed by the read/write head that moves laterally over the surface of the disk—giving the drive its random-access capabilities.

Although floppy disk drives are inexpensive, they are too slow to serve as the main secondary storage medium for today's personal computers; for business applications, a minimum configuration is one hard disk and one floppy disk drive. (The floppy disk drive is needed to copy software and disk-based data onto the system and for backup operations.) See *floppy disk, random access, read/write head,* and *secondary storage.*

disk drive controller   The circuitry that controls the physical operations of the floppy disks and/or the hard disks that are directly connected to the computer.

Until recently, most disk drive controllers were plug-in adapters, but now there is a clear trend toward including this circuitry on the computer's motherboard. With the advent of the Intelligent Drive Electronics (IDE) standard, which transfers much of the controller circuitry to the drive itself, the inclusion of the remaining circuitry on the motherboard has become much more simple.

Wherever it is positioned, the disk drive controller circuitry performs two functions: it employs an interface standard (such as ST-506/ST-412, ESDI, or SSCI) to establish communication with the drive's electronics, as well as a data encoding scheme (such as MFM, RLL, or ARLL) to encode information on the magnetic surface of the disk. See *Advanced Run-Length Limited (ARLL)*, *Enhanced System Device Interface (ESDI)*, *Modified Frequency Modulation (MFM)*, *Run-Length Limited (RLL)*, *Small Computer System Interface (SCSI)*, and *ST-506/ST-412*.

disk operating system   See *operating system*.

disk optimizer   See *defragmentation*.

diskless workstation   In a local area network, a workstation that has a CPU and RAM but lacks its own disk drives.

Do diskless workstations signal the decline of the personal computing ethos? Personal computing, after all, is about the distribution of computing *decision-making* to end users, who are free to choose their own applications and to develop their own, unique computing style. In large organizations, data processing managers have typically viewed the personal computing ethos as if it were tantamount to anarchy; far better, they believe, to let professionals choose the software, and impose a single standard on everyone, so that everyone produces and uses compatible data. An additional argument: personal computers raise serious security issues for organizations. Anyone can come into your office and, if you are not around and have not secured your system, copy a disk containing valuable information.

The rise of personal computer-based local area networks signalled a move away from the decentralism of personal computing and back toward the sharing of software and data, but from the data processing manager's point of view, LANs didn't go far enough. The diskless workstation returns the personal computer's control to the hands of system administrators and resolves security issues, but at the cost of suppressing virtually all the distributed computing advantages that have made personal computing so valuable in modern organizations.

display   See *monitor*.

display type   A typeface, usually 14 points or larger and differing in style from the body type, that is used for headings and subheadings. See *body type*.

distributed processing system   A computer system designed for multiple users that provides each user with a fully functional computer. Unlike a standalone system, however, a distributed system is designed to make communication among the linked computers and shared access to central files easier.

In personal computing, distributed processing takes the form of local area networks, in which the personal computers of a department or organization are linked via high-speed cable connections.

Distributed processing offers some advantages over multiuser systems because each user is given a fully functional workstation instead of a remote terminal without processing circuitry. If the network fails, you can still work. You also can select software tailored to your needs. A distributed processing system can be started with a modest initial investment; you need only two or three workstations and, if desired, a central file server. More workstation nodes can be added as needed.

A multiuser system, however, requires a major initial investment in the central computer, which must be powerful enough to handle system demands as the system grows. Multiuser systems have advantages such as point-of-sale terminals, in which little is to be gained by distributing processing power and much to be gained by making sure that all information is posted to a central database. See *file server, local area network (LAN),* and *multiuser system*.

dithering   In color or gray-scale printing and displays, the mingling of dots of several colors to produce what appears to be a new color. With dithering, 256 colors can be combined to produce what appears to be a continuously variable color palette, but at the cost of sacrificing resolution.

document base font   The default font that a word processing program uses, unless you override the program by choosing a different font. Unlike an initial base font that affects all documents, the document base font affects only one document.

You can choose Times Roman as the initial base font for all documents, for example, but override this choice by choosing Helvetica as the document base font for a letter you are currently writing. You can choose other fonts within this letter, but the program uses Helvetica unless you give an explicit command to the contrary. See *initial base font*.

document comparison utility   A utility program that compares two documents created with a word processing program. If the two documents are not identical, the program displays the differences between them, line-by-line.

document format   In a word processing program, a set of formatting choices that affects the page layout of all pages of the document you are currently working on. Examples of document formats include margins, headers, footers, page numbers, and columns.

document processing   The application of computer technology to every stage of the in-house production of documents, such as instruction manuals, handbooks, reports, and proposals.

A complete document processing system includes all the software and hardware needed to create, organize, edit, and print such documents. Because these documents generally are reproduced from camera-ready copy, a document processing system's word processing software should be able to generate indexes and tables of contents. See *word processing program* and *desktop publishing (DTP)*.

document window   In Microsoft Windows, a window within an application program's window that displays a document you are creating or altering. You can open more than one document window within an application window. See *Microsoft Windows*.

documentation   The instructions, tutorials, and reference information that provide users with the information required to use a computer program or computer system effectively. Documentation can appear in printed media or in on-line help systems

DOS   See *MS-DOS*.

DOS prompt   In DOS, a letter representing the current disk drive and the greater-than symbol (C>) that informs the user when the operating system is ready to receive a command. This default DOS prompt can be changed. See *prompt*.

dot-matrix printer   An impact printer that forms text and graphics images by pressing the ends of pins against a ribbon.

   A dot-matrix printer forms an image of text or graphics by hammering the ends of pins against a ribbon. The ends of these wires form a character made up of a pattern (a matrix) of dots. Dot-matrix printers are fast, but the output they produce is generally poor quality because the character is not fully formed. These printers also can be extremely noisy. Some dot-matrix printers use 24 pins instead of 9, and the quality of their output is better.

   Many of today's dot-matrix printers offer a near-letter quality (NLQ) mode that sacrifices speed to produce substantially improved output. In the NLQ mode, the printer passes over a line several times, offsetting the dots to form a solid character.

   Better dot-matrix printers can produce printout in more than one type style and size (called a font). Fonts are measured in points ($\frac{1}{72}$ of an inch). A standard type size is 12 points, producing 6 lines per vertical inch on the page, but you usually can choose sizes ranging from 8 to 24 points.

   ▲ **Caution:** In IBM PC-compatible computing, no widely accepted standard exists for printer control commands. De facto standards have been established by Epson and IBM. Many dot-matrix printers recognize the Epson or IBM commands, but others do not. If you plan to purchase a dot-matrix printer, make sure that your software includes a printer driver for the model. See *impact printer, near-letter quality (NLQ),* and *nonimpact printer.*

dot pitch   The size of the smallest dot that a monitor can display on-screen. Dot pitch determines a monitor's maximum resolution.

To keep the electron beam from spilling over and activating the wrong part of the screen, color monitors use a shadow mask, a metal sheet with fine perforations. These perforations are arranged so that the beam strikes one hole at a time, corresponding to one dot on-screen. The smaller the hole in the shadow mask, the higher the resolution.

→ **Tip:** High-resolution monitors use dot pitches of approximately 0.31 mm or less; the best monitors use dot pitches of 0.28 mm or less.

dot prompt   In dBASE, the prompt—a lone period on an otherwise empty screen—for the command-driven interface of the program.

dots per inch (dpi)   A measure of screen and printer resolution that counts the dots that the device can produce per linear inch.

→ **Tip:** In expressing the resolution of display devices, the custom is to state the horizontal measurement before the vertical one. A Super-VGA monitor with a resolution of 1024 x 768, for example, can display 1024 dots per inch horizontally and 768 dots per inch vertically.

double-click   To click the mouse button twice in rapid succession. In many programs, double-clicking extends the action that results from single-clicking; double-clicking on a word, for example, selects the whole word rather than just one character. Double-clicking also is used not only to select an item, but also to initiate an action. In a file list, for example, double-clicking a file name selects and opens the file.

double density   A widely used recording technique that packs twice as much data on a floppy or hard disk as the earlier single-density standard. See *high density, Modified Frequency Modulation (MFM) recording, Run-Length Limited (RLL),* and *single density*.

Dow Jones News/Retrieval Service   An on-line information service from Dow Jones, the publishers of the *Wall Street Journal* and *Barron's*, that offers a computer-searchable index to financial and business publications and up-to-date financial information (such as stock quotes). See *on-line information service*.

downloadable font   A printer font that must be transferred from the computer's (or the printer's) hard disk drive to the printer's random-access memory before the font can be used.

Often called soft fonts, downloadable fonts are the least convenient of the three types of printer fonts you can use. See *bit-mapped font, built-in font, cartridge font, downloading utility, font, font family, outline font, page description language (PDL)* and *Post-Script*.

downloading   The reception and storage of a program or data file from a distant computer through data communications links. See *file transfer protocol* and *modem*.

downloading utility   A utility program that transfers downloadable fonts from your computer's (or printer's) hard disk to the printer's random-access memory (RAM).

Downloading utilities usually are provided free by the publishers of downloadable fonts. You may not need the utility if the word processing or page layout program you are using has downloading capabilities built in, such as WordPerfect, Microsoft Word, Ventura Publisher and PageMaker.

downward compatibility   Hardware or software that runs without modification when used with earlier computer components or software versions. VGA monitors, for example, are downwardly compatible with the original IBM PC, if you use an 8-bit VGA adapter that fits in the PC's 8-bit expansion bus.

dpi   See *dots per inch (dpi)*.

drag   To move the mouse pointer while holding down the mouse button.

DRAM   See *dynamic random-access memory (DRAM)*.

draw program   A computer graphics program that uses object-oriented graphics to produce line art.

A draw program stores the components of a drawing, such as lines, circles, and curves, as mathematical formulas rather than as a configuration of bits on-screen. Unlike images created with paint programs, line art created with a draw program can be sized and scaled without introducing distortions.

Draw programs differ from paint programs in another way: they produce output that prints at a printer's maximum resolution. Popular draw programs include MacDraw and SuperPaint for the Macintosh. See *object-oriented graphic* and *paint program*.

draw tool   In any program that includes graphics capabilities, a command that transforms the cursor into a "pen" for creating object-oriented (vector) graphics. Draw tools typically include options for creating lines, circles, ovals, polylines, rectangles, and Bézier curves. See *object-oriented graphics*.

drive   See *disk drive*.

drive designator   In DOS and OS/2, an argument that specifies the drive to be affected by the command. For example, the command FORMAT B: instructs DOS to format the disk in drive B.

driver   A disk file that contains information needed by a program to operate a peripheral such as a monitor or printer. See *device driver*.

drop cap   An initial letter of a chapter or paragraph enlarged and positioned so that the top of the character is even with the top of the first line and the rest of the character descends into the second and subsequent lines. See *stickup initial*.

drop-down list box   In the industry-standard and graphical user interfaces, a list of command options that doesn't appear until you select the command. After you "drop down" the list, you can choose one of the options. The drop-down list box enables a programmer to provide many options without taking up a lot of space on the screen. See *graphical user interface (GUI)* and *industry-standard user interface*.

drop out type   White characters printed on a black background.

drop shadow   A shadow placed behind an image, slightly offset horizontally and vertically, that creates the illusion that the topmost image has been lifted off the surface of the page.

dual y-axis graph   In presentation and analytical graphics, a line or column graph that uses two y-axes (values axes) when comparing two data series with different measurement scales.

Dual y-axis graphs are useful when you are comparing two different data series that must be measured with two different values axes (apples and oranges). See *paired bar graph*.

dumb terminal   See *terminal*.

dump   To transfer the contents of memory to a printing or secondary storage device.

Programmers use memory dumps while debugging programs to see exactly what the computer is doing when the dump occurs. See *screen dump*.

duplex   See *full duplex* and *half duplex*.

duplex printing   Printing or reproducing a document on both sides of the page so that the verso (left) and recto (right) pages face each other after the document is bound.

A document begins on an odd-numbered recto page; verso pages have even numbers. See *binding offset*.

Dvorak keyboard   An alternative keyboard layout in which 70 percent of the keystrokes are made on the home row (compared to 32 percent with the standard QWERTY layout).

The home row is the row of keys your fingers rest on when you are ready to start typing. Ideally, most of the characters you type are positioned on the home row, but not in the QWERTY method. Because you can configure a computer keyboard any way you want, you can equip your computer with a Dvorak keyboard.

→ **Tip:** If you are just learning how to touch-type, consider a Dvorak keyboard because it is easier and faster. Every time you use a QWERTY keyboard, however, you must go back to the hunt-and-peck method.

dynamic data exchange (DDE)   In Microsoft Windows and OS/2 Presentation Manager, a channel through which correctly prepared programs can actively exchange data and control other applications. To be capable of DDE, the programs must conform to Microsoft Corporation's specifications.

dynamic link   A method of linking data shared by two programs. When data is changed in one program, the data is likewise changed in the other when you use an update command. See *hot link*.

dynamic random-access memory (DRAM)   A random-access memory (RAM) chip that represents memory states by using capacitors that store electrical charges.

Because the capacitors eventually lose their charges, DRAM chips must refresh continually (hence "dynamic").

Dynamic RAM chips vary in their access time, the speed with which the central processing unit (CPU) can obtain information encoded within them. These access times are rated in nanoseconds (billionths of a second); a chip marked –12, for example, has an access time of 120 ns. Such access times may seem remarkably fast, but they actually may be insufficient for today's fast microprocessors that must be programmed with wait states so that memory can catch up.

→ **Tip:** If you are using an Intel 80286- or 80386-based computer with a fast clock speed (such as 25 or 33 MHz), you need the fastest DRAM chips you can obtain. Chips rated 120 ns are too slow; make sure that your computer is equipped with chips rated at 80 ns or better.

See *central processing unit (CPU), Intel 80286, Intel 80386, nanosecond (ns), static random-access memory (RAM),* and *wait state.*

e

E-mail See *electronic mail.*

EBCDIC See *Extended Binary Coded Decimal Interchange Code (EBCDIC).*

echoplex An asynchronous communications protocol in which the receiving station acknowledges and confirms the reception of a message by echoing the message back to the transmitting station. See *full duplex* and *half duplex.*

Edit mode A program mode that makes correcting text and data easier.

In Lotus 1-2-3, for example, you type EDIT to correct a cell definition. After you type EDIT, the program echoes the current cell definition on the entry line, and you can use editing keys to correct errors or add characters.

editor See *text editor.*

edits In a word processing program, the changes made to a document (including insertions, deletions, block moves, and formatting).

EDLIN Pronounced "ed'-lin". In DOS, the line editor provided with the operating system for light text-creation and editing duties.

A line editor is a primitive word processing program that forces you to work with text line-by-line. Although EDLIN may be suitable for creating a small batch file, EDLIN is cumbersome and difficult to use. For most purposes, a word processor is better for creating text files.

EGA See *Enhanced Graphics Adapter (EGA)*.

EISA See *Extended Industry Standard Architecture (EISA)*.

electronic mail The use of electronic communications media to send textual messages (such as letters, memos, and reports).

Electronic mail may involve a one-to-one communication, in which one person sends a private message to another person; or a one-to-many communication, in which one person sends a message to many people connected to the network.

Electronic mail is a store-and-forward technology; unlike a telephone call, the recipient need not be present. The system stores the message and, if the system is a good one, informs the recipients that a message is waiting when they log on to the system.

Electronic mail services are provided privately and publicly. Private electronic mail is possible in local area networks. Mail can be exchanged only among users of the network. Public electronic mail is provided by an on-line information service such as CompuServe or GEnie, or an electronic mail service such as MCI Mail. Mail can be exchanged among users who can log on to the information service using a modem and a communications program. See *communications program, local area network (LAN),* and *modem*.

elite A typeface that prints twelve characters per inch. See *pitch*.

em dash A continuous dash equal in width to one em, the width of the capital letter M in a given typeface.

Em dashes often are used to introduce parenthetical remarks. The following sentence contains an em dash: The butler—or someone who knows what the butler knows—must have done it. See *en dash*.

em fraction   A single-character fraction that occupies one em of space and uses a diagonal stroke (¼).

Em fractions are used when fractions appear occasionally within body text, but they are not available in some fonts. A true em fraction is one character and should be distinguished from a piece fraction made from three or more characters (1/4). See *en fraction*.

embedded formatting command   A text formatting command placed directly in the text to be formatted that does not affect the appearance of the text on-screen.

Considered by many to be an undesirable formatting technique in word processing programs, embedded commands cannot be seen until the document is previewed on-screen or printed. Studies in work environments show that using word processors with embedded commands may take longer to produce documents than using typewriters. Synonymous with *off-screen formatting*. See *hidden codes, on-screen formatting,* and *what-you-see-is-what-you-get (WYSIWYG)*.

EMM386.EXE   A DOS (Version 5 and later) device driver that simulates expanded memory on an 80386 or higher computer equipped with extended memory. EMM386.EXE also enables the user to load device drivers and programs into the upper memory area. See *expanded memory, extended memory,* and *upper memory area*.

emphasis   The use of a non-Roman type style, such as underlining, italic, bold typefaces, and small caps, to highlight a word or phrase.

Word processing and page layout programs provide many more ways to emphasize text than typewriters do, but with the increase in options has come an increase in abuse. Emphasis often is overused by inexperienced writers.

Good taste in page layout design calls for restraint in the use of emphasis. Because underlining is a signal to the typesetter to set the text in italic, underlining is redundant in documents prepared using desktop publishing techniques. Many programs include outline and shadow characters that should be used only rarely. See *type style*.

EMS   See *Lotus-Intel-Microsoft Expanded Memory Specification (LIM EMS)*.

emulation   The duplication of the functional capability of one device in another device.

     In telecommunications, for example, a personal computer emulates a dumb terminal for on-line communication with a distant computer. See *terminal*.

en   A unit of measurement in typesetting that equals half the width of an em space, the width of the capital letter M in the current typeface.

en dash   A continuous dash equal in width to one half em, the width of the capital letter M in the current typeface.

     En dashes are used in place of the English words to or through, as in pp. 63–68 or January 9–14. See *em dash*.

en fraction   A single-character fraction that occupies one en of space and uses a horizontal stroke. See *em fraction*.

Encapsulated PostScript (EPS) file   A high-resolution graphic image stored using instructions written in the PostScript page description language.

     The EPS standard enables the device-independent transfer of high-resolution graphic images between applications. EPS graphics are of outstanding quality and can contain subtle gradations in shading, high-resolution text with special effects, and graceful curves generated by mathematical equations.

     The printout resolution is determined by the printing device's maximum capabilities; on laser printers, EPS graphics print at 300 dpi, but on Linotronic typesetters, resolutions of up to 2540 dpi are possible. EPS images can be sized without sacrificing image quality.

The major drawback of EPS graphics is that a PostScript-compatible laser printer is required to print them.

encryption The process of enciphering or encoding data so that the data cannot be read by users who do not possess the necessary password. See *decryption*.

End key A key on IBM PC-compatible keyboards with varying functions from program to program.

Frequently, the End key is used to move the cursor to the end of the line or the bottom of the screen, but the assignment of this key is up to the programmer.

end user The person who benefits, directly or indirectly, from the capabilities of a computer system and uses these capabilities to perform a professional, managerial, or technical task, such as analyzing a company's finances, preparing a publication-quality report, or maintaining an inventory of items in stock.

In corporate data processing during the 1950s and 1960s, end users typically had little or no data processing or computer expertise themselves and were kept at arm's length from computer resources. One significant outcome of the personal computer has been to distribute computer tools to people who previously could not gain access to such tools.

With the distribution of tools has come the distribution of computer expertise. Today's end user possesses sufficient expertise to carry out routine system maintenance tasks and to run application programs. Increasing numbers of end users modify application programs by writing macros and using software command languages.

endnote A footnote positioned at the end of the document rather than the bottom of the page.

Many word processing programs enable the user to choose between footnotes and endnotes.

Enhanced Expanded Memory Specification (EEMS) A technique to expand the memory of IBM PC-compatible computers running under DOS with a 640K limitation on random-access memory.

EEMS was introduced by AST, Quadram, and Ashton-Tate to improve the performance of the Lotus-Intel-Microsoft (LIM) Expanded Memory Specification. The introduction of LIM Version 4.0, however, has resolved many of the performance issues that motivated the release of EEMS, and the LIM standard is the dominant one. See *extended memory* and *Lotus-Intel-Microsoft Expanded Memory Specification (LIM EMS)*.

Enhanced Graphics Adapter (EGA) A color, bit-mapped, graphics display adapter for IBM PC-compatible computers that displays up to 16 colors simultaneously with a resolution of 640 pixels horizontally by 350 pixels vertically.

Enhanced Graphics Display A color digital monitor designed to work with the IBM Enhanced Graphics Adapter (EGA).

Enhanced System Device Interface (ESDI) An interface standard for hard disk drives. Drives using the ESDI standard transfer data at 10 megabits per second, twice as fast as the earlier ST-506/ST-412 interface standard. See *interface standard* and *ST-506/ST-412*.

➜ **Tip:** ESDI drives are substantially more expensive than drives conforming to other interface standards. If your system uses an 80286, 80386, or 80486 microprocessor, and if the system's clock speed is approximately 12 (MHz) or higher, an ST-506 drive may slow down your system's performance.

Enter/Return A key that confirms a command, sending the command to the central processing unit (CPU). In word processing, the Enter/Return key starts a new paragraph.

➜ **Tip:** On early IBM PC keyboards, this key is labeled with a hooked left arrow. On more recent IBM keyboards, and the keyboards of most IBM PC compatibles, Enter or Return is printed on the key.

▲ **Caution:** Most IBM PC-compatible keyboards have two Enter/Return keys. The first is located to the right of the typing area, and the second is located at the lower left of the numeric keypad. These two keys have identical functions in most, but not all programs. Synonymous with *carriage return*.

entry line In a spreadsheet program, the line in which the characters you type appear. The program does not insert the characters into the current cell until you press Enter.

If the cell has contents, the entry line displays the current cell definition.

envelope printer A printer designed specifically to print names, addresses, and USPS Postnet bar codes on business envelopes.

Most envelope printers can print USPS Postnet bar codes. Businesses that use the bar codes receive an attractive discount on postal rates. The use of Postnet bar codes, which are printed on envelopes and automatically read by Postal Service computer equipment, means faster and more accurate delivery of your business correspondence.

→ **Tip:** If you have a laser printer, you may not need an envelope printer because laser printers are capable of printing Postnet codes. Envelope printers, however, do a better job of handling high-volume printing jobs.

environment The hardware and/or operating system for application programs, such as the Macintosh environment.

EOF Acronym for *end of file*.

EOL Acronym for *end of line*.

equation typesetting Embedded codes within a word processing document that cause the program to print multi-line equations, including mathematical symbols such as integrals and summation signs.

The best word processing programs, such as WordPerfect and Microsoft Word, provide commands and symbols that enable technical writers to create multiline equations. You write the equation by embedding special codes for such symbols as radicals and integrals. You then use a command that displays the equation on-screen as it will print.

erasable optical disk drive A read/write secondary storage medium that uses a laser and reflected light to store and retrieve data on an optical disk.

Unlike CD-ROM and write-once, retrieve-many (WORM) drives, erasable optical disk drives can be used like hard disks are used; you can write and erase data repeatedly. Storage capacities are enormous; current drives store up to 650 megabytes of information.

However, erasable optical disk drives are expensive and much slower than hard disks and are not expected to displace magnetic secondary storage media soon. Like CD-ROM, erasable optical disk drives are used in organizations that need on-line access to huge amounts of supplementary information, such as engineering drawings or technical documentation. See *CD-ROM disk drive, optical disk, secondary storage,* and *write-once, read-many (WORM).*

erasable programmable read-only memory (EPROM) A read-only memory (ROM) chip that can be programmed and reprogrammed.

The erasability of EPROM chips matters to computer manufacturers, who often find that they need to reprogram ROM chips containing bugs. PROM chips, which cannot be reprogrammed, must be discarded when a programming error is discovered.

EPROM chips are packaged in a clear plastic case so that the contents can be erased using ultraviolet light. To reprogram the EPROM chip, a PROM programmer is necessary. See *programmable read-only memory (PROM)* and *read-only memory (ROM).*

➔ **Tip:** Because of the slight possibility that EPROM chips may be damaged by ultraviolet light, you should avoid exposing your computer's innards to bright sunlight.

ergonomics   The science of designing machines, tools, and computers so that people find them easy and healthful to use.

error handling   The way a program copes with errors, such as the failure to access data on a disk or a user's failure to press the appropriate key.

   A poorly written program may fail to handle errors at all, leading to a system lockup. The best programmers anticipate possible errors and provide information that helps the user solve the problem. See *error trapping*.

error message   In interactive computing, an on-screen message informing the user that the program is unable to carry out a requested operation.

   Early computing systems assumed users to be technically sophisticated, and frequently presented cryptic error messages such as

EXECUTION TERMINATE-ERROR 19869087

Applications for general use should display more helpful error messages that include suggestions about how to solve the problem, such as

You are about to lose work you have not saved.
Click OK if you want to abandon this work. Click
Cancel to return to your document.

error trapping   A program or application's capability to recognize an error and perform a predetermined action in response to that error.

Esc   A key that can be implemented differently by application programs. Esc usually is used to cancel a command or an operation.

escape code   A combination of the Esc code and an ASCII character that, when transmitted to a printer, causes the printer to perform a special function, such as print characters in boldface type.

EtherNet   Pronounced "ee´-thur-net." A local area network hardware standard, originally developed by Xerox Corporation, capable of linking up to 1,024 nodes in a bus network.

A high-speed standard using a baseband (single-channel) communication technique, EtherNet provides for a raw data transfer rate of 10 megabits per second, with actual throughputs in the 2 to 3 megabits per second range. EtherNet uses carrier sense multiple access/collision detection techniques (CSMA/CD) to prevent network failures when two devices attempt to access the network at the same time. See *AppleTalk, bus network,* and *local area network (LAN)*.

▲ **Caution:** Several firms such as 3Com and Novell manufacture local area network hardware that uses EtherNet protocols, but the products of one firm often are incompatible with the products of another.

EtherTalk   An implementation of EtherNet local area network hardware, jointly developed by Apple and 3Com, designed to work with the AppleShare network operating system. A network with a bus topology, EtherTalk transmits data via coaxial cables at the EtherNet rate of 10 megabits per second, in contrast to AppleTalks much slower rate of only 230 kilobits per second. An EtherTalk network requires that each networked Macintosh be equipped with a compatible network interface card.

ETX/ACK handshaking   See *handshaking*.

even parity   In asynchronous communications, an error-checking technique that sets an extra bit (called a parity bit) to 1 if the number of 1 bits in a one-byte data item adds up to an even number. The parity bit is set to 0 if the number of 1 bits adds up to an odd number. See *asynchronous communication, odd parity,* and *parity checking*.

event-driven program   A program designed to react to user-initiated events, such as clicking a mouse, rather than forcing the user to go through a series of prompts and menus in a predetermined way.

Macintosh application programs are event-driven. Unlike conventional programs that have an algorithm for solving a problem, the central feature of a Mac program is the main event loop that forces the program to run in circles while waiting for the user to do something like click the mouse.

execute   To carry out the instructions in an algorithm or program.

expandability   The ability of a computer system to accommodate more memory, additional disk drives, or adapters.

Computers vary in their expandability. The Macintosh IIsi, for instance, offers much of the functionality of the more expensive IIci, but it has only one expansion slot. Inexpensive 386 computers may offer only two or three expansion slots and room for only one or two megabytes of RAM on the motherboard; with a little comparison shopping, you can get a machine with more slots available and room for 8M of RAM.

→ **Tip:** Consider expandability when you're shopping for a computer. What accessories are you likely to add to your system? A modem? A fax adapter? Additional disk drives? As for memory, remember that what seems adequate now will prove woefully insufficient in the future. If you're planning to use Windows, and particularly if you're planning to run more than one application, you may need as much as 4M or more RAM.

expanded memory   In IBM PC-compatible computers, a method of getting beyond the 640K DOS memory barrier by swapping programs and data in and out of the main memory at high speeds.

Expanded memory uses a programming trick to get beyond the 640K RAM barrier. A peephole of 64K of RAM is set aside so that program instructions and data can be paged in and out in 64K chunks. When the computer requires a 64K chunk not currently paged in, expanded memory software finds and inserts the chunk into the peephole. Such swapping (bank switching) occurs so quickly that the computer seems to have more than 640K RAM.

If your computer uses the 8088, 8086, or 80286 microprocessor and you want to take advantage of expanded memory, equip your computer with an expanded memory board conforming to the Lotus-Intel-Microsoft Expanded Memory System. If you are using an 80386 or 80486 computer with more than one megabyte of extended RAM, you can take advantage of this additional RAM under DOS by using a memory management program such as Quarterdeck's Expanded Memory Manager (QEMM/386) or Microsoft Expanded Memory Manager 386. See *extended memory* and *Lotus-Intel-Microsoft Expanded Memory System (LIM EMS)*.

▲ **Caution:** Software cannot work with expanded memory unless designed to do so. Most popular application packages such as WordPerfect and Lotus 1-2-3 work with LIM 4.0 expanded memory, but less popular programs and shareware may not function in EMS unless you are using a windowing environment such as Quarterdeck's DESQview or Microsoft Windows.

expanded memory board An adapter that adds expanded memory to an IBM-compatible computer. See *expanded memory*.

expanded memory emulator A utility program for '386 and '486 IBM-compatible computers that uses extended memory to simulate expanded memory.

Expanded memory provided a means to prolong the useful life of 8086- and 8088-based personal computers. When IBM-compatible computers based on the 80286 and later microprocessors became available, it became possible to equip these computers with 16 megabytes (80286) or more (80386) of extended memory, which is superior to expanded memory. But DOS still couldn't use this memory; DOS runs these microprocessors in real mode, which restricts programs to the same old 640K conventional memory space. Expanded memory emulators address this problem by configuring extended memory as if it were expanded memory. With an expanded memory emulator, there's no need for an expensive expanded memory adapter board. See *expanded memory* and *extended memory.*

expanded memory manager   A utility program that manages expanded memory in an IBM-compatible computer equipped with an expanded memory board. See *expanded memory* and *expanded memory board.*

Expanded Memory Specification (EMS)   See *Lotus-Intel-Microsoft Expanded Memory Specification (LIM EMS).*

expanded type   Type that has been increased laterally so that fewer characters are contained per linear inch.

expansion bus   An extension of the computer's data bus and address bus that includes a number of receptacles (slots) for adapter boards.

Because each generation of microprocessors has a wider data bus, the expansion bus of IBM PC-compatible computers has changed. The original IBM Personal Computer and XT, based on the 8/16-bit 8088 chip, used an expansion bus with 62-pin expansion slots; the IBM Personal Computer AT, based on the 16-bit 80286, uses the same 62-pin expansion slot plus a supplemental, 36-pin expansion slot.

Non-IBM PC compatibles based on the 32-bit Intel 80386 microprocessor require a 32-bit data bus structure to connect with primary storage. Because even these computers use 16-bit peripherals such as disk drives and video displays, however, some of them set aside adequate room for memory expansion on the motherboard and use the standard, AT-style expansion bus for peripherals. Some machines have expansion slots for full 32-bit memory boards.

With the advent of true 32-bit microprocessors such as the Intel 80386, the 32-bit data bus is extended throughout the machine, and the full performance benefits of 32-bit chips are realized. However, two competing standards have emerged for 32-bit expansion buses. See *address bus, bus, Extended Industry Standard Architecture (EISA), Micro Channel Bus, microprocessor,* and *motherboard.*

expansion card   See *adapter*.

expansion slot   A receptacle connected to the computer's expansion bus, designed to accept adapters. See *adapter*.

exploded pie graph   A pie graph in which one or more of the slices has been offset slightly from the others. See *pie graph*.

export   To output data in a form that another program can read.

Most word processing programs can export a document in ASCII format, which almost any program can read and use. See *import*.

Extended Binary Coded Decimal Interchange Code (EBCDIC)
A standard computer character set coding scheme used to represent 256 standard characters.

IBM mainframes use EBCDIC coding, and personal computers use American Standard Code for Information Interchange (ASCII) coding. Communications networks that link personal computers to IBM mainframes must include a translating device to mediate between the two systems.

extended character set   In IBM PC-compatible computing, a 254-character set based in the computer's read-only memory (ROM) that includes, in addition to the 128 ASCII character codes, a collection of foreign language, technical, and block graphics characters.

The characters with numbers above ASCII code 128 sometimes are referred to as higher-order characters.

▲ **Caution:** You can produce the foreign language, technical, and graphics characters on-screen by holding down the Alt key and typing the character's code on the numeric keypad. But, you may not be able to print these characters unless your printer is designed to print the entire IBM extended character set. The popular Epson printers do not print higher-order characters because they use that space for italic characters.

Extended Graphics Array (XGA)   A high-resolution graphics standard developed by IBM and intended as the successor to the Video
Graphics Array (VGA) standard. XGA video boards and displays
are capable of a 1024 by 768 pixel resolution, but they require
IBM's proprietary Micro Channel Architecture. See *Extended Industry Standard Architecture (EISA)* and *Micro Channel*.

Extended Industry Standard Architecture (EISA)   A 32-bit expansion bus design introduced by a consortium of IBM PC-
compatible computer makers to counter IBM's proprietary Micro
Channel Bus.

   Unlike Micro Channel, the EISA bus is downwardly compatible
with existing 16-bit peripherals such as disk drives and display
adapters. See *Micro Channel Bus* and *expansion bus*.

extended memory   In '286 or later IBM-compatible computers, the
random-access memory (RAM), if any, above 1 megabyte.

   Personal computers based on the Intel 8088 and 8086 microprocessors are limited to 1 megabyte of random-access memory (RAM),
of which DOS is able to access 640K. PCs based on the 80286,
80386, and 80486 microprocessors can directly address more than
1 megabyte of RAM. An 80826-based computer can address up to
16M of main memory directly, while an 80386-based computer can
address a whopping 4 gigabytes.

   The term *extended memory* often is confused with *expanded
memory,* but the distinction is important. Extended memory is
RAM above 1M that usually is installed directly on the motherboard of 80286 and later computers and is all directly accessible to
the microprocessor. Expanded memory, in contrast, is a tricky way
of getting beyond the 640K barrier using a technique called bank
switching. A bank of conventional memory is set aside to be
swapped in and out as needed, providing up to 8 megabytes of apparent RAM. But the bank switching technique results in memory
access times that are slower than true, extended memory. With expanded memory, a program must wait until the memory circuits
swap the correct bank of memory into conventional memory.

With 8088 and 8086 machines, your only option for memory expansion is expanded memory. With '286 and later machines, you can add extended memory. That's the good news. The bad news is that your DOS applications probably can't use this memory without help. Even if you have 5 megabytes of RAM installed in your computer, DOS can use only the first 640K, called conventional memory.

What personal computing has needed, ever since the introduction of '286-based computers, is a set of standards and an operating environment that enable all programs to access extended memory.

Microsoft Windows 3, coupled with the eXtended Memory Specification (XMS), provides a much-needed solution to this problem. A DOS application designed in accordance with XMS guidelines can, with the assistance of a utility program known as an extended memory manager, use the extended memories (if any) of '286 and later machines. An extended memory manager (HIMWM.SYS) is provided with DOS 5.0 and Microsoft Windows 3, currently the most popular operating platform for extended memory access. In Window's standard and 386 enhanced modes, Windows allows DOS applications to use all the extended memory available, provided that these applications are written in conformity to the XMS guidelines. Most popular applications now observe the XMS guidelines.

Sometimes you see *extended memory* defined as "the memory above 640K." For example, many '386 computers sold with 1M of RAM are said to contain 640K of conventional memory and 384K of extended memory. (Microsoft Windows' documentation defines extended memory this way.) Technically, this definition is incorrect; extended memory begins at 1,024K (1M). However, many extended memory managers can configure the upper memory area, the memory between 640K and 1M, as if it were extended memory, and allow programs to access a portion of this memory. From the user's viewpoint, this upper memory area is an important extended memory resource. See *conventional memory, expanded memory, extended memory manager, eXtended Memory Specification (XMS), Microsoft Windows,* and *upper memory area.*

→ **Tip:** If you have a '286 or later personal computer and you are contemplating additional memory, skip expanded memory. The expanded memory option is, at best, an option of last recourse for owners of 8088 and 8086 systems who would prefer not to upgrade. With a '286 or later machine, the extended memory option costs less, provides better performance, and prepares your system for Microsoft Windows and Windows applications.

extended memory manager   A utility program that enables DOS programs written to conform to the XMS standard to access extended memory. See *conventional memory, extended memory,* and *eXtended Memory Specification (XMS)*.

eXtended Memory Specification (XMS)   A set of rules for programmers to follow so that DOS programs can access extended memory in an orderly way. The device driver HIMEM.SYS, or an equivalent memory management program, must be present in your computer's CONFIG.SYS file before XMS memory can be accessed. The specification was jointly developed by Lotus Development Corporation, Intel Corporation, Microsoft Corporation, and AST. See *CONFIG.SYS, extended memory, eXtended Memory Specification (XMS), HIMEM.SYS,* and *memory-management program*.

extensible   Able to accept new, user-defined commands.

extension   A three-letter suffix to a DOS file name that describes the file's contents.

→ **Tip:** Use extensions to categorize files, not to name them. Because DOS gives you only eight characters for file names, you may be tempted to use the extension as part of the name (LETTER-3.JOE). Doing so, however, makes grouping files more difficult for backup and other operations. If all your document files have the same extension (DOC or TXT, for example), you can use the DOS wild-card feature to back up all these files with one command.

external hard disk   A hard disk equipped with its own case, cables, and power supply. External hard disks generally cost more than internal hard disks of comparable speed and capacity.

external modem   A modem equipped with its own case, cables, and power supply. External modems are designed to plug into the serial port of a computer. See *internal modem*.

external table   In Lotus 1-2-3 Release 3, a database created with a database management program (such as dBASE III) that Lotus 1-2-3 directly can access using the /Data External command.

extremely low-frequency (ELF) emission   The magnetic field generated by commonly used electrical appliances such as electric blankets, hair dryers, food mixers, and computer display monitors, and extending one to two meters from the source. ELF fields are known to cause tissue changes and fetal abnormalities in laboratory test animals, and may be related to reproductive anomalies and cancers among frequent users of computer displays.

The debate over the health implications posed by computer displays illustrates the challenges citizens face as they try to sort out the conflicting claims made by scientists, government regulators, Congressional committee reports, employers, and equipment manufacturers. In the mid-1970s, two *New York Times* copy editors were found to have developed ocular opacities (the predecessor of cataracts) after intensive use of computer displays. After a newspaper union charged that the displays posed a health threat to workers, the National Institute of Occupational Safety and Health (NIOSH) conducted a study of the emissions produced by these and other displays. NIOSH concluded that these and other emissions fell below the measurement threshold of the equipment used and could not be distinguished from background radiation, and therefore posed no hazards to public health. Subsequent charges state that the equipment used to perform these tests was not appropriate and that the data confirming strong magnetic fields was dismissed inappropriately as an experimental anomaly.

Despite repeated assurances by employers, computer manufacturers, Federal officials, and scientific researchers that computer displays were safe, evidence continued to accumulate of reproductive disorders among pregnant computer workers. A 1981 Congressional inquiry, however, concluded that the preponderance of evidence suggested no cause for linking the use of computer displays to reproductive disorders or other health issues. During the hearings, computer manufacturers were unanimous in insisting that their products posed no hazards to users.

Subsequently, scientific researchers worldwide were beginning to document serious tissue changes and abnormalities in laboratory animals after exposure to ELF fields, but very few of these results appeared in North American newspapers. The dearth of coverage continued well into the late 1980s, despite additional reports of reproductive anomalies and additional scientific studies affirming a link between ELF fields and tissue abnormalities. These studies suggested that computer display use in excess of 20 hours per week brought about a significant increase in the miscarriage rate among pregnant women, and that the risk of cancer increased by 30 percent among children who used electric blankets. When such evidence was brought before government regulators or industry spokesmen, the position was taken that these studies had serious methodological flaws or that they failed to provide a theoretical explanation that could draw a link between ELF and living cell abnormalities.

A study conducted by the U.S. Environmental Protection Agency, originally scheduled for release in November, 1990, concluded that the overall weight of the evidence suggested "modestly elevated" risks of cancer (especially leukemia, lymphoma, and cancer of the nervous system) after prolonged exposure to ELF fields. However, the release of the study was held up on the insistence of administration officials who added qualifiers to the study's claims. In the meantime, a study jointly conducted by Columbia University and Hunter College demonstrated a link between ELF fields and a dramatically increased rate of DNA transcription in living cells, thus suggesting the missing theoretical link between ELF emissions and cancer.

▲ **Caution:** Although a link between computer display usage and cancer has not been proven beyond doubt, sufficient evidence exists to suggest that computer users should take steps to reduce their exposure to ELF fields. Contrary to what you might suppose, a computer display's ELF emissions are weakest in front of the screens; emissions from the back and sides are stronger. If your desk is positioned back to back with another, so that you are close to the side or back of another computer display, you should move your desk away. To reduce exposure to the emissions coming from the display's screen, remain an arm's length away from the screen.

→ **Tip:** Here's an excellent argument for investing in a Windows or Macintosh system, preferably with a large, full-page or two-page display. Because these systems can display font sizes on-screen, you can define a 14- or 18-point font size as the normal font for writing and editing purposes. You can easily read such a font from a distance of two or three feet. When it's time to print the document, switch to 12-point or 10-point type. Another strategy: Sweden has instituted tough new emissions standards for computer displays, and displays are now available on the U.S. market that meet or exceed these standards. You may be able to replace your current display with a low-emissions model that meets the Swedish standards. Another alternative is to use a laptop or notebook computer with an LCD or gas-plasma display; neither emit an ELF field.

f

facing pages   The two pages of a bound document that face each other when the document is open.

The even-numbered page (verso) is on the left, and the odd-numbered page (recto) is on the right. See *recto* and *verso*.

FAT   See *file allocation table (FAT)*.

fault tolerance The capability of a computer system to cope with internal hardware problems without interrupting the system's performance. Fault tolerant designs typically use back-up systems automatically brought on-line when a failure is detected.

The need for fault tolerance is indisputable whenever computers are assigned critical functions, such as guiding an aircraft to a safe landing or ensuring a steady flow of medicines to a patient. Fault tolerance also is beneficial for noncritical, everyday applications.

fax The transmission and reception of a printed page between two locations connected via telecommunications.

Short for FACSimile, fax has taken the business world by storm. A fax machine scans a sheet of paper and converts its image into a coded form that can be transmitted via the telephone system. A fax machine on the other end receives and translates the transmitted code and prints a replica of the original page.

fax board An adapter that fits into the expansion slot of a personal computer, providing much of the functionality of a fax machine at a significantly lower cost.

Compared to fax machines, fax boards have advantages and disadvantages. The advantages include lower cost, crisper output, and convenience, but the disadvantages are significant, too. What's so convenient about a fax machine is that it accepts as input anything that can be represented on paper, including handwriting, graphics, and text. To send a fax through a fax board, you must first get the material to be faxed into the computer—and unless your system is equipped with a scanner, this restriction all but rules out sending handwriting and graphics. For the most part, you will send text files. Some fax boards are send-only. Other machines, however, receive anything anyone can send to you via a fax machine.

→ **Tip:** Don't settle for a fax board that supports 4800 bps transmission speeds; 9600 bps boards aren't much more expensive and provide twice the transmission speed.

fax server   In a local area network, a PC or a self-contained unit that contains fax circuitry accessible to all the workstations in network. See *fax board* and *local area network (LAN)*.

feathering   Adding an even amount of space between each line on a page or column to force vertical justification.

female connector   A computer cable terminator and connection device with receptacles designed to accept the pins of a male connector. See *male connector*.

femto   Prefix indicating one quadrillionth, or a millionth of a billionth (10^{-15}).

field   See *data field*.

field definition   In a database management program, a list of the attributes that define the type of information that the user can enter into a data field. The field definition also determines how the field's contents appear on-screen.

In dBASE, the field definition includes the following:

- Field name. A 10-character, one-word field name that appears as a heading in data tables and as a prompt on data-entry forms.
- Data type. A definition that governs the type of data you can enter into a field.
- Field width. The maximum number of characters the field accommodates.
- Number of decimal places. The number of decimal places to appear if the field is a numeric field.
- Index attribute. If you turn on the index attribute, the program includes this field when constructing an index to the database.
- Field mask.

See *data type* and *field template*.

field name   In a database management program, a name given to a data field that helps you identify the field's contents.

→ **Tip:** Field names are important from the user's standpoint, because they describe the data contained in each data field. You see the field names on data-entry forms and data tables. Ideally, the field names you choose are descriptive—if you name a field MX-388SMRPS, nobody will know what the name means.

In dBASE, field names are restricted to one word consisting of a continuous series of characters. You can write two- or three-word field names by separating the words with underscore characters as in the following:

        FIRST_NAME
        LAST_NAME
        PHONE_NO

In dBASE, field names are limited to 10 characters. Some programs do not impose such stringent limitations. Even so, you should keep field names short. When you display data in a columnar format, therefore, you see more columns of data on-screen. However, do not make the names so short that they become cryptic.

field privilege   In a database management program, a database definition that establishes what a user can do with the contents of a data field in a protected database. See *data field* and *file privilege*.

field template   In database management programs, a field definition that specifies which kind of data can be typed in the data field. If you try to type data into a field that does not match the field template, the program displays an error message. Synonymous with *data mask*. See *data type*.

→ **Tip:** Field templates should be used as often as possible. They help to prevent users from adding inappropriate information to the database.

In dBASE, you can specify the following field templates for each character field in the database structure:

X	Accepts any character
A	Accepts alphabetic letters (a-z, A-Z)
#	Accepts numbers (0–9)
N	Accepts alphabetic letters, numbers, or an underscore character
Y	Accepts Y (for Yes) or N (for No)
L	Accepts T (for True) or F (for False)
!	Converts all inputted characters to uppercase

For numeric fields, you can specify the following templates:

9	Accepts numbers and + or − signs, and requires the user to type the number of characters specified (for example, 99999 requires that the user type five numbers)
#	Accepts numbers, space, and + or − signs
*	Displays leading zeros as asterisks
$	Displays leading zeros as dollar signs
,	Displays numbers larger than 999 with commas
.	Displays a decimal point

file   A named collection of information stored as an apparent unit on a secondary storage medium such as a disk drive.

  Although a file appears to be whole, the operating system may distribute the file among dozens or even hundreds of noncontiguous sectors on the disk, storing the linkages (chains) among these sectors in a file allocation table. To the user, however, files appear as units on disk directories and are retrieved and copied as units. See *file allocation table (FAT)* and *secondary storage*.

file allocation table (FAT)   A hidden table on a floppy disk or hard disk that stores information about how files are stored in distinct (and not necessarily contiguous) sectors. See *file fragmentation*.

file attribute   A hidden code stored with a file's directory that contains its read-only or archive status and other information about the file. See *archive attribute*, *invisible file*, *locked file*, and *read-only attribute*.

file compression utility   A utility program that compresses and decompresses infrequently used files so that they take up 40 to 50 percent less room on a hard disk. The utility decompresses these files when they are needed. File compression utilities commonly are used for two purposes: to decompress files that have been downloaded from a bulletin board system (BBS) and to make room on a hard disk by compressing all files opened for a specified period (such as one week). See *archive*.

file conversion utility   A utility program that converts files created with one program so that the files can be read by a program that employs an incompatible file format. One popular word processing conversion utility is Word for Word, which can convert files among 30 file formats. File conversion utilities are available for graphics as well as word processing file conversion.

Increasingly, word processing programs include conversion utilities to facilitate the exchange of formatted documents with other users. IBM's Signature, for example, can read and write to a wide variety of file formats, including WordStar, Microsoft Word, WordPerfect, and DisplayWrite. File conversion utilities also are increasingly found in graphics programs due to the existence of a host of incompatible graphics file formats.

file defragmentation   See *defragmentation*.

file deletion   The removal of a file name from a directory without actually removing the contents of the file from the disk.

You should understand how personal computers erase files for two reasons: security and the recovery of accidentally deleted files.

When you erase a file with a DEL or ERASE statement, the operating system does not actually destroy the data or program instructions stored on the disk; the operating system merely deletes the name of the file from the disk directory so that the space the file occupies is made available for future storage operations.

This procedure brings up the security angle: others can recover sensitive data from your system, even if you think you have erased the information. To prevent the recovery of such data, you can use a shareware program such as Complete Delete (Macintosh) that totally erases the information on disk.

The fact that file deletions do not actually erase the data on disk can be helpful if the deletion was accidental. An undelete utility, widely available as shareware and in utility program packages such as Symantec Utilities (Macintosh environment) and Norton Utilities (IBM PC-compatible environment), can restore a deleted file if no other information has been written over the file.

→ **Tip:** If you accidentally delete a file, stop working. Do not perform any additional operations that write information to the disk. Use an undelete utility immediately. See *shareware, undelete utility,* and *utility program.*

file extension   See *extension.*

file format   The patterns and standards a program uses to store data on disk.

Few programs store data in ASCII format; most use a proprietary file format that other programs cannot read. For example, Microsoft Word cannot read files created with WordPerfect, and WordPerfect cannot read files created with Microsoft Word. The use of proprietary file formats stems from marketing strategy (ensuring that customers continue to use the company's program). Proprietary file formats also enable programmers to include special features that standard formats may not allow.

→ **Tip:** If you are stuck with some documents your program cannot read, you can use a data conversion service or a file conversion utility. To locate a data conversion service, look in the Yellow Pages or in the back advertising sections of popular personal computer magazines. See *file conversion utility, native file format,* and *proprietary file format.*

file fragmentation   The inefficient allocation of files in noncontiguous sectors on a floppy disk or hard disk. Fragmentation occurs because of multiple file deletions and write operations.

When DOS writes a file to disk, the operating system looks for available clusters. If you have created and erased many files on the disk, few files are stored in contiguous clusters; the disk drive's read/write head must travel longer distances to retrieve the scattered data. A process known as defragmentation can improve disk efficiency by as much as 50 percent by rewriting files so that they are placed in contiguous clusters. See *defragmentation*.

file locking   In a local area network, a method of concurrency control that ensures the integrity of data. File locking prevents more than one user from accessing and altering a file at a time. See *concurrency control* and *local area network (LAN)*.

file management program   See *flat-file database management program*.

file name   A name assigned to a file so that the operating system can find the file. You assign file names when the files are created. Every file on a disk must have a unique name.

In DOS and early versions of OS/2, file names have two parts: the file name and the extension. These names must conform to the following rules.

- Length. You may use up to eight characters for the file name and up to three characters for the extension. The extension is optional.
- Delimiter. If you use the extension, you must separate the file name and extension by typing a period (no spaces).
- Legal characters. You may use any letter or number on the keyboard for file names and extensions. You also may use the following punctuation symbols:

         ' ~ ! @ # $ ^ & ( ) _ - { }

▲ **Caution:** One of the shortcomings of DOS and the early versions of OS/2 is the eight-character restriction on file names. (OS/2 Versions 1.2 and 2 enable you to use lengthier file names.) You are given little room to express the contents of a file. Yet, the file name must express the file's contents well enough so that you recognize the file in a disk directory. Obviously, a file name such as @12AX-97.TBT is not going to mean much to you a few months later. Good file-naming practice restricts the use of extensions to describe the type of file (not the contents). Files labeled with the extensions COM and EXE are program files. Files labeled DOC and TXT are word processor or text files. Files labeled WK1 or WKS are spreadsheet (worksheet) files, and so on.

In the Macintosh environment, you can use up to 32 characters for file names, and file names can contain any character (including spaces) with the exception of the colon (:). The colon is restricted because the Mac's Hierarchical File System (HFS) uses the colon to construct path names. For example, the path name Proposals: Foundations:Proposal No. 1 describes the location of the file Proposal No. 1. This file is in the Foundations folder within the Proposals folder.

→ **Tip:** The Mac's Open and Save dialog boxes can display only 22 characters; the last 10 characters of longer file names are truncated. Because seeing the entire file name when retrieving or saving files is convenient, knowledgeable Mac users restrict file names to 22 characters.

file privilege   In dBASE, an attribute that determines what a user can do with a protected database on a network. The options are DELETE, EXTEND, READ, and UPDATE. See *field privilege*.

file recovery   The restoration of an erased disk file. See *undelete utility*.

file server   In a local area network, a PC that provides access to files for all the workstations in the network.

In a peer-to-peer network, all workstations also are file servers, because each workstation can provide files to other workstations. In the more common client/server network architecture, a single, high-powered machine with a huge hard disk is set aside to function as the file server for all the workstations (clients) in the network.

Crucial to the file server's functions is the network operation system (NOS), which accepts incoming requests from client workstations and responds with the requested files or data. From the user's point of view at each workstation, the file server's resources appear as if they were just another hard disk that is directly connected to the workstation itself.

filespec In DOS, a complete specification of a file's location, including a drive letter, path name, file name, and extension, such as C:\REPORTS\REPORT1.WK1.

file transfer protocol In asynchronous communications, a standard that governs the error-free transmission of program and data files via the telephone system. See *asynchronous communication, Kermit,* and *XMODEM.*

file transfer utility A utility program that transfers files between different hardware platforms, such as the IBM Personal Computer and the Macintosh, or between a desktop and a laptop computer.

Popular file transfer utilities include MacLink Plus, which links PCs and Macs via their serial ports, and Brooklyn Bridge, which links desktop IBM computers with IBM PC-compatible laptops.

FILES In DOS, a configuration command that specifies the number of files that can be open simultaneously.

By default, DOS can work with up to eight files at a time. However, some applications require a CONFIG.SYS statement, such as FILES=15, that increases this number. Usually, the program's installation software adds such a statement to your CONFIG.SYS file or creates the file if it does not exist.

fill In spreadsheet programs, an operation that enters a sequence of values (numbers, dates, times, or formulas) in a worksheet.

In Lotus 1-2-3, you use the /Data Fill command to fill a range with values, beginning with the start value (the number Lotus 1-2-3 uses to start filling the range), the step value (the number Lotus 1-2-3 uses to increment each number placed in the range), and the stop value (the highest number placed in the range).

→ **Tip:** You can use /Data Fill to enter a column or row of dates automatically. If you enter **@DATE(91,11,1)** as the start value, **14 (days)** as the step value, and **@DATE(92,10,1)** as the stop value, 1-2-3 enters dates at two-week intervals between November 1, 1991 and October 1, 1992 in the column or row.

Finder   A file and memory management utility, provided by Apple, for Macintosh computers. This utility enables you to run one application at a time. See *MultiFinder*.

Often mistakenly referred to as the Macintosh's operating system, the Finder is nothing more than a shell that can be replaced by other shell programs such as XTreeMac. Although the Finder's intuitive and easy-to-use icons and menus have contributed to the Mac's success, the program's limitations quickly become apparent on systems equipped with large hard disks. A new version of the Finder, to be shipped with System 7, is expected to solve many problems.

firmware   Broadly, the system software permanently stored in a computer's read-only memory (ROM) or elsewhere in the computer's circuitry. Firmware cannot be modified by the user.

fixed disk   See *hard disk*.

fixed numeric format   In spreadsheet programs, a numeric format in which values are rounded to the number of decimal places you specify. See *numeric format*.

flame   In electronic mail, to lose one's self-control and write a communication that uses derogatory, obscene, or inappropriate language. (Slang term.)

flat-file database management program   A database management program that stores, organizes, and retrieves information from one file at a time. Such programs lack relational database management features. See *data integrity* and *relational database management*.

flatbed scanner   An optical graphics digitizer that can transform a full-page (8½-by-11-inch) graphic into a digitized file. See *scanner*.

flicker   A visible distortion that occurs when you scroll the screen of a video monitor that employs a low refresh rate.

floating graphic   A graph or picture that has not been fixed in an absolute position on the page, so that it moves up or down on the page as you delete or insert text above the graphic.

floating-point calculation   A method for storing and calculating numbers so that the location of the decimal is not fixed but floating (the decimal moves around as needed so that significant digits are taken into account in the calculation). Floating-point calculation can be implemented in numeric coprocessors or in software, improving the accuracy of computer calculations.

▲ **Caution:** Floating-point notation helps computers perform calculations more accurately. But an inherent limitation to any computer's capability to deal with large and small numbers still exists. Some programs set aside more memory than others for number storage; any program has a range of numbers that it can handle accurately. One program can handle any number from 10^{-20} to 10^{20}, but smaller or larger numbers produce erroneous results.

A good program states the range of acceptable numbers in the manual. Some programs do not inform you what the range is and enable you to enter numbers that are truncated without your knowledge. These programs can produce erroneous results when used for any calculation involving very large or small numbers. See *numeric coprocessor*.

floppy disk A removable and widely used secondary storage medium that uses a magnetically sensitive flexible disk enclosed in a plastic envelope or case.

Floppy disks are the usual way in which programs and text files are communicated from one computer to another. At one time, they also were the only medium for secondary storage for personal computers, but the availability of inexpensive hard disks has relegated floppy disks to the sidelines.

Hard disks are preferred for many reasons: floppy disk drives are slower, and the disks are damaged more easily and offer less storage. However, floppy disks are essential for getting programs and data into your computer and for backup purposes.

A floppy disk is a magnetically coated, flexible disk of plastic. The disk rotates within a flexible or firm plastic envelope. The access hole (head slot) provides an opening so that the drive's read/write head can perform recording and playback operations on the disk's surface, within the magnetically-encoded tracks and sectors created when disks are formatted. You can use the write-protect notch to keep the drive from erasing the data on the disk; when the notch is covered, the drive cannot perform erase or write operations.

Most floppy disks used in personal computing come in two sizes: 5¼ and 3½ inches. Floppy disks are available in single-sided or double-sided and standard double density or high density. Single-sided disks are rarely used, and high density disks are becoming more popular than double-density disks. 5¼-inch disks, with flimsy sleeves and open access holes, are more susceptible to damage; 3½-inch disks come in rigid plastic cases and have a sliding door that covers the access hole. (The drive opens the door after you insert the disk.)

▲ **Caution:** 5¼-inch disks are more susceptible to damage than 3½-inch disks; avoid pressing down hard with a ball-point pen as you label the disk and be wary of fingerprints on the actual surface of the disk (easy to touch through the open access hole). Always keep 5¼-inch disks in protective envelopes when they are not being used and do not leave the disk in the drive when the computer is turned off; the disk may accumulate dust. Although less susceptible than 5¼-inch disks, 3½-inch disks can be damaged. Keep both types of disks away from moisture, dust, and strong magnetic fields. See *access hole, double density, hard disk, high density, read/write head, single-sided disk,* and *write-protect notch.*

flow   To import text into a specific text area on a page layout so that the text wraps around graphics and fills in specified columns. Page layout programs can import text in this way. See *page layout program.*

flow chart   A chart that contains symbols referring to computer operations, describing how the program performs.

flush left   In word processing, the alignment of text along the left margin, leaving a ragged right margin. Flush left alignment is easier to read than right-justified text.

flush right   In word processing, the alignment of text along with right margin, leaving a ragged left margin. Flush right alignment is seldom used except for decorative effects or epigrams.

folder   In the Macintosh Finder, an on-screen representation of a file folder on the desktop into which the user can place files so that the display is not overly cluttered with files.

Folders are analogous to subdirectories in the DOS world, but with an unfortunate difference: with the exception of HyperCard, you cannot define default paths for the system to follow as it attempts to locate program and data files. A DOS user can set up a hard disk using PATH statements in the AUTOEXEC.BAT file, and if done correctly, you only rarely need to explore the disk manually in search of a file. Macintosh users, in contrast, must frequently open and scroll through folders in search of a file.

font   Pronounced "fahnt." One complete collection of letters, punctuation marks, numbers, and special characters with a consistent and identifiable typeface, weight (Roman or bold), posture (upright or italic), and font size.

Technically, font still refers to one complete set of characters in a given typeface, weight, and size, such as Helvetica italic 12. But the term often is used to refer to typefaces or font families.

Two kinds of fonts exist: bit-mapped fonts and outline fonts. Each comes in two versions, screen fonts and printer fonts. See *bit-mapped font, font family, outline font, posture, printer font, screen font, typeface, type size,* and *weight.*

Font/DA Mover   A utility program provided with Macintosh system software that adds fonts and desk accessories to the System file of the computer's startup disk. See *desk accessory (DA)* and *startup disk.*

font downloader   See *downloading utility.*

font family   A set of fonts in several sizes and weights that share the same typeface.

The following list describes a font family in the Helvetica typeface:

Helvetica Roman 10
Helvetica bold 10
Helvetica italic 10
Helvetica Roman 12
Helvetica bold 12
Helvetica italic 12
Helvetica bold italic 12

font ID conflict   In the Macintosh environment, a system error caused by conflicts between the identification numbers assigned to the screen fonts stored in the System Folder.

The Macintosh System and many Macintosh applications recognize and retrieve fonts by the identification number assigned to them, not by name. But, the original Macintosh operating system enabled you to assign only 128 unique numbers to fonts, so that you inadvertently could assemble a repertoire of screen fonts with conflicting numbers, causing printing errors. With System 6.0, a New Font Numbering Table (NFNT) scheme was introduced that enables you to assign 16,000 unique numbers, reducing—but not ruling out—the potential for font ID conflicts.

font metric   The width and height information for each character in a font. The font metric is stored in a width table.

font smoothing   In high-resolution laser printers, the reduction of aliasing and other distortions when text or graphics are printed.

font substitution   Substituting an outline font for printing in place of a bit-mapped screen font.

In the Macintosh environment, the LaserWriter printer driver substitutes the outline fonts Helvetica, Times Roman, and Courier for the screen fonts Geneva, New York, and Monaco. However, spacing may be unsatisfactory. Better results are obtained by using the screen font equivalent to the printer font.

footer   In a word processing or page layout program, a short version of a document's title or other text positioned at the bottom of every page of the document. See *header*.

footnote   In a word processing or page layout program, a note positioned at the bottom of the page.

Most word processing programs with footnoting capabilities number the notes automatically, and renumber them if you insert or delete a note. The best programs can float lengthy footnotes to the next page so that no more than half the page is taken up by footnotes.

→ **Tip:** If you are writing business reports or scholarly work that requires excellent footnoting capabilities, make sure that you can format the footnotes properly. For example, many publishers require double-spacing of all text, even footnotes, and some word processors cannot perform this task. See *endnote*.

footprint   The space occupied by a computer's case on a desk.

forced page break   A page break inserted by the user; the page always breaks at this location.

forecasting   Using a spreadsheet program, a method of financial analysis that involves the projection of past trends into the future.

▲ **Caution:** Implementing a forecast with a spreadsheet program is easy, but beware that a forecast is only a model of reality, and any model is only as good as the assumptions that it is based on. Your forecast may project stable or slightly declining revenues into the next three months, but you may have failed to take into account a seasonal variable that could stimulate sales. Your forecast may lead you to underestimate the inventory you actually need.

foreground task   In a computer capable of multitasking, a job done in priority status before subordinate, or background, tasks are executed. The foreground task generally is the one you see executing.

format   Any method of arranging information for storage, printing, or displaying.

The format of floppy disks and hard disks is the magnetic pattern laid down by the formatting utility. Programs often use proprietary file formats for storing data on disk. Because of these special formats, some programs cannot read files saved by other programs. WordPerfect, for example, cannot read files prepared with Microsoft Word.

In a spreadsheet program, the format is the style and physical arrangement of labels, values, and constants in a cell. Numeric formats include the display of decimal places, and currency symbols. Alignment formats for labels include flush left, centered, and flush right.

In a database management program, the format is the physical arrangement of field names and data fields in a data entry form are displayed on-screen. In a word processing program, document formats include the style and physical arrangement of all document elements, including characters (typeface, type size, weight, posture, and emphasis), lines and paragraphs (alignment, leading), and page design elements (folios, margins, headers, and footers).

In a graphics program, the format is the way in which text and numbers are displayed within charts and graphs and the way in which graphics are stored on disk. See *browse mode, Edit mode,* and *graphics mode.*

format file In dBASE, a file that stores the formats you have chosen for a custom data-entry form.

formatting An operation that establishes a pattern for the storage or printing of data.

In operating systems, an operation that prepares a floppy disk for use in a particular computer system by laying down a magnetic pattern. See *format, high-level format,* and *low-level format.*

formula In a spreadsheet program, a cell definition that defines the relationship between two or more values. In a database management program, an expression that instructs the program to perform calculations on numeric data contained in one or more data fields.

To enter values in a spreadsheet formula, you enter constants, cell references, or a combination. For example, $+2+2$ is a valid formula, as is $+A2+A4$ and $+4+38.9$.

To express the formula in a way that most spreadsheets can recognize, you must convert the formula to spreadsheet notation. Spreadsheet notation differs from mathematical formulas.

One key difference between the usual way you write formulas and spreadsheet notation lies in the operators, the symbols that indicate the arithmetic operation, such as addition, subtraction, multiplication, and division. The operators for addition and subtraction are the same: plus $(+)$ and minus $(-)$. However, you indicate multiplication by using an asterisk (*) and division by using a slash (/). You type a caret (^) before an exponent. See *calculated field, cell definition, precedence,* and *value.*

FORTH A high-level programming language that offers direct control over hardware devices.

Developed in 1970 by an astronomer named Charles Moore to help him control the equipment at the Kitt Peak National Radio Observatory, FORTH—short for FOuRTH-generation programming language—quickly spread to other observatories but has been slow to gain acceptance as a general-purpose programming language. The language is highly extensible—one FORTH programmer's code may be unintelligible to another FORTH programmer. FORTH sometimes is preferred for laboratory data acquisition, robotics, machine control, arcade games, automation, patient monitoring, and interfaces with musical devices. See *high-level programming language*.

FORTRAN A high-level programming language well suited to scientific, mathematical, and engineering applications.

Developed by IBM in the mid-1950s and released in 1957, FORTRAN—short for FORmula TRANslator—was the first compiled high-level programming language. The nature of FORTRAN shows the predominance of scientific applications in the early history of computing; the language enables you to describe and solve mathematical calculations. Still highly suited to such applications, FORTRAN is widely used in scientific, academic, and technical settings. For anyone familiar with BASIC, FORTRAN is immediately recognizable. Indeed, FORTRAN was BASIC's progenitor. FORTRAN shares BASIC's unfortunate limitations as a general-purpose programming language (such as the tendency to produce spaghetti code). However, recent versions of FORTRAN are more structured and have fewer limitations. See *BASIC, high-level programming language, modular programming,* and *structured programming*.

fragmentation See *file fragmentation*.

frame In desktop publishing and word processing, a rectangular area that is absolutely positioned on the page. The frame can contain text, graphics, or both.

free-form text chart   In presentation graphics, a text chart used to handle information difficult to express in lists, such as directions, invitations, and certificates. See *text chart*.

freeware   Copyrighted programs that have been made available without charge for public use. The programs may not be resold for profit. See *public domain software* and *shareware*.

frequency division multiplexing   In local area networks, a technique for transmitting two or more signals over one cable by assigning each to its own frequency. This technique is used in broadband (analog) networks. See *broadband, local area network (LAN)*, and *multiplexing*.

frequency modulation (FM) recording   An early, low-density method of recording digital signals on computer media such as tape and disks. Synonymous with *single-density recording*. See *Modified Frequency Modulation (MFM)* and *single density*.

friction feed   A printer paper-feed mechanism that draws individual sheets of paper through the printer using pressure exerted on the paper by the platen.

Friction-feed mechanisms usually require you to position the paper manually. For a document of more than one or two pages in length, however, manual feeding can be tedious. See *cut-sheet feeder* and *tractor feed*.

front end   The portion of a program that interacts directly with the user. In a local area network, this portion of the program may be distributed to each workstation so that the user can interact with the back end application on the file server. See *back end* and *client/server architecture*.

full duplex   An asynchronous communications protocol in which the communications channel can send and receive signals at the same time. See *asynchronous communication, communications protocol, echoplex*, and *half duplex*.

full justification   The alignment of multiple lines of text along the left and the right margins. See *justification*.

▲ **Caution:** Word processing programs justify both margins by placing extra spaces between words. Because such spacing irregularities destroy the color of a block of text, full justification is rarely advisable. Research also has shown that text formatted with a ragged right margin is more readable than fully justified text. See *color*.

full-motion video adapter   A video adapter that is capable of displaying moving TV images, both prerecorded and live, in a window that appears on the computer's screen.

To display TV images, the adapter is connected to a videocassette recorder, laser disc player, or a camcorder (for live images). Most full-motion video adapters come with software that enables the development of a multimedia presentation, complete with wipes, washes, fades, animation, and sound. Full-motion video applications are expected to play a growing role in corporate and professional presentations and training applications.

full-page display   A computer video monitor that is capable of displaying a full page of text at a time.

Some computer users believe that a full-page display should be considered a minimal system configuration. With a full-page display, you can view and edit an entire page of text, figures, or graphics at a time. For this reason, you can get a better grasp of the overall structure and organization of your document.

▲ **Caution:** If you're thinking about equipping your DOS system with a full-page display, be aware that not all the programs you're using can take advantage of it. Check your programs' documentation.

→ **Tip:** If you're still planning your system and you want to use a full-page display, consider a Macintosh or Windows system. The Mac's Finder supports a full-page display for most Macintosh applications; Windows supports a full-page display for most Windows applications.

full-screen editor A word processing utility designed for application program development, which is often included in programming environments and application development systems.

The term full screen refers to the utility's ability to enable cursor movement and editing within text that has already been created. Unlike a word processing program, which is designed for creating and printing documents such as letters and reports, a typical full-screen editor lacks most of the formatting and printing capabilities of word processing software. A full-screen editor is designed specifically for creating and editing computer programs. It therefore includes special features for indenting lines of program code, searching for non-standard characters, and interfacing with program interpreters or compilers.

Full-screen editing is no big deal to any user of a word processing program, but it's a major improvement over the line editors (such as the notorious EDLIN of MS-DOS) that usually are provided as part of an operating system's programming environment. With version 5.0 of DOS, a good full-screen editor (MS-DOS Editor) has finally become part of the operating system's standard equipment. See *application development system, line editor,* and *programming environment.*

function key A programmable key (conventionally numbered F1, F2, and so on) that provides special functions, depending on the software you are using.

g

gamut In computer graphics, the range of colors that can be displayed on a color monitor.

gas plasma display   See *plasma display*.

gateway   In distributed computing, a device that connects two dissimilar local area networks or that connects a local area network to a wide-area network, a minicomputer, or a mainframe. A gateway has its own processor and memory and may perform protocol conversion and bandwidth conversion.

Gateways typically are found in large organizations in which more than one local area network protocol is installed. For example, a gateway called FastPath (Kinetics) provides a link between AppleTalk and EtherNet networks. See *bridge* and *local area network (LAN)*.

general format   In most spreadsheet programs, the default numeric format in which values are displayed with all significant (nonzero) decimal places, but without commas or currency signs.

general-purpose computer   A computer whose instruction set is sufficiently simple and general that a wide variety of algorithms can be devised for the computer.

GEnie   An on-line information service developed by General Electric that, like CompuServe, offers many of the attractions of a bulletin board system (BBS) and up-to-date stock quotes, home shopping services, and news updates. See *on-line information service*.

giga   A prefix indicating one billion (10^9).

gigabyte   A unit of memory measurement approximately equal to one billion bytes (1,073,741,824). One gigabyte equals 1,000 megabytes.

global backup   A hard disk backup procedure. Everything on the hard disk, including all program files, is backed up onto a medium such as floppy disks. See *incremental backup*.

global format In a spreadsheet program, a numeric format or label alignment choice that applies to all cells in the worksheet. With most programs, you can override the global format by defining a range format for certain cells.

→ **Tip:** If you are working on a financial spreadsheet, the values in your worksheet may require dollar signs and two decimal places. You should choose this global format, therefore, when you begin the worksheet. You can override the global format in sections of the worksheet in which dollar signs are not required by creating a range format. See *label alignment, numeric format,* and *range format.*

glossary In a word processing program, a storage utility that stores frequently used phrases and boilerplate text and inserts them into the document when needed. See *boilerplate.*

grabber hand In graphics programs and HyperCard, an on-screen image of a hand that you can position with the mouse to move selected units of text or graphics from place to place on-screen.

graphical user interface (GUI) A design for the part of the program that interacts with the user and takes full advantage of the bit-mapped graphics displays of personal computers. Like the industry-standard interface that is increasingly common in DOS applications, a GUI employs pull-down menus and dialog boxes. But on-screen graphics are required to display a GUI's icons (pictorial representations of computer resources and functions) as well as a variety of visually attractive on-screen typefaces. The use of a graphical user interface requires a computer with sufficient speed, power, and memory to display a high-resolution, bit-mapped display. See *check box, dialog box, drop-down list box, Macintosh, Microsoft Windows, mousable interface, pull-down menu, radio button,* and *scroll bar/scroll box.*

graphics In personal computing, the creation, modification, and printing of computer-generated graphic images.

The two basic types of computer-produced graphics are object-oriented graphics (also called vector graphics) and bit-mapped graphics (often called raster graphics).

Object-oriented graphics programs, often called draw programs, store graphic images in the form of mathematical representations that can be sized and scaled without distortion. Object-oriented graphics programs are well suited for architecture, computer-aided design, interior design, and other applications in which precision and scaling capability are more important than artistic effects.

Bit-mapped graphic programs, often called paint programs, store graphic images in the form of patterns of screen pixels. Unlike draw programs, paint programs can create delicate patterns of shading that convey an artistic touch, but any attempt to resize or scale the graphic may result in unacceptable distortion. See *bit-mapped graphic, draw program, object-oriented graphic,* and *paint program.*

graphics character In a computer's built-in character set, a character composed of lines, rectangles, or other shapes. Graphics characters can be combined to form block graphics: simple images, illustrations, and borders. See *block graphics* and *character-based program.*

graphics file format In a graphics program, the way in which information needed to display the graphic is arranged and stored on disk.

Little standardization exists for graphics file formats. Your graphics program may be unable to read the files created by another graphics program. The situation is in many ways similar to the profusion of file formats among word processing programs. Many popular programs such as AutoCAD, GEM Draw, Lotus 1-2-3, Windows Paint, and PC Paintbrush generate files in proprietary file formats that other programs can read only if they have been specially equipped to do so.

The Macintosh environment has a standard file format called PICT that uses routines drawn from the Mac's QuickDraw toolbox, a set of image-producing programs stored in the Mac's read-only memory (ROM). But, this format is not satisfactory for many applications. Additional formats include the MacPaint file format for 72 dpi bit-mapped graphics, tagged image file format (TIFF) files for scanned images stored at up to 300 dpi, and Encapsulated PostScript (EPS) Graphics that produce high-resolution graphics on PostScript laser printers.

In the IBM PC environment, many programs can recognize TIFF and EPS files. The graphics file format of Lotus 1-2-3 charts and graphs, stored in files with the PIC extension, is widely recognized by presentation graphics packages; many of these programs are designed to read and enhance charts created with Lotus 1-2-3.

Also widely recognized is the Hewlett-Packard Graphics Language (HPGL), a graphics format created for HP plotters, and some programs recognize the Computer Graphics Metafile (CGM) format. Microsoft Windows and OS/2, unlike DOS, establish graphics file format conventions, and programs designed to run under Windows or OS/2 must adhere to this format. See *Encapsulated PostScript (EPS) file, file format, QuickDraw,* and *Tagged Image File Format (TIFF)*.

Graphics mode   In IBM and IBM-compatible computers, a mode of graphics display adapters in which the computer can display bit-mapped graphics. See *character mode, display adapter,* and *graphics view*.

graphics scanner   A graphics input device that transforms a picture into an image displayed on-screen.

graphics spreadsheet   A spreadsheet program that displays the worksheet on-screen, using bit-mapped graphics instead of relying on the computer's built-in character set.

Graphics spreadsheets such as Lotus 1-2-3/G and Microsoft Excel make available desktop publishing tools such as multiple typefaces, type sizes, rules, and screens (grayed areas). Printouts also can combine spreadsheets and business graphs on one page. See *Lotus 1-2-3* and *Microsoft Excel*.

graphics tablet A graphics input device that enables you to draw with an electronic pen on an electronically sensitive table. The pen's movements are relayed to the screen.

graphics view In some non-Windows DOS applications, a mode in which the program switches the display circuitry to its Graphics mode. In the Graphics mode, the computer is capable of displaying bit-mapped graphics. See *character view*.

→ **Tip:** On all except the fastest computers, Graphics mode is significantly slower than character mode.

gray scale In computer graphics, a series of shades from white to black.

gray-scale monitor A monitor (and compatible display adapter) capable of displaying a full range of shades from white to black on-screen.

→ **Tip:** True gray-scale monitors are expensive and, in comparison to color monitors, offer few benefits to most users. They're essential, however, for a few applications, such as photographic image processing and retouching. A VGA monitor may suffice; it can display a minimum of 64 gray-scale levels.

Greek text A block of simulated text or lines used to represent the positioning and point size of text in a designer's composition of a design.

Greek text is used to simulate the appearance of the document so that the aesthetics of the page design can be assessed. Standard Greek text used by typesetters actually looks more like Latin:

> Lorem ipsum dolor sit amet . . .

Some word processing and page layout programs use a print preview feature analogous to greeking.

greeking Displaying a simulated version of a page on-screen with lines or bars instead of text so that the overall page layout design is apparent.

group   In Microsoft Windows, a collection of program item icons that are stored together under a group icon. When you open the group icon, you see a window showing the program item icons in the group. Examples of groups include the Accessories, Main, and Games groups.

group icon   In Microsoft Windows, an icon that represents a group (a collection of program item icons). When you open the group icon, you see a group window, which contains the program item icons.

groupware   Application programs that increase the cooperation and joint productivity of small groups of co-workers.

   An example of groupware is ForComment (Broderbund Software), designed to make collaborative writing easier. The program enables each member of the group to insert comments and make changes to the text, subject to the other members' approval.

guide   In a page layout program, a nonprinting line that appears as a dotted line on-screen, showing the current location of margins, gutters, and other page layout design elements.

gutter   In word processing and desktop publishing, an additional margin that is added for two-sided printing to allow room for the binding. An extra margin is added to the left side of odd-numbered (recto) pages and to the right side of even-numbered (verso) pages.

GW-BASIC   A version of the BASIC programming language often licensed to PC-compatible computers.

   GW-BASIC is nearly identical to the BASIC interpreter distributed with IBM PCs, but each manufacturer is free to customize the language.

h

hacker   A technically sophisticated computer enthusiast who enjoys making modifications to programs or computer systems.

Hackers can be seen at virtually any college or university computer lab, where they spend inordinate amounts of time trying to master a computer system. Often described as addicted to computers, hackers nevertheless learn skills that prove valuable to organizations.

half duplex   An asynchronous communications protocol in which the communications channel can handle only one signal at a time. The two stations alternate their transmissions. Synonymous with *local echo*. See *asynchronous communication, communications protocol, echoplex,* and *full duplex*.

half-height drive   A disk drive that occupies half of the standard space allotted for a disk drive in the original IBM Personal Computer.

halftone   A copy of a photograph prepared for printing by breaking down the continuous gradations of tones into a series of discontinuous dots. Dark shades are produced by dense patterns of thick dots, and lighter shades are produced by less dense patterns of smaller dots.

A black-and-white photograph is a continuous-tone image of varying shades of gray. Photographs do not photocopy well; the fine gradations of gray tones are lost. To print a photograph in a newspaper or magazine, the photograph is copied using a halftone screen in front of the film. The screen breaks up the image into patterns of dots of varying size, depending on the intensity of the light coming from the photograph.

Halftones are usually superior to digitized photographs for professional-quality reproduction. Even professionals who use the latest desktop publishing technology may prefer to leave space for halftones and paste them in after printing the document. See *scanner* and *Tagged Image File Format (TIFF)*.

handle In an object-oriented graphics program, the small black squares that surround a selected object, enabling you to drag, size, or scale the object. See *draw program* and *object-oriented graphic*.

handshaking A method for controlling the flow of serial communication between two devices, so that one device transmits only when the other device is ready.

In hardware handshaking, a control wire is used as a signal line to indicate when the receiving device is ready to receive a transmission; software handshaking uses a special control code.

Hardware handshaking is used for devices such as serial printers, because the device is nearby and a special cable can be used. For long-distance serial communication, software handshaking must be used when the telephone system is involved. (Because the telephone system uses only two wires, hardware handshaking is impossible). The two software handshaking techniques are ETX/ACK, which uses the ASCII character Ctrl-C to pause in data transmission, and XON/XOFF, which uses Ctrl-S to pause and Ctrl-Q to resume transmission.

hanging indent A paragraph indentation in which the first line is flush with the left margin, but subsequent lines (called turnover lines) are indented.

hard card A hard disk and disk drive controller that are contained on a single plug-in adapter.

You easily can add a hard disk to a system using a hard card: you just press the adapter into the expansion slot, as you would any other adapter.

hard copy Printed output, distinguished from data stored on disk or in memory.

hard disk   A secondary storage medium that uses several nonflexible disks coated with a magnetically sensitive material and housed, together with the recording heads, in a hermetically sealed mechanism. Typical storage capacities range from 10 to 140M.

A hard disk is a complex storage subsystem that includes the disks, the read/write head assembly, and the electronic interface that governs the connection between the drive and the computer.

The disks, numbering from three to five, revolve 60 times per second (3600 rpm); the read/write head floats on a thin pocket of air just above the magnetically encoded surface of the disk, so that no wear occurs on the disk itself. Less expensive hard drives use 5¼-inch disks, but the trend is toward 3½-inch disks, because the read/write heads have shorter distances to move. The technology used to position the read/write heads in the least expensive hard disks uses stepper motors that move the heads one step at a time over the disk. However, stepper motors gradually lose their alignment, necessitating an annual reformatting procedure to make sure that the disk remains aligned with the read/write heads. More expensive drives use voice coil motors that are more reliable and less likely to go out of alignment.

Hard drive interface standards include ST506, IDE, ESDI, and SCSI. With typical storage spaces of 20M to 40M, hard disks have ample room for storing several major application programs, system software, and data files. Because most hard disks are not removable, however, you should develop a regular backup procedure. Hard disks occasionally fail, and they may take the data with them.

Some hard drives use removable cartridges, a significant advantage over normal hard drives. See *access time, Bernoulli box, Enhanced System Device Interface (ESDI), Intelligent Drive Electronics (IDE), Run-Length Limited (RLL), secondary storage,* and *Small Computer System Interface (SCSI)*.

hard disk backup program   A utility program that backs up hard disk data and programs onto floppy disks.

→ **Tip:** The best backup programs perform incremental backups, in which the program backs up only those files that have changed since the last backup procedure. See *utility program*.

hard disk interface   An electronic standard for the connection of a hard disk to the computer. See *Enhanced System Device Interface (ESDI), hard disk, intelligent drive electronics (IDE),* and *Small Computer System Interface (SCSI)*.

hard drive   See *hard disk*.

hard hyphen   A hyphen specially formatted so that a program does not introduce a line break between the hyphenated words.

Hyphenated proper nouns, such as Radcliffe-Brown and Evans-Pritchard, should not be interrupted with line breaks. A hard hyphen prevents the insertion of a line break between the two hyphenated words. Synonymous with *nonbreaking hyphen*. See *soft hyphen*.

→ **Tip:** Use a hard hyphen for hyphenated names, even if the names are not positioned near the end of a line. Remember, you may add or delete text in the paragraph later, and these changes are likely to push the name to the end of the line.

hard page break   See *forced page break*.

hard space   In a word processing program, a space specially formatted so that the program does not introduce a line break at the space's location.

hardware   The electronic components, boards, peripherals, and equipment that make up your computer system—distinguished from the programs (software) that tell these components what to do.

hardware platform   A computer hardware standard, such as IBM PC-compatible or Macintosh personal computers, in which a comprehensive approach to the computer solution of a problem can be based. See *device independence* and *platform independence*.

hardware reset   A warm boot performed by pressing a restart button after the computer system has been turned on. See *programmer's switch* and *warm boot*.

Hayes command set   A standardized set of instructions used to control modems.

Common Hayes commands include the following:

AT	Attention (used to start all commands)
ATDT 322-1234	Dial the number with touch tones
+++	Enter command mode during communication session
ATH	Hang up

See *modem*.

Hayes-compatible modem   A modem that recognizes the Hayes command set. See *Hayes command set* and *modem*.

head   See *read/write head*.

head crash   The collision of a hard disk drive's read/write head with the surface of the disk, resulting in damage to the disk surface (and possibly to the head as well).

▲ **Caution:** Most disk drives can withstand some jostling, but you should avoid moving your computer or bumping its case while the drive is running.

head seek time   See *access time*.

header   Repeated text (such as a page number and a short version of a document's title) that appears at the top of each page in a document.

Some programs include odd headers and even headers, enabling you to define mirror image headers for documents printed with duplex printing (both sides of the page). For example, you may want to place the page number on the outside corner of facing pages.

Word processing programs vary significantly in the flexibility of header commands. The best programs, such as WordPerfect and Microsoft Word, enable you to suppress the printing of a header on the first page of a document or a section of a document and to change headers within the document. Synonymous with *running head*. See *footer*.

Hercules Graphics Adapter   A single-color display adapter for IBM PC-compatible computers. The Hercules Graphics Adapter displays text and graphics on an IBM monochrome monitor with a resolution of 720 pixels horizontally and 320 pixels vertically.

▲ **Caution:** The Hercules (and Hercules-compatible) display adapter works only with graphics software that includes drivers for its non-IBM display format. Software designed to work with the Color Graphics Adapter (CGA), for example, does not display graphics on systems equipped with Hercules cards unless the software specifically includes a Hercules driver. Many shareware, public-domain, and low-priced graphics programs do not include the necessary driver and do not work with Hercules-equipped systems. However, Hercules display adapters work with all programs that display monochrome text. See *monochrome display adapter (MDA)*.

hertz (Hz)   A unit of measurement of electrical vibrations; one Hz equals one cycle per second. See *megahertz (MHz)*.

heuristic   A method of solving a problem by using rules of thumb acquired from experience. Heuristics rarely are stated formally in textbooks, but they are part of the knowledge human experts use in problem solving. See *expert system* and *knowledge base*.

Hewlett-Packard Graphics Language   A page description language (PDL) and file format for graphics printing with the HP LaserJet line of printers, and now widely emulated by HP-compatible laser printers. See *Hewlett-Packard Printer Control Language (HP-PCL)*.

Hewlett-Packard Printer Control Language (HPPCL)   The proprietary printer control language introduced by Hewlett-Packard in 1984 with the company's first LaserJet printer. Like the Hayes command set in the modem world, HPPCL has become a standard. See *LaserJet* and *printer control language*.

hexadecimal   A numbering system that uses a base (radix) of 16.

Unlike decimal numbers (base 10), hexadecimal numbers require 16 digits: 0, 1, 2, 3, 4, 5, 6, 7, 8, 9, A, B, C, D, E, and F. When counting in hexadecimal, you don't carry over to the next place until you reach the first number past F (in decimal, you carry over when you reach the number past 9).

Programmers use hexadecimal numbers as a convenient way of representing binary numbers. Using binary numbers is inconvenient because they use a base or radix of 2, and you must carry over to the next place when you reach the first number past one. Binary numbers, therefore, grow in length quickly. In binary, for example, the decimal number 16 requires four places (1111).

Binary numbers are ideally suited to the devices used in computers, but these numbers are hard to read.

For any four-digit set of binary numbers, you have 16 possible combinations of 1s and 0s. Hexadecimal numbers, therefore, provide a convenient way for programmers to represent four-digit clumps of binary numbers

Binary	Hex	Binary	Hex
0000	0	1000	8
0001	1	1001	9
0010	2	1010	A
0011	3	1011	B
0100	4	1100	C
0101	5	1101	D
0110	6	1110	E
0111	7	1111	F

hidden file   A file with file attributes set so that the file name does not appear on the disk directory. You cannot display, erase, or copy hidden files.

Hierarchical File System (HFS)   A Macintosh disk storage system, designed for use with hard disks, that enables you to store files within folders so that only a short list of files appears in the dialog boxes.

The previous Macintosh Filing System (MFS) enabled you to organize files into ·folders in the Finder. In Open and Save dialog boxes, the names of all the files on the disk appeared without any hierarchical organization.

HFS is analogous to the directory/subdirectory organization of DOS disks but with one important exception: with DOS, you can define default paths that applications follow to locate data files and program files. In HFS, no such path definition facilities exist, with the exception of the System Folder consulted when an application searches for a data or program file. Mac users, therefore, must guide applications manually through the structure of nested folders when a program cannot find a file.

high density   A storage technique for secondary storage media such as floppy disks. This technique requires the use of extremely fine-grained magnetic particles. High-density disks are more expensive to manufacture than double-density disks. High-density disks, however, can store one megabyte or more of information on one 5¼- or 3½-inch disk. Synonymous with *quad density*.

high-density disk   See *floppy disk*.

high-level format   A formatting operation that creates housekeeping sections on a disk. These sections, including the boot record and file allocation table, track free and in-use areas of the disk.

When you use the DOS FORMAT command to format a floppy disk, the computer performs a low-level format in addition to the logical format. When you use a hard disk, however, DOS performs just the logical format.

If a low-level format has not been performed at the factory, you must run a program (probably provided on a floppy disk that comes with the hard disk) that performs the absolute format. See *boot record, file allocation table (FAT)*, and *low-level format*.

high-level programming language   A programming language such as BASIC or Pascal that crudely resembles human language.

Each statement in a high-level language corresponds to several machine language instructions. Therefore, writing programs more quickly in a high-level language than in a low-level language like Assembly is possible. However, programs written in a high-level language run slower. See *assembly language, low-level programming language,* and *machine language*.

high/low/close/open graph   In presentation graphics, a line graph in which a stock's high value, low value, closing price, and average value are displayed. The x-axis (categories axis) is aligned horizontally, and the y-axis (values axis) is aligned vertically.

Another application for a high/low/close graph is a record of daily minimum, maximum, and average temperatures. Synonymous with HLCO chart. See *column graph* and *line graph*.

high memory   See *upper memory area*.

high memory area (HMA)   In a DOS computer, the first 64K of extended memory above 1 megabyte. Programs that conform to the eXtended Memory Specification (XMS) can use HMA as a direct extension of conventional memory. See *conventional memory, extended memory,* and *eXtended Memory Specification (XMS)*.

high resolution   In computer monitors and printers, a visual definition that is sufficient to produce well-defined characters even at large type sizes, as well as smoothly-defined curves in graphic images. A high-resolution video adapter and monitor can display 1,024 pixels horizontally by 768 pixels vertically; a high-resolution printer can print at least 300 dots per inch (dpi). See *low resolution*.

highlight   A character, word, text block, or command displayed in reverse video on-screen. This term sometimes is used synonymously with *cursor*.

HIMEM.SYS   A DOS device driver, supplied with Microsoft Windows and DOS, that configures the upper memory area, extended memory, and the high memory area so that properly-written programs can access it. The programs must conform to the eXtended Memory Standard (XMS). See *CONFIG.SYS, device driver, eXtended Memory Standard (XMS), high memory area (HMA),* and *upper memory area.*

    If you use Microsoft Windows, the Windows Setup program automatically installed HIMEM.SYS in the CONFIG.SYS file of your computer's hard disk.

histogram   A stacked column graph in which the columns are brought together to emphasize variations in the distribution of data items within each stack.

    By stacking the data items in a column, you emphasize the contribution each makes to the whole (as in a pie graph). By placing the columns adjacent to one another, the eye is led to compare the relative proportions of one data item as the item varies from column to column.

home computer   A personal computer specifically designed and marketed for home applications, such as educating children, playing games, balancing a checkbook, paying bills, and controlling lights or appliances.

    A home computer usually has less memory, less secondary storage, and a slower microprocessor than a business computer.

Home key   A key on IBM PC-compatible keyboards that has varying functions from program to program.

    Frequently, the Home key is used to move the cursor to the beginning of the line or the top of the screen, but the assignment of this key is up to the programmer.

horizontal scroll bar   See *scroll bar/scroll box*.

host   In a computer network, the computer that performs centralized functions such as making program or data files available to workstations in the network.

hot link   A method of copying information from one document (the source document) to another (the target document) so that the link remains active; if you change the information in the source document, the change is automatically reflected in the target document.

In Microsoft Windows, you can create a hot link between an Excel source document and a Word target document using the Paste/Link command. After the hot link has been established, Windows will automatically update the Word document if you make a change in the Excel spreadsheet.

In the Macintosh System 7, the metaphor used to describe hot linkage is drawn from publishing rather than editing. You select data for hot linkage and choose Publish from the Edit menu. In a second application, you choose Subscribe to establish the hot link. See *dynamic data exchange (DDE)*.

HP LaserJet   See *LaserJet*.

HPGL   See *Hewlett-Packard Graphics Language*.

hung system   A computer that has experienced a system failure sufficiently grave to prevent further processing, even though the cursor may still be blinking on the screen; the only option in most cases is to restart the system, which entails loss of any unsaved work.

→ **Tip:** If you are experiencing computer crashes frequently, eliminate any terminate-and-stay-resident (TSR) programs (called inits in the Mac world) you're using. These programs sometimes conflict with one another or with application programs, producing hung systems. Add the programs again, one by one, to determine which one of them (if any) is causing the problem. In addition, check the documentation provided with TSRs or inits to determine whether a given program must be loaded last. Some TSRs and

INITS operate in an unstable fashion unless they are the last program to be loaded at the time of system startup. See *INIT* and *terminate-and-stay resident (TSR) program*.

HyperCard   An authoring language bundled with the Macintosh that makes storing and interactively retrieving on-screen cards containing text, bit-mapped graphics, sound, and animation easier.

A HyperCard application, a stack, is a collection of one to several thousand cards. On each card, you find a background layer, consisting of buttons, graphics, and fields that several or all cards in the stack share and the card layer that contains the buttons, graphics, and fields unique to the card.

You interact with the stack by clicking the buttons. Each button has an associated script, written in HyperTalk, that specifies the procedure to follow when a button is clicked. Clicking a button may display another card in the stack or initiate an animation sequence that may include sound.

HyperCard comes with several prewritten stacks, but the program's significance is that it provides you with a way to create your own HyperCard applications.

The Macintosh is a formidable machine even for accomplished programmers, and the Mac received a great deal of criticism from hobbyists and users who wanted to develop their own applications without spending inordinate amounts of time. HyperCard answers these criticisms by providing a complete application development environment for nonprogrammers.

The range of applications is limited to those that can be displayed as HyperCard stacks. However, what many people would like to do with computers is related to the storage and retrieval of textual and graphic information, and HyperCard provides excellent tools for such applications.

The result is not a database management system in the traditional sense, but what Apple calls hypermedia, a way of displaying information by embedding linkages within the system and giving people the tools to explore these links interactively.

Because HyperCard is so well suited to the creation of instructional software, one could call HyperCard an authoring language. A major area of application development lies in the use of Hyper-Card as a front end for huge external information resources encoded on CD-ROM and interactive laser disks.

HyperCard also is serving as the platform for the development of multimedia applications, many with an educational emphasis. However, HyperCard can be used to create stand alone applications. Commercial applications include a musical composition program, an appointment/calendar system, an employee payroll and check-writing program, and a game that enables you to explore a huge labyrinth of interconnected rooms. See *authoring language, front end, hypermedia, HyperTalk, script,* and *stack.*

hypermedia A computer-assisted instructional application such as HyperCard that is capable of adding graphics, sound, video, and synthesized voice to the capabilities of a hypertext system.

In a hypertext system, you select a word or phrase and give a command to see related text. In a hypermedia system, such a command reveals related graphics images, sounds, and even snippets of animation or video. See *hypertext.*

HyperScript The software command language provided with Wingz, an innovative Macintosh spreadsheet program developed by Informix, Inc. Using HyperScript, even a novice programmer can develop spreadsheets by using on-screen buttons containing scripts for specific, customized spreadsheet functions. These scripts are the equivalent of macros in programs such as Lotus 1-2-3, but they are much easier to develop and use.

HyperScript resembles HyperTalk, the object-oriented programming language supplied with HyperCard. See *HyperCard, HyperTalk,* and *object-oriented programming language.*

HyperTalk A software command language for the Macintosh HyperCard application that fully implements object-oriented programming principles. See *object-oriented programming language.*

hypertext The nonsequential retrieval of a document's text. The reader is free to pursue associative trails through the document by means of predefined or user-created links.

A hypertext application seeks to break away from a sequentially oriented text presentation of information and to provide the reader with tools to construct his own connections among the component texts of the document. A hypertext application is a form of non-sequential writing.

In a true hypertext application, the user can highlight virtually any word in a document and immediately jump to other documents containing related text. Commands also are available that enable the user to create his own associative trails through the document.

Computer technology helps when constructing a hypertext application. If this book were presented in hypertext format, for example, you could click your mouse on one of the cross references, and a window would pop up displaying the cross-referenced entries.

hyphen ladder A formatting flaw caused by the repetition of hyphens at the end of two or more lines in a row.

Hyphen ladders attract the eye and disrupt the text's readability.

→ **Tip:** If you insert hyphens throughout a document, proofread the results carefully. Hyphenation utilities cannot prevent hyphen ladders. If hyphen ladders occur, adjust word spacing and hyphenation manually.

hyphenation In word processing and page layout programs, an automatic operation that hyphenates words on certain lines to improve word spacing.

When used with caution and manual confirmation of each inserted hyphen, a hyphenation utility can improve the appearance of a printed work by improving the line spacing. Automatic hyphenation is especially helpful with newspaper columns or narrow margins. An unhyphenated, lengthy word such as "collectivization" can introduce ugly word spacing irregularities into your document.

▲ **Caution:** Do not count on automatic hyphenation utilities to do the job perfectly; you should confirm each hyphen. Some programs break fundamental hyphenation rules, such as leaving fewer than two characters on one side of the hyphen or hyphenating a one-syllable word. No automatic hyphenation utility can cope effectively with homographs, two words spelled the same but that have different meanings and pronunciations. See the following:

in-val'-id	in'-va-lid
min'-ute	mi-nūte'
put'-ting	pŭtt'-ing

Watch out for hyphen ladders, an unsightly formatting error that occurs when three or more sentences in a row are hyphenated. You may need to use additional, manual hyphenation to finish the job. The automatic hyphenation utility consults an on-disk hyphenation database, but this file probably contains only a fraction of the words in your manuscript. See *hard hyphen, hyphen ladder,* and *soft hyphen.*

Hz   See *hertz (Hz).*

i

I-beam pointer   In Macintosh and Windows applications, a mouse pointer that appears when you're editing text.

In Macintosh and Windows applications, the cursor does not appear *on* a character, as it does in DOS applications; it appears *between* characters at all times. The I-beam pointer is thin enough to enable you to position the pointer between characters with precision.

IAC   See *inter-application communication (IAC).*

IBM 8514/A display adapter   A video adapter for IBM Personal System/2 computers that, with the on-board video graphics array

(VGA) circuitry, produces a resolution of 1024 dots horizontally and 768 dots vertically. The adapter also contains its own processing circuitry that reduces demand on the computer's central processing unit (CPU).

For IBM PC compatibles using the 16-bit AT bus rather than IBM's proprietary Micro Channel Bus, VGA adapters are available with the 1024-by-768 high-resolution mode. See *Super VGA* and *video adapter*.

IBM PC-compatible computer   A personal computer—dubbed a clone by industry analysts—that runs all or almost all the software developed for the IBM Personal Computer (whether in PC, XT, or AT form) and accepts the IBM computer's cards, adapters, and peripheral devices. See *clone*.

IBM Personal Computer   A personal computer based on the Intel 8088 microprocessor.

Personal computers existed before the IBM Personal Computer, but the release of the IBM PC in 1981 legitimized the fledgling personal computer industry and ensured the technology's acceptance in the business community.

No longer a plaything for hobbyists, the personal computer became a serious business tool—or so many people concluded, because those magic three letters, IBM, appeared on the nameplate.

The story of the PC's development is an interesting chapter in technological innovation. IBM had been burned in the past by failing to recognize the market potential of small computers. The company thought that no market existed for minicomputers, leaving the market open for start-up firms such as Digital Equipment Corporation (DEC) and Hewlett-Packard (HP). Both companies cashed in under the umbrella created by IBM's disinterest in small-scale computer technologies.

IBM was not about to permit this setback to occur again and made an early decision to move into the personal computer market (then dominated by Apple Computer, Radio Shack, and 8-bit CP/M computers). Recognizing that a bureaucracy can frustrate an innovation effort, the team assigned to develop the PC was given substantial autonomy. Looking at the success of the Apple II, the team decided to emulate Apple's example by creating an open bus, open architecture system that would attract droves of third-party suppliers.

The computer developed by this team (at the Entry Level Systems Division in Boca Raton, Fla.) was by no means a state-of-the-art device. The PC used the Intel 8088 microprocessor instead of the faster Intel 8086, largely because the 8088 can take advantage of the numerous and inexpensive 8-bit peripherals and microprocessor support chips that worked with the 8088 (but not with the 8086).

IBM also did not attempt to develop an operating system for the new computer. Instead, the firm hired Microsoft Corporation to develop an operating system that would enable CP/M programs to be quickly and easily modified to run on the new PC, because hundreds of business programs were available for CP/M computers.

Microsoft bought an operating system under development by a small Seattle firm, and dubbed the system MS-DOS (Microsoft Disk Operating System). Few people realized that MS-DOS is little more than a clone of CP/M. Therefore, the IBM PC fairly may be said to represent the technology of the late 1970s, not the early 1980s.

The future of IBM PC-compatible computing is much in doubt due to the limitations of MS-DOS. The 1981 machine is almost laughable by today's standards. It was released with a total of 16K of random-access memory (RAM), expandable to 64K on the motherboard. The monochrome display adapter (MDA) and monochrome monitor are incapable of displaying bit-mapped graphics—only the 254 characters (including block graphics characters) in the extended character set can be displayed. The disk drive held 160K of data—much more than the 50K to 90K drives in widespread use at the time.

Recognizing the limitations of the original IBM PC, the company introduced the PC-2 in 1983. This model came with 64K of RAM expandable to 256K on the motherboard without additional memory cards. Its disk drives used both sides of disks (they stored

320K). Also introduced was the Color Graphics Adapter (CGA) and an RGB color monitor.

IBM's choice of an open architecture and open bus for the PC quickly engendered a huge support industry as third-party vendors created memory cards, video adapters, and other accessories for the system. A major step forward was the Hercules Graphics Adapter that displayed bit-mapped graphics on the monochrome monitor.

By 1984, clones (non-IBM computers that claimed compatibility with the IBM PC) had appeared on the market, and because of their lower price, quickly gained market share. IBM countered with enhanced versions of the PC called the IBM Personal Computer XT in 1983 and the IBM Personal Computer AT in 1984.

These models were not successful in stemming the tide of clones, however, and in 1987, IBM introduced the IBM PS/2 line, abandoning the open bus architecture of the PC in favor of the proprietary Micro Channel Bus.

Because few clone manufacturers have decided to obtain the necessary license to create Micro Channel machines, the world of IBM PC-compatible computing has split into two camps: on one side is IBM, with its proprietary technology, and on the other is a consortium of clone manufacturers (led by Compaq Corporation) that continues to advocate the open architecture and open bus principles of the original IBM PC. See *Apple II, clone, Extended Industry Standard Architecture (EISA), Micro Channel Bus, open architecture,* and *open bus.*

IBM Personal Computer AT   A personal computer, based on the Intel 80286 microprocessor, that was introduced in 1984.

The AT (short for Advanced Technology) significantly improved on the performance of PCs and XTs. Using the 80286 microprocessor and a 16-bit data bus, the computer's throughput was approximately 50 to 75 percent better than the fastest XT's.

Widely emulated by clones, the AT standard lives on in the form of AT compatibles, now available at bargain prices. See *Intel 80286.*

IBM Personal Computer XT   A personal computer, based on the Intel 8088 microprocessor and including a hard disk, that was introduced in 1983.

In addition to its hard disk, the XT (short for eXtended Technology) added a heftier power supply, additional expansion slots, and room for up to 640K of random-access memory (RAM) on the motherboard.

The XT standard lives on in 8088-based compatible machines called Turbo XTs because they offer a clock speed of approximately 10 MHz, twice that of the original XT. See *Intel 8088*.

IBM Personal System/2   A series of personal computers introduced in 1987 based on the Intel 8086, 80286, and 80386 microprocessors. Most PS/2s contain a proprietary expansion bus format. See *Micro Channel Bus*.

icon   In a graphical user interface, an on-screen symbol that represents a program file, data file, or some other computer entity or function.

IDE   See *Intelligent Drive Electronics (IDE)*.

IDE drive   A hard disk for '286, '386, and '486 computers that contains most of the controller circuitry within the drive itself. Designed to connect to computers containing an IDE interface on their motherboards, IDE drives combine the speed of ESDI drives with the intelligence of the SCSI hard drive interface. This performance is offered at a price lower than most ESDI and SCSI drives. Moreover, IDE drives present themselves to the computer electronically as if they were standard ST506 drives, for which the '286 and '386 were originally designed. See *Intelligent Drive Electronics (IDE)*.

→ **Tip:** If you are shopping for a '286 or '386 computer and value is uppermost in your mind, look for a machine that includes an IDE interface and IDE drive. You need an ESDI or SCSI drive only if you run applications that demand the highest possible performance from your computer.

identifier   In database management, an identifier is used to specify the uniqueness of the information contained in the data record.

For example, the descriptor Norway appears in the data record of the only travel film that depicts scenery from that country.

illegal character   A character that cannot be used according to the syntax rules of command-driven programs and programming languages. Such characters usually are reserved for a specific program function.

For example, with DOS, you cannot assign a file name to a file if the name includes an asterisk (*). The asterisk is reserved for use as a wildcard symbol. Commas also are illegal characters for file names. DOS uses commas as an argument separator in commands requiring two or more arguments.

image compression   The use of a compression technique to reduce the size of a graphics file (which can consume inordinate amounts of disk space).

A single gray-scale TIFF file, for instance, can consume more than 100K of disk space—but the file can be reduced by as much as 96 percent for storage or telecommunications purposes.

image processing   In computer graphics, the use of a computer to enhance, embellish, or refine a graphic image. Typical processing operations include contrast enhancement or reduction, outlining of shapes, alteration of colors so that the image is more easily analyzed, correction of underexposure or overexposure, and the outlining of objects so that they can be identified.

imagesetter   A professional typesetting machine that generates very high-resolution output on photographic paper or film.

If you have a PostScript-compatible word processor or page layout program, you can take a disk to a service bureau that owns one of these machines to obtain high-resolution output. See *PostScript* and *service bureau*.

imaging model The method of representing output on-screen.

In character-based programs, a connection may not exist between the screen and printer fonts. The screen font appears to be a monospaced typewriter font, but the printer font in use may be a proportionally spaced font with a different typeface.

In a graphical user interface, the goal is to use a unified imaging model, so that the text displayed on-screen closely resembles the text printed. See *graphical user interface (GUI)* and *screen font*.

impact printer A printer that forms an image by pressing a physical representation of a character against an inked ribbon, forming an impression on the page.

Impact printers are noisy, but they can produce multiple copies of business forms using carbons. See *dot-matrix printer, letter-quality printer,* and *nonimpact printer*.

import To load a file created by one program into a different program.

Harvard Graphics, for example, can import the PIC files created by Lotus 1-2-3.

incremental backup A backup procedure in which a hard disk backup program backs up only the files changed since the last backup procedure. See *archival backup*.

incremental update See *maintenance release*.

indentation The alignment of a paragraph to the right or left of the margins set for the entire document.

index In database management programs, a compact file containing information (called pointers) about the physical location of records in a database file. When searching or sorting the database, the program uses the index rather than the full database. Such operations are faster than sorts or searches performed on the actual database.

In word processing programs, an index is an appendix that lists important words, names, and concepts in alphabetical order, with the page numbers where the terms appear. With most word processing programs, you must mark terms to be included in the index the program constructs. See *active index, concordance file, sort,* and *sort order.*

index hole In a floppy disk, a hole in the disk that is electro-optically detected by the drive to locate the beginning of the first sector on the disk. See *floppy disk* and *sector.*

industry-standard user interface An IBM standard for the organization of on-screen computer displays that is part of the company's Systems Application Architecture (SAA). The standard, called Common User Access (CUA), calls for the use throughout a computing system of many of the user interface features that are found in graphical user interfaces: pull-down menus, dialog boxes with check boxes and option buttons, and highlighted accelerator keys for rapid keyboard selection of commands.

The CUA standard is now widely found in character-based DOS applications, and it's bringing a new uniformity to the previously chaotic world of DOS user interfaces, typified by WordPerfect's idiosyncratic function key assignments and menus. The CUA interface isn't strictly speaking, a graphical user interface (GUI), because it runs in the character mode and doesn't use the on-screen pictorial representation of computer resources in the form of icons. But the CUA interface has just about every other GUI benefit, including a refreshing commonality of key assignments and procedures across applications: F1 brings up Help, F3 cancels or exits, F10 displays the menu, and so on.

Anyone hoping to avoid the big investment needed to run Windows and Windows applications can set up a very nice, near-GUI system by choosing a library of CUA-compliant DOS applications and running a CUA-compliant DOS shell (such as the new DOS shell provided with DOS 5.0). See *application program interface (API), graphical user interface (GUI), Microsoft Windows,* and *mousable interface.*

infection   The presence within a computer system of a virus or Trojan Horse. The infection may not be obvious to the user; many viruses, for example, remain in the background until a specific time and date, when they display prank messages or erase data.

information service   See *bibliographic retrieval service, bulletin board system (BBS),* and *on-line information service.*

INIT   In the Macintosh environment, a utility program that executes during a system start or restart.

Examples of INITs are SuperClock, which displays the current system date and time in the menu bar, and Adobe Type Manager, which uses outline-font technology to display Adobe screen fonts.

initial   In typography, an enlarged letter at the beginning of a chapter or paragraph.

Initials set down within the copy are drop caps, and initials raised above the top line of the text are stickup caps.

initial base font   The default printer font used by word processing programs to print all documents unless you instruct otherwise.

You can override the initial base font for a particular document by choosing a document base font, and you can override this choice by formatting individual characters or blocks of characters within the document. See *document base font.*

initialization   The process of formatting a disk so that it is ready for use. See *format.*

initialize   See *format.*

inkjet printer   A nonimpact printer that forms an image by spraying ink from a matrix of tiny jets.

Inkjet printers are quiet and can produce excellent results. Hewlett-Packard's DeskJet and DeskWriter printers can produce text and graphics at resolutions of 300 dpi, rivaling the output of laser printers to the untrained eye. See *nonimpact printer.*

▲ **Caution:** The ink used by most inkjet printers is water-soluble and smears easily.

input   The information entered into the computer for processing purposes.

input device   Any peripheral that assists you in getting data into the computer, such as a keyboard, mouse, trackball, voice recognition system, graphics tablet, or modem.

input/output (I/O) system   One of the chief components of a computer system's architecture, the channels and interfaces that make the flow of data and program instructions into and out of the central processing unit (CPU) go smoothly.

Ins key   In IBM PC-compatible keyboards, a programmable key frequently (but not always) used to toggle between the insert mode and overtype mode in applications with text entry. See *Insert mode* and *Overtype mode*.

Insert mode   In word processing programs, a program mode (usually toggled with the Ins key) that makes inserted text push the existing text right and down. See *Overtype mode*.

insertion point   In Macintosh and Windows applications, the vertical bar that shows the point at which text will appear when you start typing. The insertion point is analogous to the cursor in DOS applications. See *cursor*.

installation program   A utility program provided with an application program that assists you in installing the program on a hard disk and configuring the program for use.

instruction   In computer programming, a program statement interpreted or compiled into machine language that the computer can understand and execute.

instruction cycle   The time it takes a central processing unit (CPU) to carry out one instruction and move on to the next.

instruction set   A list of keywords describing all the actions or operations that a central processing unit (CPU) can perform. See *complex instruction set computer (CISC)* and *reduced instruction set computer (RISC)*.

integer   A whole number without any decimal places.

integrated circuit   A semiconductor circuit that contains more than one transistor and other electronic components.

ENIAC, the first North American electronic computer, occupied a room of 1,500 square feet, about the size of a three-bedroom apartment. Weighing in at a hefty 30 tons, the 1946 machine required 18,000 vacuum tubes that functioned as the main switching devices.

Vacuum tubes once were common in radios and televisions, in which they amplified a signal. Within the tube, a weak current (such as one retrieved from a radio broadcast) acts to shape a stronger one. Vacuum tubes also are useful as switching devices—and are called valves in Britain—which is how they were used in the ENIAC.

But vacuum tubes have many liabilities: they get hot; they burn out frequently; and they draw huge amounts of current. When the ENIAC's power was switched on, the computer drew so much current that the lights throughout the neighborhood dimmed. The only way technicians could keep the computer running was to have teams of university students running around with shopping carts full of vacuum tubes, ready to replace the tubes that blew during processing sessions.

By the late 1950s, the vacuum tube gave way to the transistor, an amplifying and switching device invented in 1947. Even in the late 19th century, scientists had known that certain substances, called semiconductors, had electronic characteristics, such as the capability to transform alternating current into direct current. Silicon and germanium are two semiconducting materials. Semiconducting materials lie on the border between conductors, which transmit electricity well, and insulating materials, which do not transmit electricity at all.

The conducting properties of semiconductors also can be altered by introducing impurities. Impurities, such as arsenic, are introduced in a process called doping. If you dope a wafer of silicon so that some areas conduct and some areas do not, you can make some interesting things happen. In fact, you can make a tiny flake of silicon behave exactly like a big, expensive, hot, and power-hungry vacuum tube.

Even transistorized computers could not solve what engineers called the tyranny of numbers: they could envision wonderfully complex electronic devices, but it was an uneconomic proposition to create one so complex that years of work were necessary just to hand-wire the transistors together.

The engineers interested in semiconductors, however, were not ready to quit. If you can dope up a chip of silicon to produce a transistor, why not go further—why not place two or more transistors and other electronic devices on the same chip?

Such a chip, an integrated circuit, debuted in 1959, but its reception was chilly. At that time, producing integrated circuits was difficult and expensive. Unless a mass market arose for the new chips, their production costs would remain prohibitive for circuit designers.

The integrated circuit may have remained a curiosity for many years if it had not been for two historical events. First, in 1957, the Soviet Union launched the first artificial satellite, Sputnik, and set off a major U.S. campaign to catch up with Soviet science and space technology. Second, in 1961, President Kennedy announced a major U.S. effort to land a human being on the moon.

Both events eventually created a huge domestic market for integrated circuits, which were necessary for the space effort. Unlike the Soviets, who developed huge booster rockets to launch crude, heavy circuitry into space, the U.S. space program was in a catch-up mode and had to make do with relatively small boosters, which meant reducing weight in every possible way. With the assistance of huge amounts of federal research funding, electronic firms invested in major research and development projects to increase the complexity of integrated circuits.

The research efforts paid off; in the early 1960s, the number of transistors possible on a chip doubled each year, and the price of integrated circuits declined rapidly. By the mid-1960s, integrated circuits were in all kinds of electronic devices, ranging from stereo amplifiers and hearing aids to spacecraft and nuclear missiles.

But what no one predicted was how far this amazing process of technological development was to go. In 1965, an engineer noted that if the number of transistors on a single chip kept doubling each year, by 1975 one chip would have 65,000 transistors. In 1965, that idea seemed ridiculous. But no one had realized how much room is in the microscopic realm within a semiconductor chip. Today's Intel 80486 packs more than a million transistors into about one-sixteenth square inch of silicon.

integrated program   A program that combines two or more software functions, such as word processing and database management.

When Symphony (Lotus Development Corp.) and Framework (Ashton-Tate) were released in 1984, many thought these programs had ushered in a new era in personal computing. Both programs contained a spreadsheet, a database management program, a word processing program, a telecommunications program, and an analytical graphics program.

Every program within each package had a consistent user interface, so that you could switch from one program to the next without having to learn a new set of commands and menus. These programs facilitated the movement of data from one program to another.

For most users, however, the gains achieved by the consistent user interface were not worth the sacrifice involved—neither package's set of programs measured up to the standards of the best stand-alone programs. Most users preferred to assemble their own repertoire of programs.

Apple Computer's Lisa and Macintosh computers introduced the idea of using an application programming interface (API) that any program can access, with built-in routines for generating screen menus, scroll bars, dialog boxes, alert boxes, and other user interface amenities. The use of an API creates an environment in which programs share a common core of identical commands and menus, departing from the core only to implement unique program functions.

Along with a copy-and-paste buffer called a clipboard, the API approach offers the advantages of software integration plus an attractive addition: the user can assemble precisely the repertoire of programs that he or she wants, and they all function together effectively and effortlessly.

With the introduction of a multiple-loading operating system for the Macintosh called MultiFinder, Macintosh users achieved precisely the level of context-switching functionality that Symphony and Framework users possessed.

The Macintosh example shows that the goal of software integration is correct, but the way to implement software integration is at the level of the operating system. With OS/2 and Presentation Manager, IBM PC-compatible computing is moving in the same direction.

One exception to this trend is the success of entry-level programs such as Microsoft Works. Such programs make operations like label printing and mail merging easier than with stand-alone programs. See *application programming interface (API)*, *clipboard*, and *Macintosh*.

Intel 8086   A microprocessor introduced in 1978 with a full 16-bit data bus structure.

Although the 8086 communicates with the rest of the computer more quickly than the 8088, the 8086 was not chosen for the first IBM Personal Computer because of the high cost of 16-bit peripherals and microprocessor support chips.

By the time such peripherals became available at low prices, however, Intel had developed the Intel 80286 microprocessor, which addresses 16 megabytes of memory (in contrast to the 8086's one megabyte).

Few personal computers, therefore, have used the 8086 chip. One exception is the use of the 8086 for the unsuccessful lower-end models of the PS/2 line, such as the Model 25. See *IBM Personal System/2*, *Intel 8088*, and *Intel 80286*.

Intel 8088   A microprocessor introduced in 1978 with an 8-bit external data bus and an internal 16-bit data bus structure used in the original IBM Personal Computer.

Although the Intel 8088 can process 16 bits at a time internally, the 8088 communicates with the rest of the computer 8 bits (1 byte) at a time. This design compromise was deliberate; Intel designers wanted to introduce 16-bit microprocessor technology and take advantage of the inexpensive 8-bit peripherals (such as disk drives) and 8-bit microprocessor support chips.

Capable of addressing up to 1 megabyte of random-access memory, the original 8088 operated at 4.77 MHz, a speed now considered too slow for business and professional applications. Later versions of the chip have pushed its clock speed to approximately 10 MHz; such chips power IBM PC-compatible computers known as Turbo XTs. See *Intel 8086*.

Intel 80286   A microprocessor introduced in 1984 with a 16-bit data bus structure and the capability to address up to 16 megabytes of random-access memory (RAM).

The Intel 80286 powered the high-performance IBM Personal Computer AT. The chip requires 16-bit peripherals that are more expensive than the 8-bit peripherals used in machines such as the original IBM PC, but by the time of the AT's introduction, such peripherals were available.

The 80286 has a split personality: in its real mode, the chip runs DOS programs in an 8086 emulation mode and cannot use more than 1 megabyte of RAM (under DOS, the limit is 640K), but in its protected mode, the 80286 can use up to 16 megabytes. However, DOS cannot take advantage of this mode.

Intel 80287/Intel 80387   Numeric coprocessors designed to work (respectively) with the Intel 80286 and 80386. See *numeric coprocessor* and *Weitek coprocessor*.

Intel 80386   A microprocessor introduced in 1986 with a 32-bit data bus structure and the capability to address up to four gigabytes of main memory directly.

The Intel 80386 represented a revolutionary advance over its predecessors. Not only did the chip introduce a full 32-bit data bus structure to IBM PC-compatible computing, the 80386 also brought technical advances like a much-improved memory architecture.

Because this full 32-bit chip requires 32-bit microprocessor support chips, computers using the 80386 are more expensive than their 16-bit predecessors.

The 80386 includes a mode that enables the operating system to divide memory into separate blocks of 640K, so that DOS applications can run concurrently. You can, for example, run Lotus 1-2-3 and WordPerfect at the same time. To use this mode, however, requires special software such as DESQview/386 or Windows/386. See *Microsoft Windows*.

Intel 80386SX   A microprocessor introduced in 1988 with all the electronic characteristics of the Intel 80386, except that the chip has a 16-bit external data bus structure that enables it to use the inexpensive peripherals developed for the Intel 80286.

The 80386SX is like the Intel 8088 because it processes data internally twice as fast as it communicates with the rest of the computer. However, this compromise enables the computer to use the significantly less expensive 16-bit peripherals and microprocessor support chips.

→ **Tip:** If you are thinking about purchasing a 286 computer, consider a 386SX computer instead. The prices are comparable, and the 386SX is equipped to handle 386 software.

Intel 80486   A microprocessor introduced in 1989 with a full 32-bit data bus structure and the capability to address 64 gigabytes of main memory directly.

The 80386 represents a technological leap over the 80286, but the 80486 is only an incremental step over the 80386. Packing more than one million transistors into one tiny silicon chip, the 80486 incorporates the mathematical processing circuitry that formerly was segregated on a coprocessor, such as the Intel 80387.

Intel 82385   A cache controller chip that governs cache memory in fast personal computers using the Intel 80386 and 80486 microprocessors. See *cache memory.*

Intelligent Drive Electronics (IDE)   A hard disk interface standard for '286, '386, and '486 computers that offers high performance at low cost. The IDE standard transfers most of the controller electronics to the hard disk mechanism. For this reason, the IDE interface can be contained on the computer's motherboard; no controller card is necessary, and no expansion slot is necessary. See *controller card, hard disk interface,* and *IDE drive.*

inter-application communication (IAC)   In the Macintosh System 7, a specification for creating hot links and cold links between applications. See *cold link, hot link,* and *System 7.*

interactive processing   A method of using the computer in which the computer's processing operations are monitored directly on a video display, so that the user can catch and correct errors before the processing operation is completed.

Interactive processing is so characteristic of personal computing that forgetting the old days, when batch processing was the only way one could use the computer, is easy. Certain features of today's programs, however, hearken back to the early days. Word processing programs, for example, sometimes require you to embed formatting commands into the text, rather than showing you their effects directly on-screen. See *batch processing.*

interactive videodisc   A computer-assisted instruction (CAI) technology that uses a computer to provide access to up to two hours of video information stored on a videodisc.

Like CD-ROM, videodiscs are read-only optical storage media, but they are designed specifically for the storage and random-access retrieval of images, including stills and continuous video.

An interactive videodisc application includes a computer program that serves as a front end to the information stored on the videodisc, a cable that links the computer to the videodisc player, and a videodisc that contains the appropriate images.

The user uses the front end program to explore the contents of the videodisc. For example, with a videodisc of paintings in the National Gallery of Art, the user can demand, "Show me all the renaissance paintings that depict flowers or gardens." A well-designed front end can lead the viewer through a series of vivid instructional experiences under the viewer's complete control.

With interactive videodisc technology, television viewing promises to become a less passive activity. See *computer-assisted instruction (CAI)* and *videodisc*.

interface   An electronic circuit that governs the connection between two hardware devices and helps them exchange data reliably. Synonymous with *port*.

interface standard   In hard disk drives, a set of specifications for the connection between the drive controller and the drive electronics. Common interface standards in personal computing include ST506, ESDI, and SCSI. See *Enhanced Small Device Interface (ESDI), Small Computer System Interface (SCSI),* and *ST-506/ ST-412*.

interleave factor   The ratio of physical disk sectors on a hard disk that are skipped for every sector actually used for write operations.

If the interleave factor is 6:1, the disk writes to a sector, skips six sectors, writes to a sector, skips six sectors, and so on. The interleave factor is set by the hard disk manufacturer, but the factor can be changed by system software capable of performing a low-level format.

An interleave factor greater than 1:1 slows down the transfer rate so that the computer can keep up with the disk drive. Synonymous with *sector interleave*.

▲ **Caution:** Do not attempt to change the interleave factor of your hard disk unless you know what you are doing. In almost all cases, the interleave factor set by the disk manufacturer is optimal for your disk drive and computer.

interleaved memory   A method of speeding access to dynamic random access memory (DRAM) chips by dividing RAM into two large banks or pages and storing bit pairs in alternate banks; the microprocessor accesses one bank while the other is being refreshed. See *page-mode RAM* and *random-access memory (RAM)*.

internal font   See *printer font*.

internal hard disk   A hard disk designed to fit within a computer's case and to use the computer's power supply.

→ **Tip:** Because internal hard disks do not require their own power supply, case, or cables, they generally cost less than external hard disks of comparable quality.

internal modem   A modem designed to fit into the expansion bus of a personal computer. See *external modem* and *modem*.

interrupt   A microprocessor instruction that halts processing momentarily so that input/output or other operations can take place. When the operation is finished, processing resumes.

In a hardware interrupt, the instruction is generated within the computer as the control unit manages the flow of signals within the machine. In a software interrupt, a program generates an instruction that halts processing so that a specific operation can take place.

invisible file   See *hidden file*.

I/O   See *input/output (I/O) system*.

j

job queue   Pronounced "cue." A series of tasks automatically executed, one after the other, by the computer. In WordPerfect, for example, you can assign a job number to several files to be printed, and the program prints them in the order you assign.

join   In a relational database management program, a data retrieval operation in which a new data table is constructed from data in two or more existing data tables.

To illustrate how a join works (and why join operations are desirable in database applications), consider a database design that minimizes data redundancy. Suppose that for your video store, you create a database table called RENTALS that lists the rented tapes with the phone number of the person renting the tape and the due date:

TITLE	PHONE_NO	DUE_DATE
Alien Beings	499-1234	05/07/90
Almost Home	499-7890	05/08/90

You also create another database table, called CUSTOMERS, in which you list the name, telephone number, and credit card number of all your customers:

PHONE_NO	F_NAME	L_NAME	CARD_NO
499-1234	Terrence	Jones	1234-4321-098
499-7890	Jake	Smith	9876-1234-980

Suppose that you want to find out whether any of your customers are more than two weeks late returning a tape. You want to know the title and due date of the movie and the phone number, name, and charge card number of the customer. You need to join information from two databases.

The following Structured Query Language (SQL) command retrieves the information you need:

```
SELECT title, due_date, phone_no
FROM rentals, customers
WHERE due_date=<05/07/90
```

This command tells the program to display the information contained in the data fields called title, due_date, and phone_no for those records in which the data field due_date contains a date equal to or earlier than May 7, 1990. The result is the following display:

TITLE	DUE_DATE	PHONE_NO
Alien Beings	05/07/90	499-1234
Almost Home	05/05/90	499-7890

joystick   A cursor-control device widely used for computer games and some professional applications, such as computer-aided design.

jumper   An electrical connector that enables an end user to customize a circuit board. The jumper is a small rectangle of plastic with two or three receptacles. You install a jumper by pushing it down on two- or three-prong pins sticking up from the circuit board's surface.

justification   The alignment of multiple lines of text along the left margin, the right margin, or both margins.

The term justification often is used to refer to full justification, or the alignment of text along both margins.

k

K See *kilobyte* (K).

Kermit 1. An asynchronous communications protocol that makes the error-free transmission of program files via the telephone system easier. 2. A public-domain communications program that contains the Kermit protocol.

Developed by Columbia University and placed in the public domain, Kermit is used by academic institutions, because unlike XMODEM, Kermit can be implemented on mainframe systems that transmit seven bits per byte. See *asynchronous communication, communications protocol,* and *XMODEM*.

kernel In an operating system, the core portions of the program that perform the most essential operating system tasks, such as handling disk input and output operations and managing the internal memory.

The kernel can be used with a variety of external shells that vary in their user-friendliness. The shell handles the task of communicating with the user.

kerning The reduction of space between certain pairs of characters in display type, so that the characters print in an aesthetically pleasing manner.

Kerning is rarely necessary for body type, but may be required for headlines and titles. Some page layout programs include an automatic kerning feature, relying on a built-in database of letter pairs that require kerning (such as AV, VA, WA, YA, and so on). Manual kerning is possible with most page layout and some word processing programs.

key assignments The functions given to specific keys by a computer program.

Most of the keys on a personal computer keyboard are fully programmable, meaning that an application programmer can use them in different ways. The best programs, however, stick to standards in key assignments.

One such standard is the use of the F1 key on IBM PC-compatible keyboards for initiating on-screen help. A program that violates these standards raises the cost of training users and restricts their ability to export their skills to other application programs.

key status indicator   An on-screen status message displayed by many application programs that informs you which, if any, toggle keys are active on the keyboard.

If you inadvertently press Num Lock, for example, the arrow keys on the numeric keypad do not control the cursor; they enter numbers instead. To make up for this oversight, many application programs provide on-screen indicators that flash when you press Num Lock, Scroll Lock, or Caps Lock.

key variable   In a spreadsheet program, a constant placed in a cell at the upper left corner of the spreadsheet and referenced throughout the spreadsheet using absolute cell references.

keyboard   The most frequently used input device for all computers.

The keyboard provides a set of alphabetic, numeric, punctuation, symbol, and control keys. When an alphanumeric or punctuation key is pressed, the keyboard sends a coded input signal to the computer, which echoes the signal by displaying a character on-screen. See *autorepeat key, keyboard layout,* and *toggle key.*

keyboard buffer   A small area of primary storage set aside to hold the codes of the last keystrokes you pressed on the keyboard so that the computer can continue to accept your typing even if the computer is busy.

keyboard layout   A personal computer's keyboard provides an excellent example of how computer technology has had to adapt to people (rather than people adapting to computers). A PC's keyboard layout uses the standard QWERTY layout that typewriters have used for a century. Another keyboard layout is the Dvorak keyboard, designed in the 1930s by August Dvorak, a professor of education at the University of Washington. The Dvorak keyboard is designed so that more than two-thirds of the words you type only require the home row keys. (For QWERTY keyboards, the figure is 32 percent.)

The world's typing speed record—170 words per minute—was set on a Dvorak keyboard. Equipping a PC with a Dvorak keyboard is easy, but surprisingly few people do so. The old QWERTY habit is still too strong.

Early IBM Personal computers used a standard 83-key layout that attracted a good deal of criticism because of the odd key layout, such as placing the backslash key between the Z and the Shift keys. Many people also considered the Enter key too small. Toggle keys such as Scroll Lock, Num Lock, and Caps Lock lacked lights, and you could not tell if one was active.

In response to this criticism, IBM introduced a new 84-key layout with the release of the IBM Personal Computer AT. The AT keyboard uses the standard Selectric typewriter key layout for the typing area, with three indicators that light up when you press Scroll Lock, Num Lock, or Caps Lock. The new 84th key, called Sys Req, is used only when you are running an operating system other than DOS.

The latest standard is an enhanced, 101-key layout. The 12 function keys (instead of 10) are lined up above the number keys. The 101-key layout also has a separate cursor-control keypad.

The 101-key standard includes a relocated Ctrl key that touch typists dislike. The Ctrl key is used with other keys to give commands. In the earlier keyboard, Ctrl was situated left of the A key, within easy reach of your left pinky. In the 101-key layout, however, Ctrl is at the lower left, requiring a contorted movement to reach it. Many IBM PC-compatible computers use a corrected 101-key layout that places the Ctrl key back beside the A.

The original Macintosh keyboard contained only 58 keys. This keyboard lacked a numeric keypad and arrow keys, which the Apple engineers thought were unnecessary because of the Mac's extensive use of the mouse.

Widely criticized, this keyboard was replaced by a 78-key keyboard for the Macintosh Plus. This keyboard included a numeric keypad and arrow keys. With the release of the Macintosh SE and Macintosh II computers, Apple created a new interface standard for input peripherals called the Apple Desktop Bus (ADB). Today's ADB keyboards include the 81-key Apple keyboard with Control and Escape keys, and the 105-key Apple Extended Keyboard, which includes function keys.

keyboard template   A plastic card with adhesive that can be pressed onto the keyboard to explain the way a program configures the keyboard.

Many applications provide keyboard templates, which are helpful when you are learning the program.

keystroke   The physical action of pressing down a key on the keyboard so that a character is entered or a command is initiated.

keyword   In programming languages (including software command languages), a word describing an action or operation that the computer can recognize and execute.

kilo   A prefix indicating one thousand (10^3).

kilobit   1,024 bits of information. See *kilobyte (K)*.

kilobyte (K)   The basic unit of measurement for computer memory, equal to 1,024 bytes.

The prefix kilo suggests 1,000, but this world contains twos, not tens: $2^{10} = 1,024$. Because one byte is the same as one character in personal computing, a memory of 1K can contain 1,024 characters (letters, numbers, or punctuation marks).

Early personal computers (mid-1970s) offered as little as 16K or 32K of random-access memory (RAM); memory chips were expensive. In IBM PC-compatible computing, 640K is considered a standard figure (the maximum under DOS); today, Macintosh computers are equipped with at least 1M of RAM.

kludge   An improvised, technically inelegant solution to a problem.

knowledge base   In an expert system, the portion of the program that expresses an expert's knowledge, often in IF-THEN rules (such as "If the tank pressure exceeds 600 pounds per square inch, then sound a warning.").

1

label   In a spreadsheet program, text or a heading placed in a cell. In DOS and OS/2 batch files, a string of characters preceded by a colon that marks the destination of a GOTO command. See *value*.

label alignment   In a spreadsheet program, the way labels are aligned in a cell (flush left, centered, flush right, or repeating across the cell).

     → **Tip:** In Lotus 1-2-3, you can control the alignment of a label as you type it by beginning the label with a prefix. Usually optional, the label prefix specifies how 1-2-3 aligns the label within the cell:

Label Prefix	Alignment
'	Flush left
^	Centered
"	Flush right
\	Repeating across the cell

See *label* and *label prefix*.

label prefix In a spreadsheet program, a punctuation mark at the beginning of a cell entry that tells the program that the entry is a label and specifies how the program should align the label within the cell.

Most programs enter the label prefix—often an apostrophe—when you begin the cell entry with an alphabetical character.

→ **Tip:** If you begin a cell entry with a number, the program interprets the number as a value rather than a label. However, you can make a number into a label by starting the entry with the label prefix. In Lotus 1-2-3, for example, if you type **'1991,** the program interprets the entry as a label and formats the label flush left.

label printer A printer that is designed specifically to print names and addresses on continuous labels.

LAN See *local area network (LAN).*

LAN-aware program Version of an application program specifically modified so that the program can function in a network environment.

In a local area network, you cannot place an application program on a file server and expect the application to function when several people try to use it at once. The licensing agreements of most applications prohibit placing the application on a file server. Network versions of programs, however, are designed for concurrent access. Network versions of transactional application programs—such as database management programs—create and maintain shared files. For example, an invoice-processing program has access to a database of accounts receivable.

The network versions of nontransactional programs—such as word processing programs—include file security features. For example, the word processor can lock files to prevent unauthorized users from gaining access to your documents. See *concurrency control, file locking, file server, LAN-ignorant program, local area network (LAN), nontransactional application,* and *transactional application.*

LAN backup program   A program that is specifically designed to back up the programs and data stored on a local area network's file server. The best LAN backup programs automatically back up the file server at scheduled times, without user intervention.

LAN-ignorant program   An application program that is designed for use as a stand-alone program only, and contains no provisions for use on a network (such as file locking and concurrency control). See *concurrency control*.

LAN memory management program   A utility program specifically designed to free conventional memory so that the user can run applications on a network workstation. Every workstation in a local area network must run network software, which can consume as much as 100K of conventional memory. The result is "RAM cram," the reduction of conventional memory to the point that the workstation may not be able to run certain memory-hungry applications. LAN memory managers address this problem by moving the network software, as well as device drivers, terminate-and-stay-resident (TSR) programs, and other utilities into the upper memory area, extended memory, or expanded memory.

   A popular and well-rated LAN management program is Net-Room (Helix Software). See *conventional memory, device driver, expanded memory, extended memory, local area network (LAN), network operating system (NOS),* and *terminate-and-stay-resident (TSR) program.*

LAN server   See *file server* and *printer server.*

landscape orientation   The rotation of a page design to print text and/or graphics horizontally across the longer axis of the page. See *portrait orientation.*

laptop computer   A lightweight, battery-powered, portable computer that uses a lightweight display device such as a liquid crystal display.

   True laptops that weigh less than twelve pounds are different from luggables, portable computers that are too heavy to be carried around like a briefcase. The better laptops use backlit or gas-plasma screens that are easier to read, but these brighter screens consume more electricity, and require more frequent recharges.

large-scale integration (LSI)   In integrated circuit technology, the fabrication on one chip of up to 100,000 discrete transistor devices. See *very large scale integration (VLSI)*.

laser font   See *outline font*.

laser printer   A high-resolution printer that uses a version of the electrostatic reproduction technology of copying machines to fuse text and graphic images to the page.

Although laser printers are complex machines, understanding how they work is not difficult. The printer's controller circuitry receives the printing instructions from the computer and, for each page, constructs a bit map of every dot on the page (about 1M of memory is required to ensure adequate storage space for graphics images). The controller ensures that the print engine's laser transfers a precise replica of this bit map to a photostatically sensitive drum or belt. Switching on and off rapidly, the beam travels across the drum, and as the beam moves, the drum charges the areas exposed to the beam. The charged areas attract toner (electrically charged ink) as the drum rotates past the toner cartridge.

In a write-black engine, the beam charges the areas that print and does so with a positive charge that attracts toner. In a write-white engine, the beam charges the areas not printed, giving the areas a negative charge that repels toner. Because of this technique, write-black engines show details of images better than write-white engines, but write-white engines print denser images. An electrically charged wire pulls the toner from the drum onto the paper, and heat rollers fuse the toner to the paper. A second electrically charged wire neutralizes the drum's electrical charge.

Alternative technologies include light-emitting diode (LED) imaging printers that use a dense array of LEDs instead of a laser to generate the light that exposes the drum, and liquid crystal shutter (LCS) printers that use a lattice-like array of liquid crystal gateways to block or transmit light as necessary. See *print engine* and *resolution*.

LaserJet A series of laser printers manufactured by Hewlett-Packard and widely used in IBM PC-compatible computing.

Introduced in 1984, the LaserJet offered only one built-in font (the monospace Courier), but its 300-dpi resolution and capability to accept font cartridges helped to launch desktop publishing. The LaserJet Plus, introduced in 1985, offered sufficient internal random-access memory (RAM) so that the printer could accept downloadable fonts, further increasing its versatility as a desktop typesetter.

The LaserJet Series II was introduced in 1987 with additional built-in fonts, a larger paper tray, and additional memory. The LaserJet IIP Personal Laser Printer was added in 1989 and brought the street cost of laser printing technology below $1,000 for the first time. A new version of Hewlett-Packard's proprietary printer control language has brought scalable (outline) font technology to middle- and high-end LaserJet printers. LaserJet's also can be equipped with PostScript cartridges, although such cartridges operate more slowly than true Postscript printers.

See *laser printer, outline font,* and *PostScript laser printer.*

LaserWriter A series of PostScript laser printers manufactured by Apple Computer and used with Macintosh and IBM PC-compatible computers.

Introduced in 1985 with a list price of nearly $8,000, the Apple LaserWriter was the first commercial laser printer to offer a built-in interpreter for the PostScript page description language. Capable of using the sophisticated and scalable outline fonts created by Adobe Systems, Inc., and other firms, the LaserWriter is well-integrated with the Macintosh family of computers because a standard PostScript-compatible printer driver is available for any application to use. (For an IBM PC compatible running DOS, an application cannot produce PostScript-compatible output unless the application includes a PostScript-compatible driver.)

Coupled with the Mac's capability of displaying screen fonts that suggest the typeface and type size changes, the LaserWriter gave the Macintosh an early lead in desktop publishing.

Designed to be connected to the Macintosh through inexpensive AppleTalk network connections, Apple envisioned the LaserWriter as a shared peripheral, designed for use by a small workgroup of four to seven individuals. A standard serial port is included, however, for direct connection to IBM PC-compatible computers.

The LaserWriter II series, introduced in 1987, featured a better print engine, more memory, and faster output. At the top of the line is the LaserWriter II NTX, which includes 11 Adobe typefaces (a total of 35 fonts), a 68020 microprocessor running at 16.7 MHz, and a SCSI output port for a dedicated hard disk. The LaserWriter II SC is not a PostScript printer and therefore relies on Apple's built-in QuickDraw technology to generate fonts. Macintoshes equipped with System 7 can print TrueType outline (scalable) fonts on the LaserWriter IISC, and also on Apple's newest and cheapest laser printer, the Apple Personal LaserWriter.

The LaserWriter has been imitated—many PostScript laser printers are functionally identical. Although LaserWriter printers are much cheaper now than they were originally, they can cost as much as or more than a well-equipped personal computer. LaserWriters will never be as inexpensive as LaserJets, because unlike LaserJets, PostScript-compatible printers must have their own microprocessing circuitry and require large amounts of RAM. Non-PostScript outline font technologies, however, promise to lower prices by circumventing Adobe Systems' licensing fees. See *Appletalk, laser printer, PostScript laser printer,* and *System 7.*

latency   In disk drives, the delay caused by the disk rotating so that the desired data is positioned under the read/write head.

launch   To start a program.

layer   In some illustration and page-layout applications, an on-screen sheet on which text or graphics can be placed independent of other sheets.

In SuperPaint, for example, you can create illustrations on two layers: a paint layer for bit-mapped graphics and a draw layer for object-oriented graphics. In FreeHand, you can draw or paint on up to 200 transparent layers. Commands typically named Bring to Front or Send to Back enable you to bring a background layer forward so that you can edit that layer.

layout   1. In desktop publishing, the process of arranging text and graphics on a page. 2. The arrangement of data items on a data record or the arrangement of page design elements, such as text and graphics, on a printed page.

LCD   See *liquid crystal display (LCD)*.

leader   In word processing, a row of dots or dashes that provides a path for the eye to follow across the page.

Leaders often are used in tables of contents to lead the readers' eye from the entry to the page number. Most word processing programs enable the user to define tab stops that insert leaders when the Tab key is pressed.

leading   Pronounced "ledding." The space between lines of type, measured from baseline to baseline. Synonymous with line spacing.

The term originated from letterpress-printing technology, in which thin lead strips were inserted between lines of type to control the spacing between lines.

leading zero   The zeros added in front of numeric values so that a number fills up all required spaces in a data field. For example, three leading zeros are in the number 00098.54.

Most of today's database management programs do not require leading zeros; they are symbolic of previous generations of software, which often forced the user to enter data to conform to the program's limitations.

LED See *light emitting diode (LED)*.

left justification The alignment of text along only the left margin. Synonymous with *ragged-right alignment*.

legend In presentation graphics, an area of a chart or graph that explains the meaning of the patterns or colors used in the presentation.

letter-quality printer An impact printer that simulates the fully formed text characters produced by a high-quality office typewriter.

The print technology used is a spin-off of office typewriter technology. Many letter-quality printers use daisywheels or printing mechanisms in which the character images are positioned on the ends of spokes of a plastic or metal hub that rotates quickly as printing occurs. You change fonts by changing the daisywheel.

A major drawback of letter-quality printers is that they cannot print graphics. This fact ensures a brisk market for dot-matrix printers that, despite their poorer quality for text output, can print charts and graphs. With the arrival of laser printers, the market for letter-quality printers has all but disappeared. See *impact printer*.

light emitting diode (LED) A small electronic device made from semiconductor materials. An LED emits light when current flows through it.

LEDs are used for small indicator lights, but because they draw more power than liquid crystal displays (LCD), they rarely are used for computer displays.

light pen An input device that uses a light-sensitive stylus to enable you to draw on-screen, on a graphics tablet, or select items from menus.

LIM EMS See *Lotus-Intel-Microsoft Expanded Memory System (LIM EMS)*.

line   1. In programming, one program statement. 2. In data communications, a circuit that directly connects two or more electronic devices.

line adapter   In data communications, an electronic device that converts signals from one form to another so that the signals can be transmitted.

A modem is a line adapter that converts the computer's digital signals to analog equivalents so that these signals can be transmitted via the telephone system.

line art   In computer graphics, a drawing that does not contain halftones so that it can be reproduced accurately by low- to medium-resolution printers. See *halftone*.

line chart   See *line graph*.

line editor   A primitive word processing utility that often is provided with an operating system as part of its programming environment. Line editors are notoriously difficult to use. Unlike a full-screen editor, you can write or edit only one line of program code at a time. See *full-screen editor* and *programming environment*.

line feed   A signal that tells the printer when to start a new line.

line graph   In presentation and analytical graphics, a graph that uses lines to show the variations of data over time or to show the relationship between two numeric variables. In general, the x-axis (categories axis) is aligned horizontally, and the y-axis (values axis) is aligned vertically. A line graph, however, may have two y-axes. See *bar graph*, *presentation graphics*, *x-axis*, and *y-axis*.

line spacing   See *leading*.

link   To establish a connection between two files or data items so that a change in one is reflected by a change in the second.

A cold link requires user intervention and action, such as opening both files and using an updating command, to make sure that the change has occurred; a warm link occurs automatically. See *cold link* and *hot link*.

linked list   See *list*.

linked pie/column chart   See *linked pie/column graph*.

linked pie/column graph   In presentation graphics, a pie graph paired with a column graph so that the column graph displays the internal distribution of data items in one of the pie's slices.

liquid crystal display (LCD)   A low-power display technology used in laptop computers and small, battery-powered electronic devices such as meters, testing equipment, and digital watches. The display device uses rod-shaped crystal molecules that change their orientation when an electrical current flows through them. When no current exists, the crystals seem to disappear. When energized, they direct light to a polarizing screen, producing a darkened area.

   LCD displays are flat and draw little power, but they are not bright enough for sustained use without causing eyestrain. A compromise design uses a backlit screen. This design improves the LCD screen's readability but draws more power.

live copy/paste   See *hot link*.

load   To transfer program instructions or data from a disk into the computer's random-access memory (RAM).

local area network (LAN)   The linkage of personal and other computers within a limited area by high-performance cables so that users can exchange information, share expensive peripherals, and draw on the resources of a massive secondary storage unit (called a file server).

   Local area networks offer the advantages of a distributed computing system in which computational power is distributed to users without sacrificing their ability to communicate.

   Ranging tremendously in size and complexity, LANs may link only a few personal computers to an expensive, shared peripheral, such as a laser printer. More complex systems use central computers called file servers and enable users to communicate with each other via electronic mail to share multiuser programs and to access shared databases.

Some of the largest and most complex LANs are found on university campuses and in large corporations. Such networks may be composed of several smaller networks interconnected by electronic bridges. Unlike a multiuser system, in which each user is equipped with a dumb terminal that may lack processing capabilities; each user in a LAN possesses a workstation containing its own processing circuitry. High-speed cable communication links connect these workstations.

LANs are not without their disadvantages when compared to multiuser systems, however. Multiuser systems may be highly appropriate for vertical applications such as point-of-sale systems, in which it is unnecessary to provide each node with its own processing circuitry and software.

In addition, much of the software developed for multiuser systems has its origins in vertical application development, such as the creation of software for hospital management, and as such, it represents the accumulation of years of experience in managing specific organizations with computers.

A set of standards (network protocols) governs the flow of information within the network. These standards determine when and how a node may initiate a message. Network protocols also handle conflicts that occur when two nodes begin transmitting at the same time. Common network protocols for personal computers include AppleTalk and EtherNet.

The basic components of a LAN are cables, a network interface card, a file server (which includes the central mass storage), a network operating system (NOS), and personal computers or workstations linked by the system.

Three alternative network topologies (methods for interconnecting the network's workstations) exist: bus networks, ring networks, and star networks. In addition, two methods for communicating information via the network's cables exist: baseband and broadband. See *AppleTalk, baseband, broadband, bus network, EtherNet, file server, multiuser system, network operating system (NOS), Novell Netware, ring network,* and *star network.*

local drive   In a local area network, a disk drive that's part of the workstation you currently are using, as distinguished from a network drive (a drive made available to you through the network).

local echo   See *half duplex.*

LocalTalk   The physical connectors and cables manufactured by Apple Computer for use in AppleTalk networks.

local printer   In a local area network, a printer directly connected to the workstation you are using, as distinguished from a network printer (a printer made available to you through the network).

locked file   In a local network, a file attribute that prevents applications or the user from updating or deleting the file.

logarithmic chart   See *logarithmic graph.*

logarithmic graph   In analytical and presentation graphics, a graph displayed with a y-axis (values axis) incremented exponentially in powers of 10.

On an ordinary y-axis, the 10 is followed by 20, 30, 40, and so on. On a logarithmic scale, however, 10 is followed by 100, 1,000, 10,000, and so on.

→ **Tip:** Use a logarithmic scale when one of the data series has very small values, and others have large values. In an ordinary graph, you almost cannot see the data series with small values; on a logarithmic chart, the small values show up much better. See *analytical graphics* and *presentation graphics.*

logic board   See *motherboard.*

logical drives   The disk drives of a computer system that present themselves to the user as identical devices which retrieve and store data using the same file-management commands. See *physical drive*.

logical format See *high-level format*.

logical operator A symbol used to specify the logical relationship of inclusion or exclusion between two quantities or concepts.

In query languages, the inclusive operator (OR) broadens the number of data records retrieved, and the exclusive operators (AND, NOT) restrict the number retrieved.

Suppose that you specify a query that asks "Show me the titles of all the videotapes in which the field RATING contains PG OR PG-13." You see a list of the titles with either rating; the program retrieves records that meet either of the criteria you specify.

To illustrate the restrictive effect of the AND operator, consider the following example: you ask, "Show me the titles of all the videotapes in which the field CATEGORY contains Adventure AND the field RATING includes PG." Only those records that meet both of the criteria you specify in your query appear on-screen.

The NOT operator is also restrictive, as in the following example: "Show me the titles of all the videotapes in which the field CATEGORY contains Adventure, but NOT the ones in which the field RATING includes R." Synonymous with *Boolean operator*.

log-in security In local area and mainframe networks, a validation process that requires users to type a password before gaining access to the system. See *local area network (LAN)* and *password protection*.

log off The process of terminating a connection with a computer system or peripheral device in an orderly way.

log on The process of establishing a connection with, or gaining access to, a computer system or peripheral device.

A log-on procedure is used to contact host computers via telecommunications or network links. In operating systems, a log on procedure is used to activate a disk drive.

log-on file   In a local area network, a batch file or configuration file that starts the network software and establishes the connection with the network when you turn on the workstation.

lookup function   A procedure in which the program consults stored data listed in a table or file.

lookup table   In a spreadsheet program, a range of cells set apart from the rest of the worksheet and dedicated to a lookup function, such as determining the correct tax rate based on annual income.

lost chain   In DOS and OS/2, a section of a file once connected with other sections, but the file allocation table (FAT) no longer contains the information needed to reconstruct the linkages.

→ **Tip:** Use the CHKDSK command to determine whether you have lost chains on your disk. If any are detected, choose the on-screen option that converts lost chains into files. Use the TYPE command to examine the files. Erase the files if they do not contain useful data.

lost cluster   A section of a file that remains on the disk, even though the file allocation table (FAT) contains no record of its linkages to the rest of the file.

Lost clusters occur when the computer is turned off (or the power fails) while a file is being written. They do not pose a problem other than consuming disk space.

→ **Tip:** Use the CHKDSK command occasionally with the /F switch to delete lost clusters. CHKDSK transforms the lost clusters into files, which you then can delete.

Lotus-Intel-Microsoft Expanded Memory Specification (LIM EMS)   An expanded memory standard that enables the programs that recognize the standard to work with more than 640K RAM under DOS.

The LIM Version 4.0 standard, introduced in 1987, supports up to 32M of expanded memory and enables programs to run in expanded memory (as well as providing space for the storage of data).

▲ **Caution:** Software cannot work with expanded memory unless specifically designed to do so. Most popular application packages such as WordPerfect, Lotus 1-2-3, and dBASE work with LIM 4.0 expanded memory, but less popular programs and shareware may not function in EMS unless you use a windowing environment such as Quarterdeck's DESQview or Microsoft Windows. See *expanded memory* and *extended memory.*

low-level format   The physical pattern of magnetic tracks and sectors created on a disk during formatting. This operation, sometimes called a physical format, is different from the high-level format that establishes the housekeeping sections that track free and in-use areas of the disk.

When you format a floppy disk using the DOS FORMAT command, the computer establishes an absolute and a relative format on the disk.

→ **Tip:** If you have just purchased a new hard disk for your system, remember that the DOS FORMAT command does not perform a physical format on a hard disk. On hard disks, FORMAT performs only a high-level format. In most cases, the factory has performed the absolute format. If you attempt to use FORMAT on the disk and the format fails, however, you first must perform a low-level format using a program that the hard disk manufacturer provides. See *high-level format.*

low resolution   In computer monitors and printers, a visual definition that is not sufficient to produce well-defined characters or smoothly defined curves in graphic images, resulting in characters and graphics with jagged edges.

The IBM Color Graphics Adapter (CGA) and monitor, for example, can display 640 pixels horizontally, but only 200 vertically, resulting in poor visual definition. See *high resolution.*

LPT   In DOS, a device name that refers to one of the parallel ports to which parallel printers can be connected.

LSI   See *large-scale integration (LSI)*.

m

M   See *megabyte (M)*.

MacBinary   A file transfer protocol for Macintosh computers that enables Macintosh files to be stored on non-Macintosh computers without losing icons, graphics, and information about the file (such as the creation date). Most Macintosh communication programs send and receive files in MacBinary.

machine language   The language recognized and executed by the computer's central processing unit (CPU). The language is symbolized by 0s and 1s and is extremely difficult for people to use and read. See *assembly language* and *high-level programming language*.

Macintosh   A family of personal computers introduced by Apple Computer in 1984 that features a graphical user interface.

During the 1970s, the Xerox Palo Alto Research Center (PARC) attracted what were unquestionably some of the greatest minds in computer design. In an organizational context well suited to technical innovation, the PARC scientists generated an astonishing series of innovations: a WYSIWYG word processor called Bravo that inspired Microsoft Word, desktop publishing with laser printers, local area networks for workgroups, and the graphical user interface with pull-down menus and a mouse.

Visiting PARC 1979, Steve Jobs of Apple Computer was so impressed that he hired several PARC scientists. At Apple, they joined a team that created the Lisa—a $10,000 computer released in 1983.

The Lisa, however, was a commercial flop. Well received and

considered a milestone in computer design, the Lisa was too expensive for its market. In the meantime, IBM was running away with Apple's market share in personal computing with the phenomenal success of the IBM personal computer.

In response, a team at Apple wanted to bring PARC-like technology to the masses, in the form of a computer named Macintosh.

The people at Apple developed the Mac with a utopian idealism and a near-religious fervor for changing the world; this computer was to be "the computer for the rest of us."

Yet, the machine the team produced departed significantly from the open-architecture and open-bus philosophy that had done so much to ensure the popularity of Apple's previous product, the Apple II. With a sealed case that users could not open without a special tool, the Mac seemed to be designed to bring user-friendly technology to people, but also to keep the market for expensive peripherals and accessories in Apple's hands.

With the release of the open-bus Macintosh II in 1987, Apple tacitly admitted that the closed-bus architecture of the early Mac was a mistake. By 1989, a healthy support industry had grown up around the Macintosh, with many suppliers providing adapters, monitors, and printers for Macintosh computers.

The earliest Mac had other problems beside the sealed case. Jobs is said to have stated that the average personal computer user did not want a fast computer or a lot of memory—and given that the original Mac was equipped with only 128K of RAM and only one 400K disk drive, the computer reflected this philosophy.

In other ways, however, the Macintosh was technologically advanced. The Mac was the first computer to offer a 32-bit microprocessor, the Motorola 68000, running at a clock speed of 7.8 MHz (a modest improvement over the Intel 8088s 4.77 MHz). A striking innovation was the original Mac's medium-resolution monitor that displayed 512-by-312 black pixels on a paper-white background. Perhaps most importantly, the Mac's application program interface (API) and mouse gave programmers a standard that reduced the learning time for programs.

Although the Macintosh sold well at first, the original Mac never found a mass market, especially in the business context. Pressures inside Apple led to Jobs' departure, and under the leadership of Apple's CEO, John Sculley, Apple made the necessary changes: the Macintosh received more memory (512K in the Mac 512 and 1M in the Mac Plus), hard disks, facilities for communication with corporate mainframes, and a library of business software.

What ensured the Mac's entrance into the business world, however, was the 1986 release of the LaserWriter printer, coupled with the PageMaker page-layout program and high-resolution outline fonts. This technology made desktop publishing possible, and with a major technological advantage over IBM PC-compatible computers, the Macintosh made significant inroads into the world of corporate computing in the closing years of the 1980s.

Because of the brisk market for inexpensive clones, however, 12 IBM PC-compatible computers existed for every Mac in use. A series of successful product innovations in 1989, including high-performance Mac II computers based on the Motorola 68030 microprocessor and the release of a portable Macintosh, ensured the computer's continuing place in organizational and home computing.

However, it became clear in 1990 that the concentration on the high end of the market had potentially disastrous implications. Inexpensive IBM PC clones were invading Apple's traditional market niches, home and school computing, and the company had not made sufficient progress in readying an inexpensive Mac for this market. In 1990, the company released an under-$1,000 Mac, the Macintosh Classic, which has sold well, and the Macintosh LC, Apple's least expensive color Macintosh. The 1991 release of System 7 continued Apple's technological lead, which is steadily narrowing as Microsoft Windows gains momentum. But Microsoft's release of Windows 3.0 demonstrated that Apple had all but lost its technological lead. See *graphical user interface (GUI)*, *Microsoft Windows*, *Macintosh Classic* and *Motorola 68000*.

Macintosh II   An open-bus, high-performance personal computer introduced by Apple Computer in 1987.

The earliest Mac II featured a Motorola 68020 microprocessor, but Mac IIs using the Motorola 68030 running at 15.67 MHz soon replaced the 68020. Current Macintosh II computers include the popular Macintosh IIci, the high-performance Macintosh IIfx, and the lowest cost color Mac, the Macintosh LC.

The Mac II was a significant departure from the Mac's previous closed-bus architecture. For the first time, users could assemble a system using video cards, monitors (including color monitors), and even keyboards derived from non-Apple suppliers. See *Motorola 68030*.

Macintosh Classic The successor to the popular Macintosh Plus and Macintosh SE, an entry-level Macintosh that employs the 68000 microprocessor running at 8 MHz.

The 1990 introduction of the Classic followed a period of management turmoil and firings within Apple as the company realized that its preoccupation with high-end products had left the market wide open to penetration by inexpensive IBM PC clones. The Classic, retailing for less than $1,000, features performance that surpasses the SE and offers an excellent value. Apple seriously underestimated the initial demand for the computer and was unable to take full advantage of the 1990 Christmas buying season.

MacPaint The first (and now widely imitated) paint program created for the original Macintosh computer. See *paint program*.

macro A stored list of two or more application program commands that, when retrieved, replays the commands to accomplish a task. Macros automate tedious and often-repeated tasks (such as saving and backing up a file to a floppy) that otherwise would require the user to press several command keys or choose several options from menus.

Some programs provide a macro-recording mode, in which the program records your keystrokes; you then save the recording and play it back when you want. Other programs provide a built-in macro editor that enables you to type and edit the macro commands instead of recording them. Such facilities often amount to a full-fledged software-command language.

Full-featured application programs such as Microsoft Word, WordPerfect, and Lotus 1-2-3 include macro capabilities.

MacroMind Director An animation-development program (Macro-Mind, Inc.) for Macintosh computers that creates animated sequences including graphics, text, and sound.

MacWrite The first Macintosh word processing program—an easy-to-use and fast program designed for novice users.

The new version, MacWrite II (from Claris Corporation, an Apple spin-off), is substantially slower, but includes many new features.

magnetic disk In secondary storage, a random-access storage medium that is the most popular method for storing and retrieving computer programs and data files. In personal computing, common magnetic disks include 5¼-inch floppy disks, 3½-inch floppy disks, and hard disks of various sizes.

The disk is coated with a magnetically sensitive material. Like a record player's arm, the magnetic read/write head moves laterally across the surface of the spinning disk, accessing locations of the disk under the disk drive's automatic control. Unlike a record, however, the information stored on a magnetic disk can be repeatedly erased and rewritten, like any other magnetic storage medium. See *3½-inch disk, 5¼-inch disk, floppy disk, hard disk,* and *random access.*

magnetic media In secondary storage, the use of magnetic techniques to store and retrieve data on disks or tapes coated with magnetically sensitive materials.

Like iron filings on a sheet of waxed paper, these materials are re-oriented when a magnetic field passes over them. During write operations, the read/write head emits a magnetic field that re-orients the magnetic materials on the disk or tape so that they are positively or negatively charged, corresponding to a bit of data. During read operations, the read/write head senses the magnetic polarities encoded on the tape.

magnetic tape In secondary storage, a high-capacity mass storage and backup medium.

Although magnetic tape drives must use slow sequential access techniques, magnetic tape is inexpensive and offers a cost-effective way to store massive amounts of data; one roll of tape can store up to 100 megabytes of data. Magnetic tape drives are available for IBM personal computers and compatibles. A 1991 price break placed tape cartridge drives within the reach of many PC users; drives became available for as little as $250. Most tape drives are used for hard disk backup purposes. See *sequential access*.

mail merge A utility common in full-featured word processing programs that draws information from a database—usually a mailing list—to print multiple copies of a document. Each copy contains one or part of one of the database records and text that does not vary from copy to copy.

The most common application of the mail merge utility is the generation of personalized form letters. A personalized form letter contains text that you send to all recipients, but mail merge has personalized the letter with the correspondent's name and address. You also may personalize the salutation.

In a mail-merge application, you use the word processing program to create the database, called the secondary file or data document, and you create a primary file (sometimes called a main document) that contains the text you want to send. In place of the correspondent's name and address, however, you type codes that refer to fields in the name-and-address database. Finally, you give a command that prints one copy of the primary file for each record in the database.

mailbox In electronic mail, a storage location that holds messages addressed to an individual until he or she accesses the system. An on-screen message informs the user that mail is waiting.

main program   In programming, the part of the program containing the master sequence of instructions, unlike the subroutines, procedures, and functions that the main program calls.

main storage   See *random-access memory (RAM)*.

mainframe   A multiuser computer designed to meet the computing needs of a large organization.

Originally, the term mainframe referred to the metal cabinet that housed the central processing unit (CPU) of early computers. The term came to be used generally to refer to the large, central computers developed in the late 1950s and 1960s to meet the accounting and information-management needs of large organizations. The largest mainframes can handle thousands of dumb terminals and use gigabytes of secondary storage.

Rather than differentiating such machines by size alone, experts increasingly differentiate them by function: a mainframe meets the computing needs of an entire organization, and a minicomputer meets the needs of a department within an organization. By accepting this definition, one must concede that a minicomputer should be termed a mainframe if a small business uses it as its sole computing resource. The boundaries between the two types of computers are blurring. See *minicomputer, personal computer,* and *workstation*.

maintenance release   A program revision that corrects a minor bug or makes a minor new feature available, such as a new printer driver. Maintenance releases are usually numbered in tenths (3.2) or hundreds (2.01), to distinguish them from major program revisions. Synonymous with *incremental update*.

male connector   In computer cables, a cable terminator and connection device in which the pins protrude from the connector's surface. See *female connector*.

management information system (MIS)   A computer system, usually based on a mainframe or minicomputer, designed to provide management personnel with up-to-date information on the organization's performance.

manual recalculation In a spreadsheet program, a recalculation method that suspends the recalculation of values after you change them until you press a key that forces recalculation to take place.

Most spreadsheet programs recalculate all values within the spreadsheet after you change the contents of an individual cell. If you are using a slow computer and creating a large spreadsheet, you may want to choose the manual recalculation mode as you enter data.

map A representation of data stored in memory. See *bit map*.

mapping The process of converting data encoded in one format or device to another format or device.

In database management, for example, the database index provides a way of mapping the actual records (which are stored on disk in a fixed order) to the display screen in ways useful to the user.

mask A pattern of symbols or characters that, when imposed on a data field, limits the kinds of characters that the user can type into the field.

In a database management program, for example, the mask Az enables the user to type any alphabetical character, uppercase or lowercase, but not numbers or other symbols.

master boot record See *boot record*.

mass storage See *secondary storage*.

master document In WordPerfect, for example, a method of linking two or more documents so that the program paginates all the documents as a unit and produces one table of contents and an index. See *chained printing*.

masthead   In desktop publishing, the section of a newsletter or magazine that gives the details of its staff, ownership, advertising, subscription prices, and so on.

math coprocessor   See *numeric coprocessor*.

maximize   To zoom or enlarge a window so that it fills the screen.
   In Microsoft Windows, you maximize a window by clicking the maximize button (the top arrow in the right corner) or by choosing Maximize from the Control menu. See *Microsoft Windows* and *minimize*.

MCA   See *Micro Channel Architecture (MCA)*.

mean time between failures (MTBF)   The statistical average operating time between the start of a component's life and the time of its electronic or mechanical failure.

mechanicals   In desktop publishing, the final pages or boards with pasted-up galleys of type and line art, sometimes with acetate or tissue overlays for color separations and notes, which you send to the offset printer. See *camera-ready copy* and *desktop publishing (DTP)*.

media   The plural of medium. See *secondary storage medium*.

mega   Prefix indicating one million.

megabyte (M)   A unit of memory measurement equal to approximately one million bytes (1,048,576 bytes).

megaflop   A benchmark used to rate professional workstations and scientific mainframe or minicomputers; a megaflop is equal to one million floating point operations per second.

megahertz (MHz)   A unit of measurement equal to one million electrical vibrations or cycles per second. Commonly used to compare the clock speeds of computers.

One million cycles per second sounds impressive, but it actually takes microprocessors three or four clock cycles to execute one instruction. A 1 MHz computer, in fact, is too slow by today's standards; even the 4.77 MHz clock speed of the original IBM personal computer is considered sluggish. Clock speeds of 16 MHz, 20 MHz, 25 MHz, and even 33 MHz are increasingly common in personal computing. See *clock speed* and *hertz (Hz)*.

membrane keyboard   A flat and inexpensive keyboard covered with a dust- and dirt-proof plastic sheet on which only the two-dimensional outline of computer keys appears.

The user presses the plastic sheet and engages a switch hidden beneath. Accurately typing on a membrane keyboard is more difficult, but such keyboards are needed in restaurants or other locations where users may not have clean hands.

memory   The computer's primary storage (random-access memory, or RAM, for example), as distinguished from its secondary storage (disk drives, for example). See *primary storage* and *secondary storage*.

memory address   A code number that specifies a specific location in a computer's random-access memory. See *random-access memory (RAM)*.

memory cache   See *cache memory.*

memory controller gate array   Synonymous with *MultiColor Graphics Array (MCGA),* a video display standard of the low-end models of IBM's Personal System/2.

memory-management program   A utility program that increases the apparent size of random-access memory (RAM) by making expanded memory, extended memory, or virtual memory available for the execution of programs.

Memory-management programs include utilities provided with expanded memory boards, windowing environments such as

Microsoft Windows, and virtual memory programs that set aside a portion of a hard disk and treat it as a RAM extension. See *expanded memory* and *extended memory*.

memory map   An arbitrary allocation of segments of a computer's primary storage that defines which areas the computer can use for specific purposes.

Although the Intel 8088 microprocessor can use 1M of RAM, a portion of this potential memory space is reserved for the system's use of such functions as the keyboard buffer and display adapters. User programs may use the remaining 640K of base memory.

This decision, although arbitrary, is irrevocable if DOS is involved, because DOS and its application programs cannot operate unless the memory map remains exactly the way it was laid out when IBM designed the personal computer.

memory-resident program   See *terminate-and-stay-resident (TSR) program*.

memory word   See *word*.

menu   An on-screen display that lists the choices available to the user. See *pull-down menu*.

menu bar   In the industry standard and graphical user interfaces, a bar stretching across the top of the screen (or the top of a window) that contains the names of pull-down menus. See *graphical user interface (GUI)*, *industry-standard user interface*, and *pull-down menu*.

menu-driven program   A program that provides you with menus for choosing program options so that you do not need to memorize commands. See *command-driven program*.

MFM   See *Modified Frequency Modulation (MFM)*.

micro   Prefix meaning one millionth, and an abbreviation (increasingly rare) for "microcomputer."

Micro Channel Architecture (MCA)   The design specifications of IBM's proprietary Micro Channel Bus. An MCA-compatible peripheral is designed to plug directly into a Micro Channel Bus, but will not work with other bus architectures. See *Micro Channel Bus*.

Micro Channel Bus   A proprietary 32-bit expansion-bus architecture introduced by IBM for its high-end PS/2 computers. The Micro Channel Bus is not downwardly compatible with previous bus architectures.

Given the achievement of 32-bit microprocessors such as the Intel 80386 and 80486, the AT expansion bus, with its 16-bit data bus structure, was destined to receive competition from a true, 32-bit expansion bus.

Almost all non-IBM 80386 computers use a 32-bit bus structure only on the motherboard, where the RAM is linked to the microprocessor. Outside the motherboard, these computers use the 16-bit AT expansion bus, for which a huge supply of cheap peripherals is available. But the improvement of PCs clearly calls for a 32-bit expansion bus. In an attempt to define a 32-bit bus standard, IBM introduced Micro Channel Architecture (MCA) in 1987 and used the Micro Channel Bus on its high-end PS/2 models.

The MCA standard is not downwardly compatible with existing peripherals and adapters designed for the AT expansion bus. Some industry analysts, therefore, believe MCA was designed primarily to recapture for IBM part of the lucrative market for peripherals and adapters. But the MCA bus has many technical advantages, including the capability of using 32-bit peripherals, higher speed, greater reliability, and even the capability of using more than one central processing unit (CPU) in one computer.

IBM has offered the technology to clone makers under a licensing scheme, but few have taken IBM up on the offer. Instead, the major manufacturers of IBM compatibles have offered their own 32-bit bus design, called Extended Industry Standard Architecture (EISA), which has most of MCA's benefits but also is compatible with peripherals and adapters designed for the AT expansion bus. See *Extended Industry Standard Architecture (EISA)*.

micro manager   The person responsible for managing the acquisition, modification, and maintenance of an organization's personal computers. The micro manager also trains users to use application programs.

micro-to-mainframe   The linkage of personal computer to mainframe or minicomputer networks.

microcomputer   Any computer with its arithmetic-logic unit (ALU) and control unit contained on one integrated circuit called a microprocessor.

When personal computers first appeared in the mid-to-late 1970s, people often referred to them as microcomputers, because their CPUs were microprocessors. Microcomputers were designed as single-user machines. For the first time, microcomputers placed the processing circuitry entirely under the end user's control. Many computing professionals, however, did not take microcomputers seriously at first. For them, "microcomputer" had the connotation of an amusing toy.

Since the mid-1980s, the distinction between minicomputers (as multiuser computers) and microcomputers (as single-user computers) has become blurry. Many microcomputers are substantially more powerful than the mainframes of just 10 years ago. You can transform some of today's more powerful microcomputers into minicomputers by equipping them with remote terminals. Also, many of today's minicomputers use microprocessors.

An attempt was made recently to put a mainframe on one large chip but failed. Theoretically, however, it is possible, and someday, someone will succeed. Technological change has made the distinction between microcomputers and minicomputers all but meaningless.

Differentiating among these machines by the function they are designed to perform makes the most sense.

Centralized Computing Systems. Designed for use by several users simultaneously, most mainframe and minicomputer systems meet the needs of an organization or a department within an organization. The emphasis in such computer systems is on keeping programs, data, and processing capabilities under central control, so that end users gain access to these systems through remote terminals.

Stand-alone Computers. Designed for single-user applications, a stand-alone computer such as a personal computer is a self-contained, stand-alone microcomputer that does not rely on external resources such as a central database. A PC is ideal for personal, home, or private use by an individual who does not need to share computing resources with other people.

Distributed Computing Systems. In a distributed system, the object is to get computing power to the user without giving up the means to share external computing resources, such as access to a central database. An example of a distributed computing system is a network of professional workstations.

A professional workstation is an advanced micro computer that contains the advanced display and processing circuitry needed by professionals such as engineers, financial planners, and architects. Because their computers are linked in a computer communication network, these professionals can send messages to each other using their computers, share expensive printers, and create a common pool of data and programs.

Today's advanced personal computers are powerful enough to migrate around these categories with ease. You can use most powerful PCs, for example, as centralized systems with remote terminals. These machines are as powerful as the professional workstations of five years ago, and can work smoothly in a distributed computing system.

microdisk   See *3½-inch disk.*

microprocessor　An integrated circuit that contains the arithmetic/ logic unit (ALU) and control unit of a computer's central processing unit (CPU). See *Intel 8086, Intel 8088, Intel 80286, Intel 80386, Intel 80386SX, Intel 80486, Motorola 68000, Motorola 68020,* and *Motorola 68030.*

Microsoft LAN Manager　An OS/2-based network operating system developed by Microsoft Corporation.

Microsoft Mouse　A mouse and associated software for IBM and IBM-compatible personal computers, including IBM's PS/1 and PS/2 computers.

By far the best selling mouse for the IBM environment, the Microsoft Mouse has established a standard that third-party mice must emulate to compete effectively. Available in both serial and bus versions, the Microsoft Mouse employs the optical-mechanical technology that most mouse users favor.

Microsoft Windows　A windowing environment and application user interface (API) for DOS that brings to IBM-format computing some of the graphical user interface features of the Macintosh, such as pull-down menus, multiple typefaces, desk accessories (a clock, calculator, calendar, and notepad, for example), and the capability of moving text and graphics from one program to another via a clipboard.

MIDI　See *Musical Instrument Digital Interface (MIDI).*

MIDI port　A port that enables a personal computer to be connected directly to a musical synthesizer.

migration　The movement of users (especially organizational users) from one hardware platform to another.

milli　Prefix indicating one thousand.

million instructions per second (MIPS)　A benchmark method for measuring the rate at which a computer executes microprocessor instructions. A computer capable of 0.5 MIPS can execute 500,000 instructions per second.

millisecond (ms)   A unit of measurement, equal to one-thousandth of a second, commonly used to specify the access time of hard disk drives. See *access time*.

minicomputer   A multiuser computer designed to meet the needs of a small company or a department. A minicomputer is more powerful than a personal computer but not as powerful as a mainframe. Typically, about 4 to 100 people use a minicomputer simultaneously.

minimize   In Microsoft Windows, to shrink a window so that it collapses to an icon on the desktop. You minimize a window by clicking the minimize button (the down arrow in the right corner) or by choosing Minimize from the Control menu.

MIPS   See *million instructions per second (MIPS)*.

MIS   See *management information system (MIS)*.

mixed cell reference   In a spreadsheet program, a cell reference in which the column reference is absolute but the row reference is relative ($A9) or in which the row reference is absolute but the column reference is relative (A$9). See *cell reference* and *relative cell reference*.

mixed column/line chart   See *mixed column/line graph*.

mixed column/line graph   In presentation and analytical graphics, a graph that displays one data series using columns and another data series using lines.

You use a line graph to suggest a trend over time; a column graph groups data items so that you can compare one to another.

mode   The operating state in which you place a program by choosing among a set of exclusive operating options. Within a given mode, certain commands and operations are available, but you may need to change modes to use other commands or operations.

mode indicator   An on-screen message that displays the program's current operating mode.

In Lotus 1-2-3, for example, the mode indicator appears in reverse video at the upper right corner of the screen.

model   A mathematical or pictorial representation of something.

The purpose of constructing the model is to gain a better understanding of the prototype in a cost-effective way. By examining or changing the characteristics of the model, you can draw inferences about the prototype's behavior.

In a spreadsheet model of a business enterprise, for example, you can explore the impact of increasing advertising expenditures on market share. Models, however, should be used with caution. A model is only as good as its underlying assumptions. If these assumptions are incorrect, or if important information is missing from the model, it may not reflect the prototype's behavior accurately.

modem   A device that converts the digital signals generated by the computer's serial port to the modulated, analog signals required for transmission over a telephone line and transforms incoming analog signals to their digital equivalents. In personal computing, people frequently use modems to exchange programs and data with other computers, and to access on-line information services such as the Dow Jones News/Retrieval Service.

Modem stands for MOdulator/DEModulator. The modulation is necessary because telephone lines were designed to handle the human voice, which warbles between 300 Hz and 3,000 Hz in ordinary telephone conversations (from a growl to a shriek). The speed at which a modem transmits data is measured in units called bits per second (technically not the same as bauds, although the terms are often used interchangeably). See *acoustic coupler, auto-dial/auto-answer modem, direct-connect modem, echoplex, external mo-*

dem, full duplex, half duplex, Hayes command set, Hayes-compatible modem, internal modem, and *Universal Asynchronous Receiver/Transmitter (UART).*

Modified Frequency Modulation (MFM)   A method of recording digital information on magnetic media such as tapes and disks by eliminating redundant or blank areas. Because the MFM data encoding scheme doubles the storage attained under the earlier frequency-modulation (FM) recording technique, MFM recording usually is referred to as double density.

MFM often is used erroneously to describe ordinary hard disk controllers, those conforming to the ST-506/ST-412 standard. MFM refers to the method used to pack data on the disk and is not synonymous with disk drive interface standards such as ST506, SCSI, or ESDI. See *data-encoding scheme, double density, interface standard,* and *Run-Length Limited (RLL).*

modular accounting package   A collection of accounting programs—one for each of the chief accounting functions (general ledger, accounts payable, accounts receivable, payroll, and inventory, for example)—designed to work together, even though they are not integrated into one program.

Modular accounting programs are computerized versions of traditional accounting practices, in which a firm keeps several ledgers—one for accounts receivable, accounts payable, and a general ledger. You update the general ledger in batches at period intervals after carefully proofing the hard copy for errors. Modular packages generally are sold with several separate programs for each of these functions, and you must follow special procedures to make sure that all the transactions are correctly updated.

These programs have not found a large market in personal computing for two reasons: first, because people with professional accounting experience designed them, these programs often do not reflect the way people in small businesses keep their books. Second, most of these programs are far from easy to use.

Some of these packages, however, are available with automatic links to point-of-sale terminals—for example, Flexware (Micro-financial Corporation) for Macintosh computers and Excalibur (Armour Systems, Inc.) for IBM PC-compatible computers.

modulation   The conversion of a digital signal to its analog equivalent, especially for the purposes of transmitting signals via telecommunications. See *demodulation* and *modem*.

monitor   The complete device that produces an on-screen display, including all necessary internal support circuitry. A monitor also is called a video display unit (VDU) or cathode-ray tube (CRT). See *analog monitor, digital monitor, Enhanced Graphics Display, monochrome monitor,* and *multisync monitor*.

monochrome display adapter (MDA)   A single-color display adapter for IBM PC-compatible computers that displays text (but not graphics) with a resolution of 720 pixels horizontally and 350 pixels vertically, placing characters in a matrix of 7-by-9 pixels. See *Hercules Graphics Adapter*.

monochrome monitor   A monitor that displays one color against a black or white background.

   Examples include the IBM monochrome monitor that displays green text against a black background and paper-white VGA monitors that display black text on a white background.

motherboard   A large, printed, computer circuit board that contains the computer's central processing unit (CPU), microprocessor support chips, random-access memory, and expansion slots. Synonymous with *logic board*.

Motorola 68000   A microprocessor that processes 32 bits internally, although it uses a 16-bit data bus to communicate with the rest of the computer.

   The 68000, with its 32-bit address bus, can address up to 32 gigabytes of random-access memory (RAM). Running at 8 MHz, the 68000 powers the entry-level Macintosh Plus computer and the Macintosh SE.

Motorola 68020 A microprocessor electronically similar to the Motorola 68000, except that this microprocessor uses a full 32-bit architecture and runs at a clock speed of 16 MHz.

The 68020 powers the original Macintosh II, displaced by newer models using the Motorola 68030 chip. Macintosh system software limits the amount of usable RAM to 8M (Apple's System 7 should boost this amount to 4 gigabytes).

Motorola 68030 A full 32-bit microprocessor capable of running at substantially higher clock speeds than its predecessors (the Motorola 68000 and 68020). The 68030 includes special features for virtual memory management.

The 68030 incorporates a chip that controls page-mode RAM, so that any 68030-equipped Macintosh can implement the advanced memory management features of System.

→ **Tip:** If you are buying a Mac, purchase a machine based on the 68030. The chip includes circuits that you need to take full advantage of the next generation of Macintosh software. See *clock speed, page-mode RAM,* and *System.*

mount To insert a disk into a disk drive.

mousable interface A program's user interface that responds to mouse input for such functions as selecting text, choosing commands from menus, and scrolling the screen.

mouse An input device, equipped with one or more control buttons, housed in a palm-sized case and designed to roll about on the table next to the keyboard. As the mouse moves, its circuits relay signals that move a pointer on-screen.

The simplest of all mouse functions is repositioning the cursor: you point to the cursor's new location and click the mouse button. You also can use the mouse to choose commands from menus, select text for editing purposes, move objects, and draw pictures on-screen.

The mouse was developed by researchers to make computers easier to use. Instead of forcing users to memorize long lists of keyboard commands, they reasoned, displaying a menu or list of commands on-screen would be easier. The user then could point the cursor at the desired command and click the mouse button.

Most people who have used a mouse agree that it makes the computer easier to use. Others, however, do not like to take their fingers away from the keyboard. Programs that use the mouse often include keyboard equivalents.

Mice are distinguished by the internal mechanism they use to generate their signal and by their means of connection with the computer. Two types of internal mechanisms are popular:

- Mechanical mouse. This mouse has a rubber-coated ball on the underside of the case. As you move the mouse, the ball rotates, and optical sensors detect the motion. (Many companies, therefore, advertise their mice as optomechanical.) You can use a mechanical mouse on virtually any surface, although a mouse pad made of special fabric usually gives the best results.

- Optical mouse. This mouse registers its position by detecting reflections from a light-emitting diode that directs a beam downward. You must have a special metal pad to reflect the beam properly, and you cannot move the mouse beyond the pad.

Mice are connected to the computer in the following three ways:

- Bus mouse. You connect a bus mouse to the computer with an adapter pressed into one of the computers expansion slots.

- Serial mouse. You connect a serial mouse to the computer with the standard serial port.

- Regular mouse. Most mice are connected to a special mouse port on the computer.

→ **Tip:** Mechanical mice are prone to collect dirt within their internal mechanisms. If too much debris accumulates, the pointer may behave erratically. You usually can clean a mechanical mouse. Turn the mouse over and rotate the ball-retainer ring. Clean the ball and the ball rollers with a cotton swab moistened in rubbing alcohol. Blow dust out of the ball chamber and reassemble the mouse.

MS-DOS   The standard, single-user operating system of IBM and IBM-compatible computers.

Introduced in 1981, MS-DOS (short for Microsoft Disk Operating System) is marketed by IBM as PC DOS; the two systems are almost indistinguishable.

MS-DOS's origins lie in CP/M—the operating system for 8-bit computers popular in the late 1970s. The original version of what was to become MS-DOS was created for experimental purposes by a small Seattle firm. Because Microsoft had landed an IBM contract to create an operating system for the IBM personal computer, Microsoft purchased and developed the program.

The similarity between MS-DOS and CP/M is no accident—MS-DOS was designed to enable an inexpensive and fast conversion of popular CP/M business programs to the new IBM personal computer. IBM analysts thought that their new computer would not succeed unless software publishers could rewrite their programs with a minimum of expense.

The chief advantages of MS-DOS over CP/M are that some commands were improved and the user could not crash the computer by removing a disk before rebooting the system. In addition, Version 2.0 of MS-DOS added UNIX-like directories and subdirectories to the system, enhancing its usefulness with hard disks. Even the most recent versions of MS-DOS are still compatible with Version 2.0.

Although the IBM personal computer architecture supports up to 640K of user RAM, the earliest IBM PCs were sold with 64K (a standard figure in 1981). MS-DOS was designed as an extremely compact operating system that could operate under severely limited memory conditions.

MS-DOS, therefore, provides little in the way of an application program interface (API) or a set of standard routines that applications can use to handle the display of information on-screen. Individual applications are free to configure the screen and keyboard as they like, and the result is a jumble of confusing and mutually incompatible user interfaces.

Operating systems that offer an API—the Macintosh System, for example—encourage the development of programs that use the same user actions and interface procedures for common operations such as selecting and deleting text, using menus, opening and closing applications, and printing.

Recognizing the advantages of an API, Microsoft developed Windows, an optional API for MS-DOS. Very few programs took advantage of the early less-powerful versions of Microsoft Windows.

MS-DOS is a command-line operating system with an interface that requires users to memorize a limited set of commands, arguments, and syntax to use MS-DOS computers successfully.

After mastering MS-DOS commands, however, users can achieve a high degree of control over the operating system's capabilities—including setting file attributes, creating automatically executed batch files, and developing semi-automated backup procedures.

The most severe limitation of MS-DOS is the 640K RAM barrier that the operating system imposes on IBM PC-compatible computing. When the system was devised, 640K seemed like a copious amount of memory. However, the creation of applications such as Lotus 1-2-3 and the advent of terminate-and-stay resident (TSR) programs soon demonstrated that 640K was barely adequate even for a stand-alone workstation.

The use of TSR programs revealed another severe limitation of MS-DOS: the system was not designed for multiprogramming, or running more than one program at a time. MS-DOS, therefore, does not prevent one program from invading the memory space used by another. Such invasions almost invariably result in crashes or unpredictable results.

Concluding that MS-DOS is about to go the way of CP/M, however, would be wrong. Microsoft has developed an operating system called OS/2 to break the 640K RAM barrier. Also, OS/2 simultaneously can run more than one program. The system includes an application-programming interface in the form of Presentation Manager, the OS/2 version of Microsoft Windows.

Software publishers, however, have been reluctant to develop programs for OS/2 because the majority of IBM PC-compatible computers that cannot run the system.

Through the use of extended memory, expanded memory, and memory-management programs, the 640K RAM barrier under MS-DOS has been broken. Microsoft Windows also gives many of OS/2's capabilities to DOS users.

In spite of the confusion about the status of MS-DOS and OS/2 in IBM PC-compatible computing, millions of computer users use MS-DOS daily; even with its limitations, MS-DOS is without question the most widely used operating system in existence. A significant 1991 upgrade, Version 5.0, addressed many of the DOS shortcomings.

DOS Features

Version Number	Features
1.25	320K floppy disk support
2.0	360K floppy disk support
	ANSI display driver
	CONFIG.SYS file
	device drivers
	file handles
	filters
	hard disk support
	hierarchical file systems
	improved batch program language
	input/output redirection
	international features
	more file attributes

Version Number	Features
	pipes print spooling volume labels
3.0	1.2M floppy disk support clock/calendar board support file locking multiple hard disk partitions network support RAM disk
3.1	network drives network file sharing
3.2	3½-inch 720K floppy disk support XCOPY command added
3.3	3½-inch 1.44M floppy disk support multiple 32M hard disk partitions
4.0	hard disk partitions to 2 gigabytes memory drivers MS-DOS Shell
5.0	2.88M floppy disk support accesses more than two hard disks device drivers in upper memory directory sorting with DIR DOS in high memory area (HMA) Doskey macros improved hard disk partition MS-DOS Editor (full-screen editor) MS-DOS QBasic (improved BASIC) MS-DOS Shell improved on-line help for DOS commands undelete command unformat command

See *application program interface (API)*, *Microsoft Windows*, *OS/2*, *MS-DOS QBASIC*, *MS-DOS Shell*, *Presentation Manager*, *protected mode*, *real mode*, *terminate-and-stay-resident (TSR) program*, and *UNIX*.

MS-DOS QBASIC An improved BASIC programming environment, supplied with DOS 5.0 and later, that includes extensive online help.

MS-DOS Shell An improved, menu-driven user interface for the DOS operating system, supplied with DOS version 5.0 and later, that conforms to the industry-standard user interface.

MS-DOS Shell provides menu-driven access to most DOS commands. Using Shell, you can copy, delete, move, and rename files; backup and restore a hard disk; format disks and recover from an accidental format of the wrong disk; undelete files that were deleted accidentally; create and remove directories; and even view and edit file attributes. MS-DOS Shell finally provides much of the functionality, in other words, that has long been missing from DOS. Users may find less need for utility packages such as PC Tools.

MultiColor Graphics Array (MCGA) A video display standard of IBM's Personal System/2. MCGA adds 64 gray-scale shades to the CGA standard and provides the EGA standard resolution of 640 x 350 pixels with 16 possible colors.

MultiFinder A utility program supplied by Apple Computer that extends the Finder's capabilities so that the Macintosh can run more than one application at a time.

The Finder is the Macintosh operating system's shell; the program that handles communication with the user. The Finder can handle only one program at a time.

With MultiFinder, the Macintosh becomes a multiple-loading operating system with some limited capabilities to perform tasks in the background, such as downloading information via telecommunications and carrying out background printing.

Contrary to common belief, MultiFinder is not a true multitasking operating system; when you activate one application, the other application freezes. See *context switching, multiple program loading, multitasking,* and *shell.*

multilaunching   In a local area network, the opening of an application program by more than one user at a time.

multilevel sort   In database management, a sort operation that uses two or more data fields to determine the order in which data records are arranged.

To perform a multilevel sort, you identify two or more fields as sort keys—fields used for ordering records, and you arrange the records in an order of primacy. The first sort key (called the primary sort key) determines the overall order in which data records are arranged.

In a library's bibliographic database, for example, the primary sort key is LAST_NAME. All records are alphabetized by the author's last name. The second sort key—FIRST_NAME—comes into play when two or more records have the same last name. A third sort key—PUB_DATE (publication date) is used when two or more records have the the same last name and the same first name. The following is a sample of the properly sorted output:

        Smith, Bill
                1986 French Soups
        Smith, Fern
                1982 Organic Gardening
        Smith, Jack
                1983 The American Space Program
                1985 The Soviet Space Program
                1987 Private Ventures into Space

→ **Tip:** Use a multilevel sort when one sort key cannot resolve the order of two or more records in your database.

multimedia   The presentation of information on a computer using graphics, sound, animation, and text. See *animation, computer-assisted instruction (CAI),* and *hypermedia.*

multiple program loading   An operating system that enables you to start more than one program at a time; only one of the programs is active at any one time, however. You switch from one program to another by pressing a key. See *context switching* and *MultiFinder*.

multiplex   To combine or interleave messages in a communications channel.

multiplexing   In local area networks, the simultaneous transmission of multiple messages in one channel.

A network capable of multiplexing can enable more than one computer to access the network at the same time. Multiplexing increases the cost of a network, however, because multiplexing devices must be included that handle the combination of signals into a single channel for transmission, and the reverse process for receiving. See *frequency division multiplexing, local area network (LAN),* and *time division multiplexing*.

multisync monitor   A color monitor capable of adjusting to a range of input frequencies so that it can work with a variety of display adapters.

multitasking   The execution of more than one program at a time on a computer system. Multitasking should not be confused with multiple program loading, in which two or more programs are present in RAM, but only one program executes at a time.

The active or foreground task responds to the keyboard, while the background task continues to run (but without your active control).

In a multitasking operating system, terminate-and-stay resident (TSR) programs are unnecessary, because you simultaneously can run any programs you want to, as long as the computer has enough memory.

Critics of multitasking operating systems say that users of stand-alone workstations have little need for multiprogramming operations. Programs that can print or download files in the background, however, hint at the power of multitasking. Imagine the capability of writing with a word processor while a spreadsheet recalculates and a database sorts.

Among the operating systems or shells that provide multitasking are OS/2 and Microsoft Windows. See *Microsoft Windows* and *multiple program loading*.

multiuser system   A computer system that enables more than one person to access programs and data at the same time.

Each user is equipped with a terminal. If the system has just one central processing unit, a technique called time-sharing provides multiple access. A time-sharing system cycles access to the processing unit among users.

Personal computers equipped with advanced microprocessors such as the Intel 80486 are sufficiently powerful to serve as the nucleus of a multiuser system. Such systems typically are equipped with the UNIX operating system, designed for multiuser systems.

Such technical advances have helped to blur the distinction between personal computers and minicomputers. If a minicomputer is a multiuser system designed to meet the needs of 4 to 100 people, multiuser computers based on 80386 and 80486 chips are legitimate minicomputers. Given such advances, the term personal computer usually is reserved for computers dedicated to stand-alone applications.

→ **Tip:** If you are considering installing a system that more than one person will use, familiarize yourself with the pros and cons of the two alternatives: multiuser systems and local area networks. See *local area network (LAN)*.

Musical Instrument Digital Interface (MIDI)   A standard communications protocol for the exchange of information between computers and musical synthesizers.

MIDI provides tools that many composers and musicians say are becoming almost indispensable. With a synthesizer and a computer equipped with the necessary software and a MIDI port, a musician can transcribe a composition into musical notation by playing the composition at the keyboard. After being placed into computer-represented form, virtually every aspect of the digitized sound—pitch, attack, delay time, tempo, and more—can be edited and altered.

n

nano   A prefix indicating one-billionth.

nanosecond (ns)   A unit of time equal to one billionth of a second.

Far beyond the range of human perception, nanoseconds are relevant to computers. For example, an advertisement for 120 ns RAM chips means that the RAM chips respond within 120 nanoseconds.

Macintosh computers with the 68030 microprocessor need faster RAM chips, 80 ns or better. See *millisecond (ms)*.

native code   See *machine language*.

native file format   The default file format an application program uses to store data on disk.

The format is often a proprietary file format that cannot be read by other programs. However, many programs can save data in several formats. See *American Standard Code for Information Interchange (ASCII)*, *file format*, and *proprietary file format*.

natural recalculation   In a spreadsheet program, a recalculation order that performs worksheet computations in the manner logically dictated by the formulas you place in cells. If the value of a formula depends on references to other cells that contain formulas, the program calculates the other cells first. See *column-wise recalculation*, *optimal recalculation*, and *row-wise recalculation*.

near-letter quality (NLQ)   A dot-matrix printing mode that prints typewriter-quality characters. As a result, printers using this mode print slower than other dot-matrix printers.

NetBIOS   See *Network Basic Input/Output System (NetBIOS)*.

NETNORTH   A Canadian wide-area network fully integrated with BITNET and that performs the same functions as BITNET.

NetWare   A network operating system, manufactured by Novell, for local area networks.

    NetWare links hardware and accommodates more than 90 types of network interface cards, 30 network architectures, and several communications protocols. Versions are available for IBM PC compatibles and Macintosh computers. See *network operating system (NOS)*.

network administrator   In local area networks, the person responsible for maintaining the network and assisting end users.

network architecture   The complete set of hardware, software, and cabling standards that specifies the design of a local area network. See *network topology*.

Network Basic Input/Output System (NetBIOS)   A system program included in DOS since version 3.1 that establishes standard methods for linking personal computers to local area networks.

network drive   In a local area network, a disk drive made available to you through the network, as distinguished from a drive connected directly to the workstation you're using.

    → **Tip:** In a DOS network, local drives are labeled with A, B, C, D, or E; network drives have a letter chosen from the rest of the alphabet.

network interface card   An adapter that enables you to hook a network cable directly to a microcomputer.

    Rather than forcing network communications to occur through

the serial port, a network interface card takes advantage of a microcomputer's internal bus to make network communications easier.

The board includes encoding and decoding circuitry and a receptacle for a network cable connection. Because data is transmitted more rapidly within the computer's internal bus, a network interface card enables the network to operate at higher speeds than it would if delayed by the serial port.

Networks using interface cards (such as EtherNet and ARCnet) can transmit information much faster than networks using serial ports (such as AppleTalk).

network operating system (NOS)   The system software of a local area network that integrates the network's hardware components. Network operating systems for personal computers typically provide facilities adequate for connecting up to approximately 50 workstations. Included, typically, are such features as a menu-driven administration interface, tape backup of file server software, security restrictions, facilities for sharing printers, central storage of network-capable applications and databases, remote log-in via modem, and support for diskless workstations.

Crucial to the network's operation, a network operating system establishes and maintains the connection between the workstations and the file server; the physical connections alone are not sufficient to support networking. A network operating system consists of two parts: the file server software and workstation software. See *file server, local area network (LAN), Microsoft LAN Manager, Novell NetWare,* and *workstation.*

▲ **Caution:** The workstation software can consume enough base memory to prevent you from running DOS applications. Microsoft's LAN Manager, for example, consumes 158K of RAM, as against 56K for Novell's popular NetWare 386. When considering a network, find out how much workstation memory is required, and whether it's possible to store some or all of it in extended or expanded memory.

network printer   In a local area network, a printer made available to you through the network, as distinguished from a local printer (a printer connected directly to the workstation you're using).

network protocol   The method by which a workstation's access to a computer network is governed to prevent data collisions. Examples include Carrier Sense Multiple Access with Collision Detect (CSMA/CD) and token passing. See *carrier sense multiple access with collision detect (CSMA/CD)* and *token passing*.

network server   See *file server*.

network topology   The geometric arrangement of nodes and cable links in a local area network.

Network topologies fall into two categories: centralized and decentralized. In a centralized topology such as a star network, a central computer controls access to the network. This design ensures data security and central management control over the network's contents and activities.

In a decentralized topology such as a bus network or ring network, no central computer controls the network's activities. Rather, each workstation can access the network independently and establish its own connections with other workstations. See *bus network, ring network,* and *star network*.

newspaper columns   A page format in which two or more columns of text are printed vertically on the page so that the text flows down one column and continues at the top of the next.

Sometimes called snaking columns to suggest the flow of text, newspaper columns differ from side-by-side columns in which paragraphs are printed in linked pairs—one to the left and one to the right.

Many word processing programs and all page-layout programs can print multiple-column text, but only the best programs can display multiple columns on-screen while you edit the text. High-end word processing programs such as Microsoft Word and WordPerfect do a good job of producing newspaper columns, but you need a page-layout program such as Ventura Publisher to justify the columns vertically so that all columns align precisely with the bottom margin.

Vertical justification is by no means necessary, but newspapers and magazines often use vertical justification to create a professional-looking effect. You can accomplish vertical justification manually with a word processing program, but the operation is tedious, and the columns may fall out of alignment if you add or delete text.

NLQ   See *near-letter quality (NLQ)*.

no parity   In asynchronous communications, a communications protocol that disables parity checking and leaves no space for the parity bit. See *asynchronous communication, communications protocol, parity bit,* and *parity checking*.

node   A connection point in a local area network that can create, receive, or repeat a message.

In personal computer networks, nodes include repeaters, file servers, and shared peripherals. In common usage, however, the term node is synonymous with *workstation*. See *network topology* and *workstation*.

noise   The extraneous or random electrical content of a communications channel, unlike the signal, which carries information. All communications channels have noise, and if the noise is excessive, data loss can occur.

Telephone lines are particularly noisy. The error-free transmission of data via telecommunications, therefore, requires communications programs that can perform error-checking operations to make sure that the data being received is not corrupted.

nonimpact printer   A printer that forms a text or graphics image by spraying or fusing ink to the page.

Nonimpact printers include inkjet printers, laser printers, and thermal printers. All nonimpact printers are considerably quieter than impact printers, but nonimpact printers cannot print multiple copies using carbon paper. See *impact printer, inkjet printer, laser printer,* and *thermal printer.*

nontransactional application   In a local area network, an application program that produces data that you do not need to record and keep in one commonly shared database so that all network participants can have access. (For example, most of the work done with word processing programs is nontransactional).

non-Windows application   A DOS application program that wasn't designed to take full advantage of Microsoft Window's application program interface, including on-screen display of fonts and the Windows user interface conventions. Microsoft Windows can run non-Windows applications just as they would run under DOS. In Windows' standard or 386 enhanced modes, you can switch from one non-Windows application to another without quitting a program. In 386 Enhanced mode, you can multitask two or more DOS applications, each in its own window. Industry experts believe that many copies of Microsoft Windows have been purchased to run DOS applications in this way. See *386 enhanced mode, application program interface (API), Microsoft Windows,* and *standard mode.*

NOS   See *network operating system (NOS).*

Novell NetWare   A network operating system for 286- and 386-based DOS computers.

With an excellent reputation for reliability, software compatibility, and system features, Novell's NetWare 286 and NetWare 386 have established a commanding lead in the local area network market for IBM PCs and PC compatibles: an estimated 70 percent of PC-based LANS use NetWare. See *local area network (LAN)* and *network operating system (NOS).*

NuBus   The high-speed expansion bus of Macintosh II computers. NuBus requires adapters specifically designed for its 96-pin receptacles.

null modem cable   A specially configured serial cable that enables you to connect two computers directly, without the mediation of a modem.

null value   In an accounting or database management program, a blank field in which the user has never typed a value, as distinguished from a value of zero that the user has deliberately entered.

Num Lock key   A toggle key that locks the numeric keypad into a mode in which you can enter numbers. When the Num Lock key is on, the cursor-movement keys are disabled.

On IBM PC-compatible keyboards, the keys on the numeric keypad are labeled with arrows and numbers. You can use these keys to move the cursor and to enter numbers. The gray Num Lock key toggles the keypad back and forth between these two modes.

number crunching   Calculation, especially of large amounts of data. (Slang term.)

numeric coprocessor   A microprocessor support chip that performs mathematical computations—specifically those using binary-coded decimal (BCD) and floating-point calculations—at speeds of up to 100 times faster than a microprocessor alone.

The Intel numeric coprocessors (8087, 80287, and 80387) are designed to work with their microprocessor counterparts (the 8087 is designed to work the 8088 and 8086, and the 80287 and 80387 are designed to work with the 80286 and 80386, respectively).

Otherwise, all three Intel numeric coprocessors are similar; they are designed to work with 80 bits at a time so that a programmer can express a number of sufficient length to ensure accurate calculations. An innovative feature of the Intel 80486 chip is the numeric coprocessor circuitry on the microprocessor chip.

numeric coprocessor socket   A push-down socket on the motherboard of many personal computers into which you or a dealer can mount a numeric coprocessor, such as the Intel 80287. The coprocessor improves the performance of the computer system when running calculation-intensive applications such as a spreadsheet.

numeric format   In a spreadsheet program, the way in which the program displays numbers in a cell.

With Lotus 1-2-3, for example, you may choose among the following numeric formatting options:

- Fixed. You specify the number of decimal places to display, ranging from 0 to 15. Lotus 1-2-3 rounds numbers that have more decimal places than you chose. If the number of digits exceeds the column width, you see a row of asterisks across the cell.

- Scientific. Displays very large or small numbers using scientific notation (12,460,000,000 appears as 1.25E+11).

- Currency. Displays values with commas and dollar signs. You choose the number of decimal places (0 to 15). If the number of digits exceeds the column width, you see a row of asterisks across the cell.

- Comma. Displays numbers larger than 999 with commas separating thousands; 1-2-3 inserts the commas automatically.

- General. Displays numbers without commas. Does not display trailing zeroes to the right of the decimal point. If the number of digits to the left of the decimal point exceeds the column width, 1-2-3 uses scientific notation. If the number of digits to the right of the decimal point exceeds the column width, 1-2-3 rounds the number.

- +/−. Converts the number to a simple bar graph appearing in the cell, with the number of plus or minus signs equaling the whole-value number of the entry (5 appears as +++++). Plus signs indicate a positive value; negative signs indicate a negative value.

- Percent. Multiplies the value by 100 and adds a percent

sign. You choose the number of decimal places (0 to 15). For example, 0.485 appears as 48.5%. If the number of digits exceeds the column width, you see a row of asterisks across the cell.

- Date. Converts a number to a date. The number 32734 is August 14, 1989.
- Text. Displays the formula instead of the value computed by the formula.
- Hidden. Makes the cell entry invisible on-screen. You can see the entry by placing the pointer in the cell and looking at the cell contents indicator. See *cell*.

numeric keypad   A group of keys, usually to the right of the typing area on a keyboard. The keypad is designed for the rapid, touch-typing entry of numerical data.

O

object code   In computer programming, the machine-readable instructions created by a compiler or interpreter from source code.

object-oriented graphic   A graphic image composed of discrete objects such as lines, circles, ellipses, and boxes, that you can move independently.

Object-oriented graphics often are called vector graphics because the program stores them as mathematical formulas for the vectors, or directional lines, that compose the image. Unlike bit-mapped graphics, you can resize object-oriented graphics without introducing distortions.

Increasing the size of a bit-mapped rectangle introduces distortions because you thicken the lines as you increase the overall size.

Moreover, the image prints using the printer's highest resolution (up to 300 dpi with laser printers). See *bit-mapped graphic*.

odd parity   In asynchronous communications, an error-checking protocol in which the parity bit is set to 1 if the number of 1 bits in a one-byte data item adds up to an odd number. The parity bit is set to 0 if the number of 1 bits adds up to an even number. See *asynchronous communication, communications parameter, communications protocol, even parity* and *parity checking*.

OEM   See *original equipment manufacturer (OEM)*.

off-line   1. Not directly connected with a computer. A device that is not hooked up to your PC is off-line. 2. In data communications, not connected with another, distant computer. Off-line refers to a workstation that you have temporarily or permanently disconnected from a local area network. 3. A printer that is not turned on or not selected and cannot receive output from the computer is off-line.

off-screen formatting   In a word processing program, a formatting technique in which formatting commands are embedded in the text so that they affect printing, but the formatting is not visible on-screen. See *embedded formatting command, on-screen formatting,* and *what-you-see-is-what-you-get (WYSIWYG)*.

office automation   The use of computers and local area networks to integrate traditional office activities such as conferencing, writing, filing, and sending and receiving messages.

Because many tasks such as filing or word processing can be performed much faster on a computer, many firms hoped to reap huge productivity gains from office automation systems. With some exceptions, these gains have not materialized.

Training employees to use the systems often is expensive and time-consuming, and after the systems are installed, perfectionists may use the technology to do a better job (rather than to do more work). In the days of typewriters, a letter may have been sent out with some imperfections, such as a minor misspelling, because too much work was required to retype the letter, but with today's technology, a secretary may spend more time correcting mistakes until the letter is perfect.

Businesses that have met with success in office automation begin by identifying a specific activity that can be done more cheaply or more rapidly on the computer, and then they develop a system—hardware and software included—for that specific application. For example, an insurance company has realized a major productivity gain by having agents fill out application data directly on portable computers. The software then uploads the applications to the company's main offices via telecommunications.

OK button In the industry standard and graphical user interfaces, a push button in a dialog box that the user can activate to confirm the current dialog box settings and execute the command.

one hundred percent (100%) column graph A column graph that resembles a pie graph in that each column displays the relative percentage of the data item compared to the total. See *stacked column graph*.

on-line 1. Directly connected with a computer. A device that you have successfully hooked up to your PC is on-line. 2. In data communications, connected with another, distant computer. On-line refers to the successful connection with a host computer in a server-client network. 3. A printer turned on, directly connected to the computer, and selected so that it is ready to accept the computer's output is on-line.

on-line help A help utility available on-screen while using a network or an application program.

on-line information service A for-profit firm that makes current news, stock quotes, and other information available to its subscribers via telecommunications linkages. See *bibliographic retrieval service, CompuServe, Dow Jones News/Retrieval Service, GEnie*, and *Prodigy*.

on-screen formatting   In a word processing program, a formatting technique in which formatting commands directly affect the text visible on-screen. See *embedded formatting command, off-screen formatting,* and *what-you-see-is-what-you-get (WYSIWYG)*.

open architecture   A computer system in which all the system specifications are made public so that other companies will develop add-on products such as adapters for the system.

open bus system   A computer design in which the computer's expansion bus contains receptacles that readily accept adapters.

An open-architecture system generally has an open bus, but not all systems with open buses have open architectures; the Macintosh is an example of the latter. See *expansion bus*.

Open System Interconnection (OSI) reference model   An international standard for the organization of local area networks (LANs) established by the International Standards Organization (ISO) and the Institute of Electrical and Electronic Engineers (IEEE).

The OSI reference model is an important contribution to the conceptual design of local area networks because this model establishes hardware independence. The model separates the communication process into distinct layers: the physical hardware (such as the cabling), the transport layer (the method by which data is communicated via the physical hardware), the presentation layer (the method by which the transmitted data interacts with application programs in each computer), and the application layer (the programs available to all users of the network).

Because each layer is at least to some extent independent of the others, you can, in theory, change the cabling (from twisted-pair cable to coaxial cable, for example) without making changes at the other layers. Of course, not all local area networks live up to this level of independence.

From the user's perspective, however, the most important point about the OSI reference model is that you can distinguish between the network hardware and the network software. For example,

TOPS, a local area network system, runs on systems physically wired with AppleTalk hardware and twisted-pair cables as well as EtherNet hardware and coaxial cables. See *local area network (LAN)*.

operating system A master control program for a computer that manages the computer's internal functions and provides you with a means to control the computer's operations.

The most popular operating systems for personal computers include DOS, OS/2, and the Macintosh System.

Operating System/2 (OS/2) A multitasking operating system for IBM PC-compatible computers that breaks the 640K RAM barrier, provides protection for programs running simultaneously, and enables the dynamic exchange of data between applications.

IBM and Microsoft Corporation jointly developed and introduced OS/2 in 1987; they designed OS/2 as a replacement for MS-DOS.

OS/2 has significant advantages over DOS. Unlike DOS, which uses a maximum of 640K of RAM, OS/2 can use up to 16M of RAM, and by using a technique known as virtual memory, which stores little-used sections of program code on disk, the memory space apparent to programs is expandable to a full 48M.

OS/2 is ideally suited to multitasking (running two or more programs simultaneously). Unlike DOS, which enables programs to invade each other's memory space (a common cause of system crashes), OS/2 takes full advantage of the protected mode of Intel 80286, 80386, and 80486 microprocessors. While running two or more programs simultaneously, moreover, the OS/2 user can move data from one program to another using a temporary parking space called a clipboard.

OS/2's command-line interface closely resembles DOS, and most DOS users do not need much retraining to work with OS/2. Beginning with Version 1.1, OS/2 shipped with Presentation Manager—a shell that resembles Microsoft Windows.

Despite OS/2's many advantages, the system has gained acceptance slowly. Few applications are available in OS/2 versions because software publishers do not want to shut themselves out of the lucrative market for applications that run on the many millions of 8088- and 8086-based personal computers, which cannot run OS/2. The applications available for OS/2, such as Lotus 1-2-3 Release 3, resemble the DOS versions, and many users have no reason to upgrade. If advanced programs that require OS/2 appear, however, this situation may change.

You can run DOS applications in a special DOS-emulation mode, but this mode has few advantages over running DOS programs under MS-DOS. In addition, OS/2 is expensive to run; the system requires approximately 2M of RAM, up to 8M of disk space, and a 80286 or later microprocessor. Few users, therefore, see a clear rationale to upgrade. Multitasking and protected-mode processing are now available for DOS applications with Microsoft Windows 3. The phenomenal success of Windows 3 has cast grave doubts on OS/2's future. See *Microsoft Windows, MS-DOS, multitasking, Presentation Manager,* and *protected mode.*

optical character recognition (OCR)   The machine recognition of printed or typed text.

optical disk   A secondary storage medium for computers in which you store information of extremely high density on a disk in the form of tiny pits, the presence or absence of which corresponds to a bit of information read by a tightly focused laser beam.

Optical storage technologies are expected to play a significant role in the secondary storage systems of the 1990s. CD-ROM disks and CD-ROM disk drives offer an increasingly economical distribution medium for read-only data and programs. Write-once read-many (WORM) drives enable organizations to create their own huge, in-house databases.

Erasable optical disk drives, such as the 256M drive included with the NeXT computer, offer more secondary storage than hard disks, and the CDs are removable.

Optical storage disk drives, however, are more expensive and much slower than hard disks. See *CD-ROM, interactive videodisc;* and *write-once, read many (WORM)*.

optimal recalculation   In Lotus 1-2-3 and other advanced spreadsheet programs, a method that speeds automatic recalculation by recalculating only those cells that changed since the last recalculation. See *automatic recalculation*.

option button   See *radio button*.

organization chart   In presentation graphics, a text chart that you use to diagram the reporting structure of a multilevel organization, such as a corporation or a club.

orientation   See *landscape orientation* and *portrait orientation*.

original equipment manufacturer (OEM)   The company that actually manufactures a given piece of hardware, unlike the value-added reseller (VAR)—the company that modifies, configures, repackages, and sells the hardware.

     For example, only a few companies such as Canon, Toshiba, and Ricoh make the print engines used in laser printers. These engines are configured and sold by VARs.

orphan   A formatting flaw in which the first line of a paragraph appears alone at the bottom of a page.

     Most word processing and page-layout programs suppress widows and orphans; the better programs enable you to switch widow/orphan control on and off and to choose the number of lines for which the suppression feature is effective. See *widow*.

OS/2   See *Operating System/2*.

outline font   A printer or screen font in which a mathematical formula generates each character, producing a graceful and undistorted outline of the character which the printer then fills in at its maximum resolution.

     Mathematical formulas, rather than bit maps, produce the graceful arcs and lines of outline characters. You can easily change the type size of an outline font. Unlike bit-mapped fonts, you can scale outline fonts up and down without introducing distortions. (You may need to reduce the weight of small font sizes by using a process called hinting, which keeps the fine detail from being lost).

Because mathematical formulas produce the characters, you need only one font in the printer's memory to use any type size from 2 to 127 points. With bit-mapped fonts, you must download a complete set of characters for each font size into the printer's memory, and you cannot use a type size that you have not downloaded.

Outline fonts are available as built-in fonts in many laser printers and as downloadable fonts provided on disk. The leading supplier of outline fonts is Adobe Systems, Inc., which encrypts these fonts (using a proprietary technique) by transforming them into instructions phrased in the Adobe's page description language (PostScript). Adobe's fonts print only on laser or high-resolution printers specifically licensed (at a fee) to contain PostScript decoders. Such fonts are called Type 1 fonts, and PostScript laser printers give these fonts priority in processing operations. See *bit-mapped font*.

outline utility   A mode of some full-featured word processing programs that assists you in planning and organizing a document by equating outline headings with document headings. The program enables you to view the document as an outline or as ordinary text.

This convenient feature is useful for anyone who writes lengthy, complex documents segmented by internal headings and subheadings (scholarly articles, technical reports, and proposals, for example). When you view the document in Outline mode, the headings and subheadings appear as they would in an outline. The text beneath the headings collapses (disappears) so that only the headings and subheadings are visible.

In Outline mode, however, you can move the headings and subheadings vertically; if you move the heading, all the hidden text positioned beneath it also moves. The Outline mode provides the tools necessary for reorganizing large text in a document with just a few keystrokes. After you switch back to Document mode, the outline format disappears, and the document appears as normal.

output The process of displaying or printing the results of processing operations. See *input*.

overlay See *program overlay*.

overstrike The printing of a character not found in a printer's character set by printing one character, moving the print head back one space, and printing a second character on top of the first.

Overtype mode An editing mode in word processing programs and other software that enables you to enter and edit text; the characters you type erase existing characters, if any.

In WordPerfect, the Overtype mode is called the Typeover mode, which you can toggle on and off by pressing the Ins key. See *Insert mode*.

overwrite To write data on a magnetic disk in the same area where other data is stored (destroying the original data).

p

packaged software Application programs commercially marketed, unlike custom programs privately developed for a specific client. Synonymous with *off-the-shelf software*.

page description language (PDL) A programming language that describes printer output in device-independent commands.

Normally, a program's printer output includes printer control codes that vary from printer to printer. A program that generates output in a PDL can drive any printer containing an interpreter for the PDL; a PDL, therefore, is device-independent. A program that generates output in the PostScript page description language, for example, can drive any printer with a PostScript interpreter—including imagesetters with 1200 dpi or better resolutions.

PDLs are technically superior to ordinary printing techniques for another reason: the burden of processing the output is transferred from the computer to the printer. To print a circle using ordinary printing techniques, the computer must transform the screen image into a bit map and send the bit map to the computer.

A circle in a PDL, however, is represented mathematically, and the printer is responsible for constructing the actual image. This technique has a drawback: to interpret the PDL output, the printer must have its own central processing unit (CPU) and random-access memory (RAM), which makes PostScript printers expensive. See *PostScript*.

page layout program   In desktop publishing, an application program that assembles text and graphics from a variety of files, with which you can determine the precise placement, sizing, scaling, and cropping of material in accordance with the page design represented on-screen.

Page layout programs such as PageMaker and Ventura Publisher display a graphic representation of the page, including nonprinting guides that define areas into which you can insert text and graphics. See *Ventura Publisher*.

page-mode RAM   A random-access memory (RAM) chip that segments stored information into a 2K page of rows and columns, and provides fast access to the row or column. Synonymous with *static random-access memory RAM*.

Page-mode RAM is one of several solutions to the problems posed by fast microprocessors outpacing slower memory chips. If the information needed by the central processing unit (CPU) is within the page, even the fastest microcomputers can access the information without wait states. See *cache memory, static random-access memory,* and *wait state*.

page orientation See *landscape orientation* and *portrait orientation*.

paint file format A bit-mapped graphics file format found in programs such as MacPaint and PC Paintbrush.

The standard paint file format in the Macintosh environment is the 72 dots-per-inch format originally used by MacPaint, which is linked to the Mac's bit-mapped screen display. In the IBM PC-compatible environment, no single standard paint format exists. Programs such as Windows Paint and PC Paintbrush create their own proprietary file formats that other programs may not be able to read.

paint program A program that enables users to paint the screen by switching on or off the individual dots or pixels that make up a bit-mapped screen display.

The first paint program (and the first program for the Macintosh) was MacPaint, the creation of Bill Atkinson at Apple Computer. MacPaint is designed to work with the Mac's bit-mapped display that has a resolution of 72 dots per inch. Graphics created with MacPaint have the same resolution when printed and look rather crude, but you can create some striking effects by varying the patterns of on-and-off pixels.

MacPaint has many imitators in the Macintosh world, such as SuperPaint (Silicon Beach Software). MacPaint-like applications also exist for IBM PC-compatible computers; a leading program in this category is PC Paintbrush. See *MacPaint*.

pair kerning See *kerning*.

paired bar graph A bar graph with two different y-axes (values axes).

A paired bar graph is an excellent way to demonstrate the relationship between two data series that share the same x-axis categories but require two different y-axis measurements. As the bars mirror each other, variations become obvious. See *dual y-axis graph*.

palette   In computer graphics, an on-screen display containing the set of colors or patterns that can be used.

parallel columns   See *side-by-side columns*.

parallel interface   See *parallel port*.

parallel port   A port that supports the synchronous, high-speed flow of data along parallel lines to peripheral devices, especially parallel printers.

Essentially an extension of the internal data bus of the computer, the parallel port provides a high-speed connection to printing devices. A parallel port also negotiates with peripheral devices to determine whether they are ready to receive data and reports error messages if a device is not ready. Unlike the serial port, the parallel port provides a trouble-free way to connect a printer to your computer; you usually can install parallel printers easily. As the length of the cable increases, however, so does the risk of crosstalk (interference between the parallel wires). Parallel printer cables, therefore, usually are no longer than 10 to 15 feet.

You can configure the systems of IBM PC-compatible computers with three parallel ports. The device names of the ports are LPT1, LPT2, and LPT3 (the LPT abbreviation stands for line printer). The device named PRN is the same as LPT1.

parallel printer   A printer designed to be connected to the computer's parallel port.

→ **Tip:** If a printer is available in serial and parallel versions, the parallel version is the better choice unless you must position the printer more than 10 feet away from the computer. Parallel printers are usually easier to install and use than their serial counterparts.

parallel processing   See *multitasking*.

parameter   A value or option that you add or alter when you give a command so that the command accomplishes its task in the way you want. If you do not state a parameter, the program uses a default value or option.

For example, most programs enable you to type the name of the file you want to work with when you start the program. If you type **WORD report1.doc,** for example, Microsoft Word and the document file called REPORT1.DOC load up at the same time. In this case, the file name is the parameter. If you do not type the file name, Word starts and opens a new, blank document file. See *argument*.

parameter RAM In the Macintosh environment, a small bank of battery-powered memory that stores user configuration choices after you switch the power off.

parent directory In DOS directories, the directory above the current subdirectory in the tree structure.

→ **Tip:** You can move quickly to the parent directory by typing **CD..** (two periods) and pressing Enter.

parity bit In asynchronous communications and primary storage, an extra bit added to a data word for parity checking.

This term becomes relevant to users attempting to use a communications program to contact another computer. For such contact to succeed, the two computers must use the same communications protocol—one of the parameters of this protocol is the parity bit setting.

→ **Tip:** If you are using a communications program, try setting the parity bit option to no parity and the data bits option to 8 bits. If these settings do not work, try even parity with 7 data bits. See *asynchronous communication* and *parity checking*.

parity checking A technique used to detect memory or data communication errors. The computer adds up the number of bits in a one-byte data item, and if the parity bit disagrees with the sum of the other bits, the computer reports an error.

When errors occur in a computer's memory or in data communications, a 50 percent chance exists that the sum of the bits in a one-byte data item will change from an odd to an even number, or vice versa.

Parity-checking schemes work by storing a one-bit digit (0 or 1) that indicates whether the sum of the 1 bits in a data item is odd or even. When the data item is read from memory or received by another computer, a parity check occurs. If the parity check reveals that the parity bit is incorrect, the computer displays an error message. See *even parity* and *odd parity.*

parity error   An error that a computer reports when parity checking reveals that one or more parity bits is incorrect, which indicates a probable error in data processing or data transmission.

park   To position a hard drive's read/write head so that the drive is not damaged by jostling during transport.

parse   To separate imported data into separate columns so that it appears correctly in a spreadsheet.

When you import data using 1-2-3's /File Import Text command, for example, the program enters each line of the data as a long label—in other words, each line of data appears in just one cell. Because Lotus 1-2-3 uses soft-cell boundaries, you can see the entire line on-screen, but you cannot use this data for calculations. To render this data usable, you must use the /Data Parse command that separates the data into distinct columns.

partition   A section of the storage area of a hard disk. A partition is set aside during initial preparation of the hard disk, before the disk is formatted.

In DOS, every hard disk has at least one DOS partition. Versions of DOS prior to 4.0 require you to set up more than one partition on a single hard disk to use a disk larger than 32M. A DOS user also can create a second partition to run another operating system (such as UNIX).

Macintosh users may partition their drives to separate the Macintosh System and the A/UX version of UNIX, but utility programs are available (such as MultiDisk) that enable the user to create several system partitions. These partitions are treated by the operating system as if they are different disks. These utilities are useful for organizing large hard disks. See *directory* and *subdirectory*.

password   A security tool used to identify authorized users of a computer program or computer network and to define their privileges, such as read-only, reading and writing, or file copying.

password protection   A method of limiting access to a program or a network by requiring the user to enter a password.

▲ **Caution:** Some programs enable you to password-protect your files, but be sure to keep a record of the password. Many users have lost work permanently because they forgot the password, and they cannot find out what the password is. (If a method for retrieving a password was included in software programs, a clever hacker would quickly discover it, and your data would not be secure.)

paste   To insert text or graphics at the cursor's location.

patch   A quick fix, in the form of one or more program statements, added to a program to correct bugs or to enhance the program's capabilities.

path   The route a program must follow to access data physically on a secondary storage device.

path name   In DOS and OS/2, the name of a DOS subdirectory expressed in a way that describes the path DOS can take through the tree structure to reach it.

PC   See *personal computer*.

PC DOS   See *MS-DOS*.

PC Local Area Network (PC LAN) Program   An IBM network operating system designed for use on IBM's Token-Ring Network. Introduced in 1986, this IBM program provides electronic mail, shared access to printers, and shared access to data and program files.

PDL See *page description language (PDL)*.

peer-to-peer file transfer A file-sharing technique for local area networks in which each user has access to the public files of all other users in the network located on their respective workstations. (Each user determines which files, if any, he or she wants to make public for network access.) See *TOPS*.

peer-to-peer network A local area network without a central file server and in which all computers in the network have access to the public files of all other workstations. See *client-server network* and *peer-to-peer file transfer*.

peripheral A device, such as a printer or disk drive, connected to and controlled by a computer but external to the computer's central processing unit (CPU).

permanent swap file In Microsoft Windows, a disk file composed of contiguous disk sectors that is set aside for the rapid storage and retrieval of program instructions or data in the program's 386 enhanced mode. This storage space is used in virtual memory operations, which use disk space as a seamless extension of random-access memory (RAM). Because the storage areas used in a permanent swap file are contiguous, storage and retrieval operations exceed the normal speed of hard disk operations, which usually distribute data here and there on the disk. The permanent swap file, however, consumes a large amount of space on the disk. See *Microsoft Windows*, *random-access memory (RAM)*, *swap file*, *temporary swap file*, and *virtual memory*.

personal computer A stand-alone computer equipped with all the system, utility, and application software, and the input/output devices and other peripherals that an individual needs to perform one or more tasks.

The idea of personal computing, at least initially, was to free individuals from dependence on tightly controlled mainframe and minicomputer resources. In a corporate setting, for example, data processing managers once had the sole authority to choose the programs and data formats people used. Even if this choice was made responsibly, it would suit some employees more than others. With the rise of personal computing, people have gained substantially more freedom to choose the applications tailored to their needs.

In recent years, ample reason has been found to reintegrate personal computers (PCs) into the data communications networks of organizations, and this goal can be achieved without forcing people to give up the autonomy that personal computing implies.

PCs can serve, for example, as ideal platforms for the use of common organizational databases, enabling users to access a huge, central-information storehouse. Smaller networks can facilitate productivity and work efficiency among members of a workgroup. By means of electronic mail, the network can serve as a new way of improving communication and exchanging information.

Because PCs increasingly are equipped with the networking and communications hardware they need to participate in such networks, the boundary between PCs and professional workstations has blurred considerably. Professional workstations are powerful, high-performance computers designed to provide professionals such as graphics designers, engineers, and architects with the computing power they need for calculation-intensive applications, such as computer-assisted design (CAD). Generally equipped with communications hardware, workstations clearly provide the model toward which high-end PCs, such as those based on the Intel 80386 and 80486 microprocessors, are evolving.

Similarly blurred is the distinction between PCs and minicomputers. At one time, PCs were synonymous with microcomputers (computers that have a microprocessor as their CPU). Many minicomputers, however, now use microprocessors. Further blurring the issue is the fact that today's high-end PCs can handle a few remote terminals if the PCs have UNIX or some other multiuser operating system. See *professional workstation*.

personal information manager (PIM)   A database-management program such as Lotus Agenda that stores and retrieves a wide variety of personal information, including notes, memos, names and addresses, and appointments.

   Unlike a database management program, a PIM is optimized for the storage and retrieval of a variety of personal information. You can switch among a variety of views of your notes, such as people, to-do items, and expenses. PIMs have been slow to gain acceptance, though, because they are hard to learn and people are often away from the computer when they need the information.

PgUp/PgDn keys   On IBM PC-compatible computer keyboards, keys that you press to move the cursor to the preceding screen or the next screen.

   Because the precise implementation of these keys is up to the programmer, their functions vary from program to program. Some word processing programs, for example, use PgUp and PgDn keys for moving to the top of the preceding of text as the page will appear when printed, rather than to the preceding screen of text.

phosphor   An electrofluorescent material used to coat the inside face of a cathode ray tube (CRT). After being energized by the electron beam being directed to the inside face of the tube, the phosphors glow for a fraction of a second. The beam must refresh the phosphor many times per second so that a consistent illumination is produced. See *cathode ray tube (CRT)* and *raster display*.

phototypesetter   See *imagesetter*.

physical drive   The disk drive actually performing the read/write operations in a secondary storage system.

   A disk drive, such as a floppy disk or a hard disk, may have unique electronic and electromechanical characteristics when compared to the other drives in the system, but these unique characteristics of the physical drive are invisible to the user. In an IBM PC-compatible computer equipped with a floppy drive and a hard disk, for example, you follow exactly the same procedure to save a file to drive A and to drive C—in spite of the fact that the two drives are different items of hardware.

From the user's perspective, you can think of all the drives as logical drives—the drives that appear to have exactly the same characteristics, even though they are physically, electronically, and electromechanically different. See *floppy disk, hard disk, logical drives,* and *secondary storage*.

physical format   See *low-level format*.

pica   In typography, a unit of measure equal to approximately ⅙ inch, or 12 points. In typewriting and letter-quality printing, a 12-point monospace font that prints at a pitch of 10 characters per inch (cpi).

Picas usually describe horizontal and vertical measurements on the page, with the exception of type sizes, which are expressed in points.

Although thinking that 6 picas equal one inch is convenient, this comparison is not accurate. In formal typography, a pica is 0.166 of an inch, and ⅙ inch is approximately .1667. Thirty picas, therefore, equal 4.98 inches—a bit less than five inches. Many word processing and page layout programs, however, break with this tradition and define one pica as exactly ⅙ inch.

PICT file format   An object-oriented graphic file format that draws on information available in the Macintosh computer's QuickDraw toolbox, which is part of the Mac's read-only memory (ROM). See *paint file format*.

pie graph   In presentation graphics, a graph that displays a data series as a circle to emphasize the relative contribution of each data item to the whole.

Each slice of the pie appears in a distinctive pattern which can produce Moiré distortions if you juxtapose too many patterns. Some programs can produce paired pie graphs that display two data series. For presentations, exploding a slice from the whole is a useful technique to add emphasis. See *linked pie/column graph* and *proportional pie graph*.

PIF   See *program information file (PIF)*.

PILOT   An authoring language for computer-assisted instruction (CAI).

John Starkweather developed PILOT (short for Programmed Inquiry Learning Or Teaching) at the University of California (San Francisco, 1968).

PILOT is exceptionally easy to learn because it has very few commands. Used primarily to develop on-screen instructional materials, PILOT is being displaced by new authoring languages that use graphical user interfaces such as HyperTalk. See *computer-assisted instruction (CAI)*.

PIM   See *personal information manager (PIM)*.

pin feed   See *tractor feed*.

pitch   A horizontal measurement of the number of characters per linear inch in a monospace font, such as those used with typewriters, dot-matrix printers, and daisywheel printers.

By convention, pica pitch (not to be confused with the printer's measurement of approximately 1/6 inch) equals 10 characters per inch, and elite pitch equals 12 characters per inch. See *monospace, pica,* and *point*.

pixel   The smallest element (a picture element) that a device can display on-screen and out of which the displayed image is constructed. See *bit-mapped graphic*.

plain text document   A document that contains nothing but the standard ASCII text and number characters. See *American Standard Code for Information Interchange (ASCII)*.

→ **Tip:** In many applications, you have the option to save a plain text document in two ways: with or without Enter keystrokes at the end of each line.

plasma display   A display technology used with high-end laptop computers. The display is produced by energizing an ionized gas held between two transparent panels. Synonymous with *gas plasma display*.

platen   In dot-matrix and letter-quality impact printers, the cylinder that guides paper through the printer and provides a surface for the impression of the image onto the page.

platform   See *hardware platform*.

platform independence   The capability of a local area network to connect computers made by different makers (such as IBM PC compatibles and Macintosh computers).

platter   Synonymous with *disk*.

plot   To construct an image by drawing lines.

plotter   A printer that produces high-quality output by moving ink pens over the surface of the paper. The printer moves the pens under the direction of the computer, so that printing is automatic. Plotters are commonly used for computer-aided design and presentation graphics.

point   1. To move the mouse pointer on the screen without clicking the button. 2. In typography, the fundamental unit of measure. 72 points equal an inch. See *pica* and *pitch*.

pointer   An on-screen symbol, usually an arrow, that shows the current position of the mouse. In database management programs, a record number in an index that stores the actual physical location of the data record. See *cursor*.

pointing device   An input device such as a mouse, trackball, or stylus graphics tablet used to display a pointer on-screen.

point-of-sale software   A program that transforms a personal computer into cash register, invoicing, and inventory-tracking system for retail businesses.

For more than a decade, large businesses have taken full advantage of computerized point-of-sale systems that employ bar-code readers and inventory databases. The advantages of such systems are significant: the person working the checkout stand uses the bar-code reader to read the product code from each item, and the system automatically looks up the item's name and price. Not only does the computer perform this task more quickly and accurately than even the best checker, but it also automatically adjusts the inventory database as each item is sold. The software warns the manager to re-order an item when stocks fall below a predetermined level and enables the manager to analyze sales patterns and trends.

With the arrival of point-of-sale software and bar-code readers for personal computers, even a small retail business can take advantage of this technology. A typical point-of-sale software package such as Retail Store Controller (Microbiz) brings virtually all the functionality of the large business systems to a single-user, PC-based point-of-sale workstation. Included are such features as automatic credit card verification, customer history tracking, bar code label printing, sales tracking by employee, reorder reports, flexible sales analysis and reports, and export links to accounting software. Available accessories include a compatible cash drawer and a receipt printer.

polarity   1. In electronics, polarity refers to the negative or positive property of a charge. 2. In computer graphics, polarity refers to the tonal relationship between foreground and background elements. Positive polarity is the printing of black or dark characters on a light or white background, and negative polarity is the printing of white or light characters on a dark or black background.

polling   In local area networks, a method for controlling channel access in which the central computer continuously asks or polls the workstations to determine whether they have a message to transmit.

With polling channel access, you can determine how often, and for how long, the central computer polls the workstations. Unlike CSMA/CD and token-ring channel-access methods, the network manager can establish a form of electronic inequality among the networked workstations, in which some nodes have more access to the network than others. See *carrier sense multiple access with collision detect (CSMA/CD)* and *token-ring network*.

pop-up menu   A menu that appears on-screen anywhere other than in the standard menu bar location (at the top of the screen). See *pulldown menu*.

port   1. An entry/exit boundary mechanism that governs and synchronizes the flow of data into and out of the central processing unit (CPU) to external devices such as printers and modems. Synonymous with *interface*. 2. Reprogramming an application so that it runs on another type of computer. See *central processing unit (CPU), interface, parallel port,* and *serial port*.

portable   Able to work on a variety of hardware platforms.

UNIX is a portable operating system. Most operating systems are designed around the specific electronic capabilities of a given central processing unit (CPU). UNIX, in contrast, is designed with a predetermined, overall structure. To work on specific systems, instructions are embedded within the program that enable the program to function on a given CPU.

portable computer   A computer designed to be transported easily from one location to another.

The first portable personal computers, such as the Osborne I and Compaq II, are best described as "luggables." These computers weigh in at well over 25 pounds and cannot be carried comfortably for more than a short distance. Today's battery-powered laptop computers are much more portable. A computer weighing over 10 pounds is too heavy to carry around all day.

portrait monitor See *full-page display.*

portrait orientation The default printing orientation for a page of text, with the longest measurement oriented vertically. See *landscape orientation.*

post In database management, to add data to a data record.

postprocessor A program that performs a final, automatic processing operation after the user has finished working with a file.

Postprocessing programs include text formatters that prepare a document for printing, and page description languages that convert an on-screen document into a set of commands the printer's interpreter can recognize and use to print the document.

PostScript A sophisticated page description language for medium- to high-resolution printing devices.

PostScript, developed by Adobe Systems, Inc., is a programming language that describes how to print a page that blends text and graphics. Because PostScript is a genuine programming language, you can learn to write PostScript instructions and embed them in documents to be printed.

For most users, however, PostScript is invisible and automatic. When you use an application program equipped with a PostScript printer driver, the program generates the PostScript code that goes to the printer. At the printer, a PostScript interpreter reads the instructions and follows them to generate an image of the page in precise accordance with these instructions. The whole operation is transparent to you.

A major benefit of PostScript is its device independence; you can print the PostScript code generated by an application on any printer with a PostScript interpreter—this includes expensive typesetting machines, such as those manufactured by Linotronic, Compugraphic, and Varityper, that are capable of resolutions of up to 2,400 dpi.

PostScript printer output always takes full advantage of the printer's maximum resolution. You can take the disk containing a document you have created with an application such as Microsoft Word or WordPerfect to a service bureau, which can print the document at resolutions equal or surpassing those found in professional publications. See *page description language (PDL)* and *PostScript laser printer*.

PostScript laser printer   A laser printer that includes the processing circuitry needed to decode and interpret printing instructions phrased in PostScript—a page description language (PDL) widely used in desktop publishing.

Because PostScript laser printers require their own microprocessor circuitry and at least 1M RAM to image each page, they are more expensive than non-PostScript printers.

PostScript laser printers such as the Apple LaserWriter have several advantages over non-PostScript laser printers such as the Hewlett-Packard LaserJet. PostScript printers can print text or graphics in subtle gradations of gray. They can use encapsulated PostScript (EPS) graphics and outline fonts, both of which you can size and scale without introducing distortions. PostScript printers also can produce special effects, such as rotation and overprinting. See *PostScript*.

power-down   To turn off the computer's power switch.

power line filter   An electrical device that smoothes out the peaks and valleys of the voltage delivered at the wall socket.

Every electrical circuit is subject to voltage fluctuations, and if these fluctuations are extreme, they may cause seemingly random computer errors and failures. Flickering lights are a good sign of uneven voltage. If you are using a computer in a circuit shared by heavy appliances, you may need a power line filter to ensure error-free operation. See *surge protector*.

power supply   The electrical component of a computer system that converts standard AC current to the lower-voltage, DC current used by the computer. The amount of current a power supply can provide is rated in amperes (amps).

   ▲ **Caution:** The power supply of early IBM PC-compatible computers (63.5 watts) often proved inadequate after users added several adapters, a hard disk, and other system upgrades. An overloaded power supply can cause erratic operations, such as read or write errors, parity errors, and unexplained system crashes. For systems with hard disks and several adapters, users should have a power supply of at least 200 watts.

power surge   A brief and often very large increase in line voltage caused by turning off appliances, by lightning strikes, or by the re-establishment of power after a power outage. See *surge*.

power-up   To switch on the computer's power switch.

power user   A computer user who has gone beyond the beginning and intermediate stages of computer use. Such a person uses the advanced features of application programs, such as software command languages and macros, and can learn new application programs quickly.

precedence   The order in which a spreadsheet program performs the operations in a formula. Typically, the program performs exponentiation (such as squaring a number) before multiplication and division; the program then performs addition and subtraction.

precision   The number of digits past the decimal that are used to express a quantity. See *accuracy*.

presentation graphics   Text charts, column graphs, bar graphs, pie graphs, and other charts and graphs, which you enhance so that they are visually appealing and easily understood by your audience. See *analytical graphics*.

presentation graphics program   An application program designed to create and enhance charts and graphs so that they are visually appealing and easily understood by an audience.

A full-featured presentation graphics package such as Harvard Graphics includes facilities for making text charts, bar graphs, column graphs, pie graphs, high/low/close graphs, and organization charts.

The package also provides facilities for adding titles, legends, and explanatory text anywhere in the chart or graph. A presentation graphics program includes a library of clip art so that you can enliven charts and graphs by adding a picture related to the subject matter (for example, an airplane for a chart of earnings in the aerospace industry). You can print output, direct output to a film recorder, or display output on-screen in a computer slide show.

Presentation Manager   A graphical user interface and application programming interface (API) for OS/2, jointly developed by Microsoft Corporation and IBM.

Presentation Manager brings to IBM PC-compatible computers running the OS/2 operating system many of the graphical user interface features associated with the Macintosh—multiple on-screen typefaces, pull-down menus, multiple on-screen windows, and desktop accessories.

Presentation Manager is not a version of Microsoft Windows. Presentation Manager clearly reflects its joint development by Microsoft and IBM. Unlike Windows, Presentation Manager conforms to IBM standards such as SAA (Systems Application Architecture). The application programming-interface standards are set by SAA, not by Windows, and programs developed for Windows do not run on Presentation Manager without very substantial modification.

The lack of an easy upgrade path from Windows applications to Presentation Manager is one of the many factors that has delayed the development of programs for OS/2. See *Microsoft Windows* and *Operating System/2 (OS/2)*.

primary storage The computer's main memory directly accessible to the central processing unit (CPU), unlike secondary storage, such as disk drives.

In personal computers, primary storage consists of the random-access memory (RAM) and the read-only memory (ROM).

print engine Inside a laser printer, the mechanism that uses a laser to create an electrostatic image of a page and fuse that image to a cut sheet of paper.

You can distinguish print engines by their resolution, print quality, longevity, paper-handling features, and speed.

Laser printers generally produce resolutions of 300 dpi, although the trend is toward 400-dpi printers.

High-end laser printers available for professional typesetting purposes are capable of resolutions of up to 600 dpi. (Professional typesetting machines called imagesetters use chemical photo-reproduction techniques to produce resolutions of up to 2,400 dpi.)

Write-white engines expose the portion of the page that does not receive ink (so that toner is attracted to the areas that print black) and generally produce deeper blacks than write-black engines, but this quality varies from engine to engine. Although dozens of retail brands of laser printers are on the market, the print engines are made by just a few Japanese original equipment manufacturers (OEM), such as Canon, Ricoh, Toshiba, and Casio. Canon engines are highly regarded within the desktop publishing industry.

Most print engines have a life of 300,000 copies, but the life span ratings among brands vary from 180,000 to 600,000 copies. Because printer longevity is estimated from heavy use over a short period of time, you should consider a printer's longevity rating only if the printer will be used in heavy-demand network applications.

Early laser printers vexed users with thin paper trays capable of holding only 50 or 60 sheets of paper. For convenient use, you should consider a paper tray capacity of at least 100 sheets; 200 or 250 is better.

Print engines often are rated (optimistically) at speeds of up to 10 pages per minute. Such speeds, however, are attained only under ideal conditions; the same sparse page of text is printed over and over, so that the bit map is kept in memory and is zapped out repeatedly. When printing a real manuscript with different text on each page, the printer must pause to construct the image and output is substantially slower. Also, if the printer encounters a graphic, printing may grind to a halt for as long as a minute.

For real-world applications, what determines a print engine's speed is the processing prowess of the controller's microprocessor. The speed demons of laser printing use third-generation microprocessors (such as the Motorola 68020) running at clock speeds of up to 16.7 MHz.

print queue A list of files that a print spooler prints in the background while the computer performs other tasks in the foreground.

print spooling program A utility program that prints a file while you continue to work with an application.

printer control language The command set used to control a printer of a given brand. Common printer control languages include the Epson command set for dot-matrix printers, the Hewlett-Packard Printer Control Language (HPPCL) for IBM-compatible laser printers, and the Diablo command set for letter-quality printers.

Printer control languages should be distinguished from page description languages such as PostScript, which are true programming languages in their own right. Printer control languages are often little more than proprietary implementations of the higher-order ASCII control codes, which programs send to the printer to toggle features such as boldfaced printing on and off.

printer driver   A file that contains information a program needs to print your work with a given brand and model of printer.

A major difference between the DOS and Macintosh environments is the way printer drivers are handled. In IBM PC-compatible computing, printer drivers are the responsibility of application programs; each program must come equipped with a printer driver for the many dozens of printers available.

These printer drivers work only with the program for which they were written. The WordPerfect printer driver for the HP DeskJet, for example, does not help Microsoft Word print with the DeskJet. If a program does not include a driver for your printer, you may be out of luck. Microsoft Windows, fortunately, cures the printing deficiencies of DOS by providing printer drivers for all Windows applications.

Printer drivers also are part of the operating environment in the Macintosh. Individual programs do not have printer drivers; instead, they are designed to take advantage of printer drivers provided at the operating system level and stored in the system folder.

A significant advantage of this method for handling printer drivers is that all programs can use the printer—not just the programs that have included a printer driver.

printer emulation   The recognition by one printer of another brand of printer's printer control language. Widely emulated are Epson, Hewlett-Packard, and Diablo printers.

printer font   A font available for printing, unlike screen fonts available for displaying text on-screen.

Ideally, screen fonts and printer fonts should be identical—only then can a computer system claim to offer what-you-see-is-what-you-get text processing. Today's systems are often far from the ideal. Character-based programs running under DOS cannot display typefaces on-screen other than those built into the computer's ROM. In WordPerfect, for example, you can choose many different printer fonts in a document, but you cannot see the font changes on-screen. Many users are quite satisfied with this technology and get excellent results. For others, seeing the fonts on-screen is necessary to avoid printing errors.

Under current windowing environments (such as Microsoft Windows, Presentation Manager, and the Macintosh System), you can display screen fonts that are bit-mapped imitations of what you will get on the printer.

The computing world is clearly headed toward the integration of screen fonts and printer fonts, using outline font technology.

Printer fonts are of three types: built-in fonts, cartridge fonts, and downloadable fonts.

printer port   See *parallel port* and *serial port*.

printer server   In a local area network, a PC that has been dedicated to receiving and temporarily storing files to be printed, which it doles out one-by-one to a printer. The printer server runs print spooler software, which establishes a print queue. The print server is accessible to all the workstations in the network. See *local area network (LAN)*, *print queue*, and *printer spooler*.

printer spooler   A utility program that temporarily stores files to be printed in a print queue and doles them out one-by-one to the printer. See *background printing*, *print queue*, *printer server*.

procedural language   A language such as BASIC or Pascal that requires the programmer to specify the procedure the computer has to follow to accomplish the task.

processing   The execution of program instructions by the computer's central processing unit (CPU) so that data is transformed in some way, such as sorting data, selecting some data according to specified criteria, or performing mathematical computations on data.

professional workstation   A high-performance personal computer optimized for professional applications in fields such as digital circuit design, architecture, and technical drawing.

Professional workstations typically offer excellent screen resolution and fast, powerful processing circuits and ample memory. Examples include the workstations made by Sun Microsystems and NeXT, Inc. Professional workstations are more expensive than personal computers, and typically use the UNIX operating system. The boundary between high-end personal computers and professional workstations, however, is eroding as personal computers become more powerful.

program   A list of instructions in a computer-programming language that tell the computer what to do. See *software*.

program generator   A program that enables non-programmers to use simple techniques to describe an application that the program generator then codes.

In database management programs, for example, program generation techniques are used to give the user a way to describe the output format graphically. The program generator then uses the user's input as a set of parameters by which the output program code is constructed.

program information file (PIF)   A file provided with many non-Windows application programs that tells Windows how to run the program. Windows can still run an application even if it lacks a PIF file. See *Microsoft Windows*, and *non-Windows application*.

program item In Microsoft Windows, an icon representing an application.

program overlay A portion of a program kept on disk and called into memory only as required.

programmable Capable of being controlled through instructions that can be varied to suit the user's needs.

programmable read-only memory (PROM) A read-only memory (ROM) chip programmed at the factory for use with a given computer.

The alternative to PROM is a ROM chip in which the information is expressed in the actual design of the circuits internal to the chip. This approach is inflexible because the chip can be modified only with difficulty, and if the programming has a bug, or if the firm decides to add a feature to the computer, redesigning and manufacturing the chip is expensive and time-consuming.

A programmable ROM chip gets around this problem by offering the computer manufacturer a write-once chip—a chip that can be programmed just once, after which the programming becomes permanent. The process of programming the chip is called burning the PROM. If it becomes necessary to change the programming, making the alterations and burning the new PROMS with the modified information is simple. See *erasable programmable read-only memory (EPROM)*.

programmer A person who designs, codes, tests, debugs, and documents a computer program.

Professional programmers often hold B.S. or M.S. degrees in computer science, but a great deal of programming (professional and otherwise) is done by individuals with little or no formal training. More than half the readers of a popular personal computer magazine, for example, stated in a survey that they regularly programmed their personal computers using languages such as BASIC, Pascal, and assembly language.

programmer's switch A plastic accessory included with all Macintosh computers that, when installed on the side of the computer, enables you to perform a hardware reset and access the computer's built-in debugger.

programming The process of providing instructions to the computer that tell the microprocessor what to do.

  Stages in programming include design, or making decisions about what the program should accomplish; coding, or using a programming language to express the program's logic in computer-readable form; testing and debugging, in which the program's flaws are discovered and corrected; and documentation, in which an instructional manual for the program is created.

programming environment A set of tools for program development, debugging, and maintenance that is commonly provided with a computer's operating system. Minimally, the tools include a line editor, a debugger, and assembler to compile assembly language programs. These tools may not be sufficient for professional program development, however, and are often replaced by an application development system. See *application development system*.

project management program Software that tracks individual tasks that make up an entire job.

  Managing a big project, like building a submarine or the World Trade Center in New York, is far from easy. Thousands of little jobs must be coordinated so that they're finished at the same time thousands of other little jobs are finished, because both groups of little jobs are prerequisites for the next phase of the project. To help project managers cope with the problems caused by having so many activities going on at once, project management techniques called CPM (critical path method) and PERT (Program Evaluation and

Review Technique) were created. Both methods try to help managers discern the critical path, that is, the jobs that must be completed on time if the whole project is to be finished on time. When the critical path becomes clear, the manager can allocate the resources necessary to complete these tasks in a timely fashion.

Project management software brings to PCs the analytical tools of CPM and PERT, but whether many personal computer users will benefit from managing projects with these techniques is doubtful. CPM and PERT are cost-effective only for large projects where a manager or team of managers cannot keep track of all the tasks involved without some record-keeping assistance. Few PC users are likely to engage in tasks of that size, and the value of CPM and PERT for smaller projects is not clear, even when a computer takes care of the formerly troublesome calculations involved in these techniques.

PROM See *programmable read-only memory (PROM)*.

PROMPT In DOS and OS/2, an internal command that customizes the system prompt.

→ **Tip:** If you are using a hard disk divided into directories, use the following command to change the system prompt to display the current directory and the current drive:

PROMPT pg

prompt A symbol or phrase that appears on-screen informing you that the computer is ready to accept input.

property In Microsoft Windows and MS-DOS Shell, an item of information associated with a program. Properties include the program's start-up directory, the application shortcut key, and a password. *See application shortcut key, Microsoft Windows,* and *MS-DOS Shell.*

proportional pie graph   In presentation graphics, a paired pie graph in which the size of the two pies is adjusted to reflect the difference in their overall magnitude.

Proportional pie graphs are useful for comparing two pies when one is significantly larger than the other.

proprietary file format   A file format developed by a firm to be used for the storage of data created by its products. A proprietary file format usually is unreadable by other firms' application programs. Microsoft Word, for example, cannot read WordPerfect files.

protected mode   In 80826 and later Intel microprocessors, an operating mode in which programs running simultaneously cannot invade each other's memory space or directly access input/output devices, preventing system failures during multitasking operations.

The default operating mode of Intel microprocessors (8088, 8086, 80286, 80386, and 80486) is called the real mode. In the real mode, a program can interfere with another program's instructions in memory, and such interference can cause the computer to crash. (That's why crashes are so frequent when you're running several terminate-and-stay resident [TSR] programs.) Worse, the programs you're running must compete for the limited, 640K conventional memory space, the maximum allowable under DOS.

With the 80286 and later microprocessors, a second operating mode, the protected mode, became available. In the protected mode, the computer can use memory beyond the 640K conventional memory barrier. The best benefits of protected mode processing, however, only become available with 80386 and higher microprocessors. To run DOS programs in this extended memory, 80386 and higher microprocessors are capable of simulating two or more 640K DOS computers, up to the limits of the available extended memory. These simulated "machines" are called virtual machines. In protected mode, each program is given what amounts to its own, 640K DOS computer in which to run, and each 640K "machine" is protected from interference by the others. Note that this mode is not available unless your system is equipped with memory management software to switch it on and manage the programs.

By far the most popular software for this purpose is Microsoft Windows 3.0, running in the 386 enhanced mode. To run your computer in 386 enhanced mode with Microsoft Windows, your computer must be equipped with a minimum of two megabytes of RAM; in practice, four or more megabytes of RAM are required. See *386 enhanced mode, extended memory, memory-management program, Microsoft Windows, real mode,* and *terminate-and-stay-resident (TSR) program.*

protocol See *communications protocol* and *file transfer protocol.*

PrtSc On IBM PC-compatible keyboards, a key that you can use to print an image of the screen display.

→ **Tip:** If the screen display is currently in a graphics mode, you must run the DOS program GRAPHICS.COM before the screen prints properly.

PS/2 See *IBM Personal System/2.*

pseudocode An algorithm expressed in English to conceptualize the algorithm before coding it in a programming language. See *algorithm.*

public domain software Software not copyrighted that can be freely distributed without obtaining permission from the programmer or paying the programmer a fee. See *freeware* and *shareware.*

pull-down menu A method of providing a command menu that appears on-screen only after you click the menu's name.

To select an option on the menu, press and hold down the mouse button and drag the mouse pointer down the menu until the option you want is highlighted.

pull-out quote   In desktop publishing, a quotation extracted from the copy of a newsletter or magazine article and printed in larger type in the column, often blocked off with ruled lines.

pushbutton   In the industry-standard and graphical user interfaces, a large option button in a dialog box that initiates actions after you choose an option. Most dialog boxes contain an OK pushbutton (which confirms your choices and carries out the command) and a Cancel pushbutton (which cancels your choices and closes the dialog box). The button representing the option you're most likely to choose, called the default button, is highlighted.

→ **Tip:** In many applications, you can press Enter to choose the default button (which is usually called OK). You can press Esc to choose the Cancel button.

q

QBasic   See *MS-DOS QBASIC*.

QEMM 386   A memory-management program (Quarterdeck Office Systems) that moves network drivers, disk cache programs, device drivers, and terminate-and-stay-resident programs to the upper memory area, thus freeing conventional memory for DOS programs. See *conventional memory* and *upper memory area*.

quad density   See *high density*.

query   In database management, a search question that tells the program what kind of data should be retrieved from the database.

The point of an effective database management system is not to display all the information the system contains but to show you only the information you need for a specific purpose.

A query specifies the criteria by which information is extracted from the database. The query guides the computer toward retrieving the required information (and eliminating information not required). See *data independence, query language,* and *Structured Query Language (SQL).*

query by example (QBE) In database management programs, a query technique that prompts you to type the search criteria into a template resembling the data record.

QBE was developed at IBM's Research Laboratory and is used in the QBE program. As a retrieval technique, QBE is emulated by some personal computer database management programs, such as Paradox.

The advantage of query-by-example retrieval is that you need not learn a query language to frame a query. When you initiate the search, the program displays a screen listing all the data fields that appear on every data record; you enter information that restricts the search to just the specified criteria. The fields left blank, however, will match anything.

Suppose that you are searching for the titles of all the Western videotapes in stock rated PG or PG-13. Using QBE techniques, you can type the following query:

CATEGORY	RATING	TITLE
Western	PG or PG-13	

This query says, "Find all records in which the field CATEGORY contains Western and the field RATING contains PG or PG-13."

The output of such a query is a list like the following:

CATEGORY	RATING	TITLE
Western	PG	Showdown
Western	PG	Tumbleweed
Western	PG-13	Not-So-OK Corral

See *database management program*, *data record*, and *query language*.

query language In database management programs, a retrieval and data-editing language that enables you to specify the criteria by which the program retrieves and displays the information stored in a database.

The ideal query language is natural language, or everyday English. Ideally, you could ask the computer, "Using the database called VIDEOS, show me all the records in which the CATEGORY field contains Western and the RATING field contains PG or PG–13."

A good query language enables you to type queries in a format that, although rigid in syntax, approximates English, as follows:

```
SELECT title
FROM videos
WHERE CATEGORY = Western
AND RATING = PG
OR RATING = PG-13
```

The dot-prompt language of dBASE is a full-fledged query language, although it has quirks and odd nomenclature that make it difficult to use. The up-and-coming query language for personal computing is Structured Query Language (SQL), already widely used for minicomputer and mainframe databases. See *database management program*, *query*, *query by example (QBE)*, and *Structured Query Language (SQL)*.

queue See *job queue*.

QuickBASIC A high-performance compiler for programs written in Microsoft BASIC. QuickBASIC recognizes modern control structures and enables programmers to omit line numbers.

QuickBASIC was designed to compile any program written in BASICA or GWBASIC, the versions of BASIC supplied with most

IBM Personal Computers and compatibles. However, the compiler enables you to create structured programs, complete with indentations and a full set of control structures.

QuickBASIC programs execute much faster than their interpreted counterparts, making the compiler suitable for the creation of commercial software. See *BASIC, compiler,* and *control structure.*

Quicken   A checkbook-management program developed by Intuit for IBM PC compatibles and Macintosh computers. Quicken is widely used as a complete system for home and small-business accounting.

Quicken simplifies home and small-business accounting by enabling you to carry out tasks such as check writing, check printing, budgeting, and tax accounting in a familiar way. Quicken screens resemble an actual checkbook register.

Recurring transactions (the payment of the same amounts every month to utilities or creditors) can be automated so that several checks are generated and posted to the register with just one keystroke. The program also can produce a wide variety of reports that enable you to track spending, assess net worth, plan for future cash needs, and list tax-deductible expenditures.

You can accomplish all of these tasks without learning accounting terminology.

QWERTY   Pronounced "kwerty." The standard typewriter keyboard layout also used for computer keyboards.

Alternative keyboard layouts, such as the Dvorak keyboard, speed typing by placing the most commonly used letters on the home row. See *Dvorak keyboard.*

r

r/w See *read/write*.

radio button In a graphical user interface, the round option buttons that appear in dialog boxes. Unlike check boxes, radio buttons are mutually exclusive; you can pick only one of the radio button options. See *graphical user interface (GUI)*.

radio frequency interference (RFI) The radio noise generated by computers and other electronic and electromechanical devices during their operation. Excessive RFI, generated by computers can severely degrade the reception of radio and television signals, while RFI generated by other sources can cover screen flickering and even data loss in poorly-shielded computers. See *FCC certification*.

ragged-left alignment In word processing and desktop publishing, the alignment of each line of text so that the right margin is even, but the left remains ragged. Synonymous with *flush right*.

ragged-right alignment In word processing and desktop publishing, the alignment of each line of text so that the left margin is even, but the right remains ragged. Synonymous with *flush left*.

→ **Tip:** Typographers say that ragged-right alignment is easier to read and more attractive than full justification, in which the left and right margins are aligned. Full justification often is chosen by personal computer users because it produces a more professional appearance, but full-justified documents may be more difficult to read.

RAM See *random-access memory (RAM)*.

RAM cache Pronounced "ram cash." A section of random-access memory (RAM) set aside to serve as a buffer between the central processing unit (CPU) and the disk drives.

Because RAM can deliver data and program instructions to the CPU hundreds of times faster than a disk drive, a computer's performance may improve significantly with a RAM cache. A RAM cache stores data and program instructions that an application is likely to require frequently so that this information can be accessed directly from RAM.

The RAM cache also speeds operations by accepting data to be written to disk as fast as the CPU can send data, rather than forcing the CPU to wait until disk-writing operations are completed at the disk's speed. See *central processing unit (CPU)*, *disk cache*, and *random-access memory (RAM)*.

RAM disk An area of electronic memory configured by a software program to emulate a disk drive. Data stored in a RAM disk can be accessed more quickly than data stored on a disk drive, but this data is erased whenever you turn off or reboot the computer.

RAMDRIVE.SYS In DOS, a configuration file provided with the operating system that sets aside part of your computer's random-access memory (RAM) so that it acts as a disk drive.

▲ **Caution:** Because virtual disk drives operate much faster than real disk drives, placing programs or data in a virtual disk drive can result in major performance improvements. However, the benefits come at a stiff price.

If you are using a 640K DOS system, you must create the virtual disk out of the available random-access memory (RAM), and because you do not have enough memory to begin with, you may not be able to run your application programs. If you have extended memory or expanded memory, however, you can place the virtual disk in the RAM above 640K, but you still are taking a big risk. When you save work to this disk, you are really writing your work to RAM, and everything in RAM is lost when you switch off the computer. Many computer users have lost hours of important work by failing to copy a document from a virtual disk to a real disk at the end of a session. Synonymous with *VDISK.SYS*, the name of the driver in IBM releases of DOS. See *configuration file*, *device driver*, *expanded memory*, *extended memory*, and *random-access memory (RAM)*.

random access   An information storage and retrieval technique in which the information can be accessed directly without having to go through a sequence of locations.

This term doesn't imply that information is stored randomly in the memory. The computer does not have to go through a sequence of items (sequential access) to get to the needed information. A better term is direct access, but "random access" has become enshrined in the acronym commonly used to describe a PC's internal memory, random-access memory (RAM).

To understand the distinction between random and sequential access, compare a cassette tape with a long-playing record. To get to the song you want on a cassette tape, you must fast forward through a sequence of songs until you encounter the one you want. To get to the song you want on a record, however, you can move the arm above the surface of the record and go to the track you want. Precisely the same principle is used in computer disk drives. See *random-access memory (RAM)* and *sequential access*.

random-access memory (RAM)   The computer's primary working memory in which program instructions and data are stored so that they are accessible directly to the central processing unit (CPU).

To perform computations at high speeds, the computer's processing circuitry must be able to obtain information from the memory directly and quickly. Computer memories, therefore, are designed to give the processor random access to the contents.

Think of RAM as a checkerboard, with each square on the board capable of holding a byte of data or program instructions. Because many personal computers can hold half a million bytes of internal memory, the computer needs some way to find a given memory location with precision. Every square on the checkerboard, therefore, has an address, like a post office box.

Because each location has a unique address, the CPU can access each memory location directly by specifying the address and activating the circuit that leads directly to that address.

RAM often is called read/write memory to distinguish it from read-only memory (ROM), the other component of a personal computer's primary storage. In RAM, the CPU can write and read data. Most application programs set aside a portion of RAM as a temporary work space for your data, enabling you to modify (rewrite) as needed until the data is ready for printing or storage on disk.

Almost all computers now use volatile semiconductor memory, which does not retain its contents when the power to the computer is switched off.

▲ **Caution:** Save your work frequently. In the event of a system failure or power interruption, you lose all work in RAM that you have not recorded (saved) on a magnetic medium such as a disk drive. See *primary storage, random access, read-only memory (ROM),* and *secondary storage.*

range   In a spreadsheet program, a cell or a rectangular group of cells.

Spreadsheet programs would be tedious to use if you could not perform operations (such as formatting) on groups of cells. For example, you can format one column of numbers with the currency format, even though the rest of the worksheet uses a general format.

All spreadsheet programs enable you to identify ranges of cells. A range can include one cell or thousands, with one restriction: the range must be rectangular in shape and consist of contiguous cells. Valid ranges include a single cell, part of a column, part of a row, and a block spanning several columns and several rows.

When using a spreadsheet program, you use range expressions

frequently in commands and formulas. A range expression gives you a way to define the boundaries of the rectangular range. See *cell*.

range expression   In a spreadsheet program, an expression that describes a range by defining the upper left cell and the lower right cell.

In Lotus 1-2-3, you write a range expression using the beginning cell..ending cell pattern as in the following example:

A9..B12

The range expression A9..B12 defines a rectangular block that begins with cell A9. Because the ending cell is B12 (one column right and three rows down) the range includes all the following cells:

A9	B9
A10	B10
A11	B11
A12	B12

See *range name*.

range format   In a spreadsheet program, a numeric format or label alignment format that applies to only a range and overrides the global format. See *global format, label alignment, numeric format,* and *range*.

range name   In a spreadsheet program, a range of cells to which you attach a distinctive name.

Remembering a range name is much easier than remembering a range expression. You can name a range of cells and then refer to the range by entering the name. For example, suppose that you create a worksheet in which range E9..E21 contains your company's sales for the first quarter of 1991. After naming the range FQ1991, you use the range name—not the range expression—in formulas. In a formula that totals the column, for example, you type

@SUM(FQ1991)

A second advantage of range naming is that after you have named the range, the name accurately and precisely refers to the entire range. If you type FQ1991, the program unfailingly equates this name with the range E9..E21. If you type this range expression over and over (rather than the range name), however, you may make a typing error, referring once to the range E9..E20 without catching your error. The program cannot detect an error of this sort, and you introduce a significant error into your spreadsheet.

→ **Tip:** To avoid errors in range references, name ranges and use the names in formulas. See *range* and *range expression*.

raster display   The display technology used in television sets and computer monitors. Dozens of times each second, the screen is scanned from top to bottom by a tightly focused electron beam that follows a zig-zag pattern as it moves line-by-line down the screen. See *vector graphics*.

raster font   See *bit-mapped font*.

raster image processor (RIP)   Pronounced "rip." In a laser printer, a device that interprets the instructions of a page description language to compose an image of a page and transfer the image to the photosensitive drum of the print engine, line-by-line.

raw data   Unprocessed or unrefined data that has not been arranged, edited, or represented in a form for easy retrieval and analysis.

RDBMS   See *relational database management system (RDBMS)*.

read   To retrieve data or program instructions from a peripheral such as a disk drive and place the data into the computer's memory.

read-only   In DOS, a file whose read-only file attribute has been set so that the file can be viewed but not deleted or modified.

→ **Tip:** In DOS, when you create a template such as a letterhead or a generic worksheet, use the ATTRIB command to turn the file's read-only attribute on. When you retrieve and modify the file, you cannot overwrite the original file accidentally; DOS requires you to save the file with a new file name. You also cannot erase the file accidentally, unless you shut off the read-only attribute. See *AT-TRIB, file attribute, locked file,* and *read/write.*

read-only attribute   In DOS and OS/2, a file attribute stored with a file's directory entry that indicates whether the file can be modified or deleted.

When the read-only attribute is on, you can display the file but cannot modify or erase it. When the read-only attribute is off, you can modify or delete the file.

The ATTRIB command is used to change a file's read-only attribute. See *file attribute.*

read-only memory (ROM)   Pronounced "rahm." The portion of a computer's primary storage that does not lose its contents when the current is switched off and contains essential system programs, which neither you nor the computer can erase.

Because the computer's random-access memory (RAM) is volatile (loses information when the current is switched off), the computer's internal memory is blank at power-up, and the computer can perform no functions unless given start-up instructions.

These instructions are provided by the ROM, which may contain only simple programs that tell the disk drive where to find and load the computer's operating system. A growing trend, however, is toward including substantial portions of the operating system on ROM chips, instead of providing the bulk of the operating system on disk.

In the Macintosh, for example, much of the Macintosh System is encoded on ROM chips, including the graphics routines (Quick-Draw) that are part of the Mac's application program interface (API). However, upgrading top ROM is more difficult and expensive than supplying new disks. See *application program interface*

(API), erasable programmable read-only memory (EPROM), programmable read-only memory (PROM).

read/write   The capability of an internal memory or secondary storage device to record data (write) and to play back data previously recorded or saved (read).

read/write file   In DOS, a file whose read-only file attribute is set so that the file can be deleted and modified. See *ATTRIB, file attribute, locked file,* and *read-only.*

read/write head   In a hard disk or floppy disk drive, the magnetic recording and playback device that travels back and forth across the surface of the disk, storing and retrieving data.

read/write memory   See *random-access memory (RAM).*

real mode   An operating mode of Intel microprocessors in which a program is given a definite storage location in memory and direct access to peripheral devices.

   Real mode is a straightforward way of allocating memory space in a single-user, stand-alone computer system but causes problems when more than one program is loaded into memory simultaneously; programs can invade each other's memory space or try to access peripheral devices simultaneously. In both situations, a system failure may result.

   Therefore, the Intel 80286, 80386, and 80486 microprocessors offer an additional operating mode, protected mode, that supervises the allocation of memory and governs access to peripheral devices. See *Intel 80286, Intel 80386, Intel 80486, memory-management program,* and *protected mode.*

real time   The immediate processing of input, such as a point-of-sale transaction or a measurement performed by an analog laboratory device.

recalculation method   In a spreadsheet program, the way the program recalculates cell values after you change the contents of a cell. See *automatic recalculation* and *manual recalculation*.

recalculation order   In a spreadsheet program, the mode currently in effect for recalculating the values in the spreadsheet after you type new values, labels, or formulas.

Early spreadsheet programs offered two recalculation modes, column-wise recalculation and row-wise recalculation. In the column-wise mode, the program recalculates all the cells in column A before moving to column B, and so on.

In row-wise recalculation, the program recalculates all the cells in row 1 before moving to the beginning of row 2, and so on. See *column-wise recalculation, natural recalculation, optimal recalculation,* and *row-wise recalculation*.

reboot   See *warm boot*.

record   See *data record*.

record-oriented database management program   A database management program that displays data records as the result of query operations, unlike a table-oriented program in which the result of all data query operations is a table. Purists argue that a true relational database management program always treats data in tabular form, and any program that displays records as the result of queries, such as dBASE, does not deserve to call itself relational even if the program can work with two or more databases at a time.

The rationale for such an attitude is partly academic; the relational model of database management is based on an elegant mathematical foundation so that any departure from its true form (in which data is represented in tables) is an affront to mathematical purity. But the rationale also is practical; a program that retrieves data records as the result of query operations confronts you with much unwanted information, and because most records take up the whole screen, you must page through them.

A table-oriented program, in contrast, succinctly summarizes data in tables displayed on-screen, eliminating all extraneous data not specifically called for in the search query. See *data retrieval, relational database management, Structured Query Language (SQL),* and *table-oriented database management program.*

record pointer   In a database management program, the record pointer is an on-screen status message that states the number of the data record currently displayed on-screen (or in which the cursor is positioned).

recover   To bring the computer system back to a previous, stable operating state or to restore erased or misdirected data. The recovery, which may require user intervention, is needed after a system or user error occurs, such as instructing the system to write data to a drive not containing a disk. See *undelete utility.*

recoverable error   An error that does not cause the program or system to crash or to erase data irretrievably.

redirection operator   In DOS and OS/2, a symbol that routes input or output directions to or from a device other than the console (the keyboard and video display).

You can use the following redirection operators in a DOS or OS/2 command:

>   Output redirection. Redirects the output of a command from the console to a file or device. The following command, for example, redirects the contents of LETTER.DOC to the printer:

>   PRN

>>   Append redirection. Redirects the output of a command from the console to an existing file and adds the output to the existing file's contents. The

following command, for example, redirects the output to DIR.DOC, and appends the information to the end of the file if DIR.DOC exists:

DIR B: > > DIR.DOC

< Input redirection. Changes the input of a command from the console to a file, so that the contents of the file are used instead of data input at the keyboard. The following command, for example, redirects SORT's input from the file TERMS.DOC:

SORT < TERMS.DOC

redlining In word processing, an attribute such as a distinctive color or double underlining that marks the text co-authors have added to a document by a workgroup. The redlined text is highlighted so that other authors or editors know exactly what has been added to or deleted from the document.

reduced instruction set computer (RISC) A central processing unit (CPU) in which the number of instructions the processor can execute is reduced to a minimum to increase processing speed.

Microprocessors, such as the Intel 80386, recognize well over one hundred instructions for performing various computations, but the more instructions a chip can handle, the more slowly it runs for all instructions.

The idea of a RISC architecture is to reduce the instruction set to the bare minimum, emphasizing the instructions that are used most of the time, and optimizing them for the fastest possible execution. The instructions left out of the chip must be carried out by combining the ones left, but because these instructions are needed far less frequently, a RISC processor usually runs 50 to 75 percent faster than its CISC counterpart.

RISC processors also are cheaper to design, debug, and manufacture because they are less complex. See *central processing unit (CPU)* and *complex instruction set computer (CISC)*.

reformat In operating systems, to repeat a formatting operation on a secondary storage disk, such as a floppy disk or hard disk. In word processing or page layout programs, to change the arrangement of text elements on the page.

refresh To repeat the display or storage of data to keep it from fading or becoming lost. The video display and random-access memory (RAM) must be refreshed constantly.

relational database management An approach to database management in which data is stored in two-dimensional data tables. The program can work with two data tables at the same time, relating the information through links established by a common column or field.

The term relational as applied to database management was introduced in 1970 by Edgar Codd to refer to the storage and retrieval of data in the form of tables, in which the table defines the relation between the items listed in rows (data records) and columns (data fields).

Codd founded his database design on an elegant mathematical theory. A true relational database, one designed solely in accordance with this theory, treats all data as tables, and the result of any query is a new table.

Suppose that a video store database lists customer's phone numbers and names in a table as follows:

```
Phone_no      Name
325-4321      Smith, Ted
325-4411      Jones, Jane
```

Another table contains the titles of rented videotapes, the phone number of the person who rented the tape, and the due date:

Title	Phone_no	Due_date
Blues	325-4321	07/16/90
Danger	325-4411	07/19/90

A query may ask, "Show me the name and phone number of customers with tapes due on or before July 19, 1990, and print the film's title." Such a query results in the following table:

Name	Phone_no	Title
Smith, Ted	325-4321	Blues
Jones, Jane	325-4411	Danger

Not all database management programs marketed as relational are true table-oriented programs. Most are record-oriented programs relational only to the extent that they can link data in two databases through a common field. dBASE is such a program; data is stored in records, not tables. However, you can use dBASE as if it were a true relational program.

relational database management system (RDBMS)   A relational database management program, especially one that comes with all the necessary support programs and documentation needed to create, install, and maintain custom database applications.

relational model   See *relational database management*.

relational operator   A symbol used to specify the relation between two numeric values.

In query languages, relational operators frequently are used in specifying search criteria. For example, a video store manager may want to ask the computer, "Show me all the telephone numbers of customers with overdue tapes—due on a date less than or equal to May 7, 1990."

In electronic spreadsheets, relational operators are used to return the number 1 if the expression is true and 0 if the expression is false. In @IF formulas, relational operators can be used to perform tests on data so that different values are displayed depending on the results of the test.

Suppose that you are computing sales bonuses. If a salesperson has sold more than $22,000 worth of merchandise, the normal bonus (5 percent) is increased to 7.5 percent. In the expression @IF(B14>22000, 0.75, 0.5), the program tests cell B14 to see whether the number (total sales) is greater than 22,000. If so, the cell displays 0.75. If not, the cell displays 0.5.

To permit the expression of logical operators in the character-based world of computing, many programs use the following conventions:

=	equal to
<	less than
>	greater than
< =	less than or equal to
= >	greater than or equal to
< >	not equal to

relative addressing See *relative cell reference*.

relative cell reference In a spreadsheet program, a formula's cell reference adjusted when you copy the formula to another cell or a range of cells.

To understand what happens when you copy a relative cell reference, you need to know how a spreadsheet program actually records a cell reference. When you type the formula @SUM(C5..C8) in cell C10, the program does not actually record "add cells C5, C6, C7, and C8" in the file. Instead, the program records a code that means, "add all the values in the next four cells above the current cell."

When you copy this formula to the next four cells to the right (D10..G10), it still reads, "add all the values in the next four cells above the current cell," and sums each column correctly. See *absolute cell reference* and *mixed cell reference*.

release number   The number, usually a decimal number, that identifies an incrementally improved version of a program, rather than a major revision, which is numbered using an integer.

A program labeled Version 5.1, for example, is the second release of Version 5 of the program (the first was Version 5.0). This numbering scheme isn't used by all software publishers, and competitive pressures sometimes encourage publishers to jump to a new version number when the program being released is in fact only an incremental improvement over its predecessor. See *version*.

reliability   The capability of computer hardware or software to perform as the user expects and to do so consistently, without failures or erratic behavior. See *mean time between failures (MTBF)*.

remark   In a batch file, macro, or source code, explanatory text ignored when the computer executes the commands. See *batch file*.

remote control program   A utility program that enables the user to link two personal computers so that one can be used to control the operation of the second.

Why would anyone want to control a distant PC? Users of popular remote control programs such as Carbon Copy Plus are using this software to train remote users, to perform tasks at the office while working at home, to install and demonstrate software on clients' computers, and to provide technical support by logging on to the remote computer and figuring out what went wrong.

remote terminal   See *terminal*.

removable mass storage   A high-capacity secondary storage medium, such as a Bernoulli box or a tape backup system, in which the magnetic disk or tape is encased in a plastic cartridge or cassette and can be removed from the drive for safekeeping.

By this definition, a high-density floppy disk qualifies as a removable mass storage medium, but the term usually is reserved for cartridge-based backup systems with many megabytes of storage capacity. See *Bernoulli box*.

removable storage media   A secondary storage device in which the actual storage medium, such as a magnetic disk, can be removed from the drive for safekeeping.

Floppy disks are removable storage media, but the term is more often applied to tape backup units and Bernoulli boxes that use cartridges which can hold dozens of megabytes of data.

rendering   In computer graphics, the conversion of an outline drawing into a fully formed, solid image.

repagination   In word processing and desktop publishing, a formatting operation in which pages are renumbered to reflect insertions, deletions, block moves, or other changes to the document's text.

Most programs repaginate automatically as the user inserts and edits text, but some programs require a manual repagination operation before the page count and specific page numbers are correctly displayed on-screen.

repeat key   A key that continues to enter the same character as long as the key is held down.

repeater   In local area networks, a hardware device used to extend the length of network cabling by amplifying and passing along the messages traveling along the network. See *local area network (LAN)*.

repeating field   A fundamental error of database design that compromises data integrity by forcing you to type the same data item repeatedly.

Consider the following database design:

TITLE	SUPPLIER_ID	SUPPLIER
Spring Rains	BVS	Big Video Supply
Prince of Doom	AD	Acme Distributors
Warp Drive	AD	Acme Distributors
Fast Buck	AD	Acme Distributors

The SUPPLIER field repeats the data in the SUPPLIER_ID field and forces you to type the SUPPLIER name more than once, because one vendor can supply more than one videotape.

The cure for this problem is to create two databases, TITLES and SUPPLIER. In the TITLES database, you see the following:

TITLE	SUPPLIER_ID
Spring Rains	BVS
Prince of Doom	AD
Warp Drive	AD
Fast Buck	AD

And in the SUPPLIER database, you see the following:

SUPPLIER_ID	SUPPLIER	ADDRESS
AD	Acme Dist.	8609 Elm Drive
BVS	Big Video Supply	123 24th St.

See *data integrity, data redundancy,* and *database design*.

repeating label   In a spreadsheet program, a character preceded by a label prefix that causes the character to be repeated across the cell.

For example, \ is used in Lotus 1-2-3 to repeat one or more characters across a cell. For example, the entry \- produces a line of hyphens across the cell.

repetitive strain injury (RSI)   A serious and potentially debilitating occupational illness caused by prolonged repetitive hand and arm movements, which may damage, inflame, or kill nerves in the hands, arms, shoulder, or neck.

Also known as cumulative trauma disorder (CTD), RSI occurs when constantly repeated motions stress tendons and ligaments, resulting in scar tissue that squeezes and may eventually kill nerves. RSI has long been observed among meat packers, musicians, and assembly-line workers who repeatedly perform the same hand movements. With the proliferation of computer keyboards, RSI is increasingly noted among white-collar office workers and poses a genuine threat to personal computer users who work long hours at the keyboard. Specific RSI disorders include carpal tunnel syndrome (CTS), which often afflicts supermarket cashiers who must drag items over price-code scanners for extended periods.

Symptoms of CTS include burning, tingling, or numbness in the hands, as well as a loss of muscle control and dexterity. Potentially incapacitating to full-time writers, secretaries, and journalists, CTS and other RSI injuries are estimated to cost U.S. corporations an estimated $27 billion per year in medical bills and lost workdays.

▲ **Caution:** The symptoms of RSI frequently occur after office hours, creating the impression that the pain, numbness, or twinges are not related to computer usage. However, they are potentially signs of a serious and debilitating disease. You should see a doctor immediately if you work at the computer for long hours and experience any of these symptoms.

→ **Tip:** RSI can be prevented. Adjust your chair height to eliminate any unnecessary extension or flexing of the wrist. Take frequent breaks, use good posture, and vary your daily activities so that you perform a variety of actions with your wrists.

replace   A text processing utility found in most word processing programs that searches for a string and replaces it with another string.

replaceable parameter   In DOS and OS/2, a symbol used in a batch file that DOS replaces with information you type. The symbol consists of a percent sign and a number from 1 through 9, such as %1.

Suppose that you create a batch file, PRINTNOW .BAT, containing the following statement:

```
COPY %1 PRN
```

Then, you type the following command:

PRINTNOW letter.doc

DOS or OS/2 replaces the %1 symbol with the file name you typed and copies LETTER.DOC to the printer. See *batch file* and *FOR*.

report   In database management, printed output usually formatted with page numbers and headings. With most programs, reports can include calculated fields, showing subtotals, totals, averages, and other figures computed from the data. See *calculated field*.

report generator   A program or program function that enables a non-programmer to request printed output from a computer data-base.

research network   A wide-area computer network, such as AR-PANET or NSFNET, developed and funded by a governmental agency to improve research productivity in areas of national inter-est.

ResEdit   Pronounced "rez edit." A Macintosh utility program, available free from Apple Computer dealers, that enables you to edit (and copy to other programs) many program features such as menu text, icons, cursor shapes, and dialog boxes.

Every Macintosh file is made up of two parts, the data fork and the resource fork. The data fork contains data, such as text or the data in a database; the resource fork contains a variety of separate program resources, such as dialog boxes, sounds, icons, menus, and graphic images.

With ResEdit, you can edit these resources, thereby customizing the program, or copy the resources to other programs, where they become available as programming resources.

▲ **Caution:** If you are modifying a program file, be sure to work on a backup copy of the program. With ResEdit, modifying icons, menus, and dialog boxes is easy, but you accidentally may make a change that corrupts the program. See *utility program*.

reserved memory   See *upper memory area*.

reset button   A button, usually mounted on the system unit's front panel, that enables you to perform a warm boot if the system has hung so badly that the reset key doesn't work. On Macintoshes, the reset button is part of the programmer's switch. Synonymous with *hardware reset*. See *programmer's switch, reset key,* and *warm boot*.

reset key   A key combination that, when pressed, restarts the computer. This key combination (Ctrl-Alt-Del on DOS machines) provides an alternative to switching the power off and on after a crash so severe that the keyboard does not respond. See *hardware reset, programmer's switch,* and *warm boot*.

resident program   See *terminate-and-stay resident (TSR) program*.

resolution   A measurement—usually expressed in linear dots per inch (dpi), horizontally and vertically—of the sharpness of an image generated by an output device such as a monitor or printer.

In monitors, resolution is expressed as the number of pixels displayed on-screen. For example, a CGA monitor displays fewer pixels than a VGA monitor, and, therefore, a CGA image appears more jagged than a VGA image.

Dot-matrix printers produce output with a lower resolution than laser printers.

response time   The time the computer needs to respond and carry out a request.

Response time is a better measurement of system performance than access time because it more fairly states the system's throughput. See *access time*.

retrieval   All the procedures involved in finding, summarizing, organizing, displaying, or printing information from a computer system in a form useful for the end user.

Return   See *Enter/Return*.

reverse video   In monochrome monitors, a means of highlighting text on the display screen so that normally dark characters are displayed as bright characters on a dark background, or normally bright characters are displayed as dark characters on a bright background. See *highlighting*.

rewrite   Synonymous with *overwrite*.

RGB monitor   A color digital monitor that accepts separate inputs for red, green, and blue, and produces a much sharper image than composite color monitors.

Although the Enhanced Graphics Display uses RGB techniques, RGB monitor is synonymous in IBM PC-compatible computing with the Color Graphics Adapter (CGA) standard. See *composite color monitor*.

Rich Text Format (RTF)   A text formatting standard developed by Microsoft Corporation that enables a word processing program to create a file encoded with all the document's formatting instructions, but without using any special codes. The RTF-encoded document can be transmitted over telecommunications links or read by another RTF-compatible word processing program, without loss of the formatting.

right justification   In word processing, the alignment of text along the right margin and the left margin, producing a superficial resemblance to professionally printed text. The results may be poor, however, if the printer is incapable of proportional spacing; in such cases, right justification can be achieved only by inserting unsightly gaps of two or more spaces between words. For readability, most graphics artists advise computer users to leave the right margin ragged.

ring network   In local area networks, a decentralized network topology in which a number of nodes (including workstations, shared peripherals, and file servers) are arranged around a closed loop cable.

Like a bus network, a ring network's workstations send messages to all other workstations. Each node in the ring, however, has a unique address, and its reception circuitry constantly monitors the bus to determine whether a message is being sent. A message sent to the node named Laser Printer is ignored by the other nodes on the network.

Unlike a bus network, each node contains a repeater that amplifies and sends the signal along to the next node. Therefore, ring networks can extend far beyond the geographic limits of bus networks that lack repeaters.

However, the failure of a single node can disrupt the entire network. Fault-tolerance schemes, however, have been devised that enable ring networks to continue to function even if one or more nodes fail.

The ring-like electronic structure of the network may not be immediately obvious from its physical layout, which may resemble a star network or multiple stars; the ring is implemented in the actual electronic connections among the computers, which may or may not be reflected in their actual geographic distribution. See *file server, local area network (LAN), network topology,* and *node*.

RIP   See *raster image processor (RIP)*.

ripple-through effect   In a spreadsheet program, the sudden appearance of ERR values throughout the cells of a spreadsheet after a change is made that breaks the linkage among formulas.

If you introduce a change into a spreadsheet that corrupts to a formula so that it evaluates to ERR (error) or NA (unavailable value), all the formulas linked to (dependent on) this one also display ERR, and you see the ERR message ripple through the spreadsheet.

If this happens, you may think that you have ruined the whole spreadsheet. But after you locate and repair the problem, all the other formulas are restored.

RLL See *Run-Length Limited (RLL)*.

RMDIR In DOS and OS/2, an internal command that deletes an empty subdirectory from a disk. See *internal command*.

ROM See *read-only memory (ROM)*.

root directory The top-level directory on a disk, the one DOS creates when you format the disk. See *directory, parent directory,* and *subdirectory.*

root name The first, mandatory part of a DOS file name, using from one to eight characters. See *extension* and *file name.*

rotated type In a graphics or desktop publishing program, text that has been rotated from its normal, horizontal position on the page. The best graphics programs, such as CorelDRAW!, permit the user to edit the type even after it has been rotated.

rotation tool In a graphics or desktop publishing program, an on-screen command option, represented by an icon, that the user can use to rotate type from its normal, horizontal position. See *rotated type*.

roughs In desktop publishing, the preliminary page layouts done by the designer using pencil sketches to represent page design ideas. Synonymous with *thumbnails*. See *desktop publishing.*

row In a spreadsheet program, a horizontal block of cells running across the breadth of the spreadsheet. In most programs, rows are numbered sequentially from the top. In a database, a row is the same as a record or data record.

row-wise recalculation   In spreadsheet programs, a recalculation order that calculates all the values in row 1 before moving to row 2 and so on.

   ▲ **Caution:** If your spreadsheet program does not offer natural recalculation, use row-wise recalculation for worksheets in which rows are summed and the totals are forwarded. Column-wise recalculation may produce an erroneous result. See *column-wise recalculation, natural recalculation, optimal recalculation,* and *recalculation order.*

RS-232   A standard recommended by the Electronic Industries Association (EIA) concerning the asynchronous transmission of computer data.

   The standard widely used in IBM PC-compatible computing is an updated one: Recommended Standard 232C. See *serial port.*

RS-422   A standard recommended by the Electronic Industries Association (EIA) and used as the serial port standard for Macintosh computers, RS-422 governs the asynchronous transmission of computer data at speeds of up to 920,000 bits per second.

RSI   See *repetitive strain injury (RSI).*

rule   In computer graphics and desktop publishing, a thin black horizontal or vertical line.

run   To execute a program.

Run-Length Limited (RLL)   A method of storing and retrieving information on a hard disk that, compared to "double density" techniques, increases by at least 50 percent the amount of data a hard disk can store.

   The improvement in storage density is achieved by translating the data into a new digital format that can be written more compactly to the disk. The translation is achieved, however, only at the cost of adding complex electronics to the storage device. Therefore, RLL drives are more expensive than their MFM counterparts. See *Advanced Run-Length Limited (ARLL)* and *Modified Frequency Modulation (MFM)*.

run-time version   A commercial version of an interpreter or windowing environment that enables the creator of a program to sell an executable version of the program.

Not all users have Microsoft Windows, for example, so some software publishers sell their Windows applications with a run-time version of Windows. This version loads each time the program is used but cannot be used with other programs. See *windowing environment*.

S

SAA   See *Systems Application Architecture (SAA)*.

safe format   A disk format that does not destroy the data on the disk if you inadvertently format the wrong disk. To format safely with DOS 5.0, use the FORMAT command *without* using the /u switch. Utility packages such as PC Tools and Norton Utilities also can perform safe formats. You can quickly and easily restore the data on disk that has been formatted safely using the UNFORMAT command (DOS 5.0 and later), as long as you haven't copied more files to the disk.

satellite   In a multiuser computer system, a terminal or workstation linked to a centralized host computer. See *host*.

sawtooth distortion   See *aliasing*.

scalable font   See *outline font*.

scaling   In presentation graphics, the adjustment of the y-axis (values axis) chosen by the program so that differences in the data are highlighted.

Most presentation graphics programs scale the y-axis, but the scaling choice may be unsatisfactory. Manually adjusting the scaling produces better results. See *presentation graphics* and *y-axis*.

scanned image   A bit-mapped, or TIFF, image generated by an optical scanner. See *Tagged Image File Format (TIFF)*.

scanner   A peripheral device that digitizes artwork or photographs and stores the image as a file that can be merged with text in many word processing and page layout programs.

Scanners use two techniques for transforming photographs into digitized images. The first technique, dithering, simulates a halftone by varying the space between the dots normally used to create a bit-mapped graphic image. Like all bit-mapped images, the digital halftone cannot be sized without introducing crude distortions, and the quality may be too crude for professional applications.

The second technique, Tagged Image File Format (TIFF), stores the image using a series of 16 gray values and produces better results, but this technique is still inferior to halftones produced by photographic methods. See *bit-mapped graphic, halftone,* and *Tagged Image File Format (TIFF)*.

scatter diagram   An analytical graphic in which data items are plotted as points on two numeric axes.

Scatter diagrams show clustering relationships in numeric data. In Lotus 1-2-3, for example, a scatter diagram (an x-y graph) shows a clear correlation between sales and advertising funds.

scatter plot   See *scatter diagram*.

scientific notation   See *floating-point calculation*.

scissoring   In computer graphics, an editing technique in which an image is trimmed to a size determined by a frame, which is sized and then placed over the graphic.

scrapbook   On the Macintosh, a desk accessory that can hold frequently used graphic images, such as a company letterhead, which can be inserted into new documents as required.

screen capture   The storage of a screen display as a text or graphics file on disk.

screen dump   A printout of the current screen display.

screen font   A bit-mapped font designed to mimic the appearance of printer fonts when displayed on medium-resolution monitors. Modern laser printers can print text with a resolution of 300 dpi or more, but video displays, except for the most expensive, professional units, lack such high resolution and cannot display typefaces with such precision and beauty. What you see isn't necessarily what you get.

In character-based IBM PC-compatible machines running under DOS, no attempt is made to suggest the printer font's typeface. In WordPerfect, for example, you type what appears to be a generic Roman typeface and attach invisible formatting instructions that control the selection of printer fonts.

In graphics-oriented windowing environments (such as Microsoft Windows, OS/2's Presentation Manager, or the Macintosh's System) a low-resolution font can be used to suggest the design of the typeface that appears when the document is printed. Such fonts usually are bit-mapped fonts, which do not resize well without introducing sawtooth and other distortions.

To avoid distortions, keep a complete font on disk for every font size you are likely to use—consuming an inordinate amount of disk space. A trend in end-user computer system design, reflected in the

NeXT computer, is the use of high-resolution displays combined with screen fonts using outline (rather than bit-mapped) font technology. See *bit-mapped font, laser printer, outline font, printer font, resolution,* and *typeface.*

screen saver utility   A utility program that prolongs the life of your monitor by blanking the screen while you are away from your computer.

Monitors degrade with use, particularly when one image is displayed on-screen continuously. Such images burn into the screen phosphors, resulting in a ghost image. Prolonged use also decreases screen sharpness.

Screen-saver utilities help to prevent burned-in images and to prolong monitor life by blanking the screen while you are away from the computer. The utility can be set so that the blanking occurs after a number of specified minutes, such as 5 or 10.

To alert you that the computer has not been turned off, screen saver utilities display a moving image (such as a clock or stars) on a black background. See *utility program.*

script   In a communications program, a file containing log-on procedures for a specific host, including dialing instructions, access codes, passwords, and initial host commands. The file can be retrieved to automate what otherwise would be a cumbersome and time-consuming procedure.

scripting   The process of creating a handler, a brief program that traps messages initiated by the user, for an object in an object-oriented programming language, such as HyperTalk.

scroll   To move the window horizontally or vertically so that its position over a document or worksheet changes.

In some programs, scrolling is clearly distinguished from cursor movement; when you scroll, the cursor stays put. In other programs, however, scrolling the screen also moves the cursor.

scroll bar/scroll box A method of providing the user with horizontal and vertical scrolling capabilities by placing rectangular scrolling areas on the right and bottom borders of the window. You scroll the document horizontally or vertically by clicking the scroll box or scroll arrows, or by dragging the scroll box.

Scroll Lock key On IBM PC-compatible keyboards, a toggle key that switches the cursor-movement keys between two different modes with most programs.

The exact function of this key varies from program to program. In one program, for example, the cursor-movement keys normally move the cursor within the screen. After pressing Scroll Lock, however, the up- and down-arrow keys bring in new lines of text at the top or bottom so that the cursor always remains within two or three lines of the screen's center—and the left- and right-arrow keys do not work at all.

SCSI See *Small Computer System Interface (SCSI)*.

search and replace See *replace*.

secondary storage A nonvolatile storage medium such as a disk drive that stores program instructions and data even when the power is switched off. Synonymous with *auxiliary storage*. See *primary storage*.

secondary storage medium The specific secondary storage technology used to store and retrieve data, such as magnetic disk, magnetic tape, or optical disk.

sector In a floppy disk or hard disk, a segment of one of the concentric tracks encoded on the disk during a low-level format.

In IBM PC-compatible computing, a sector usually contains 512 bytes of information. See *cluster*.

sector interleave factor See *interleave factor*.

seek   In a secondary storage device, to position the read/write head so that data or program instructions can be retrieved.

seek time   In a secondary storage device, the time it takes the read/write head to reach the correct location on the disk. See *access time*.

select   To highlight text so that the program can identify the text on which you want the next operation to be performed.

selection   1. A unit of text, ranging from one character to many pages, highlighted in reverse video for formatting or editing purposes. 2. In programming, a branch or conditional control structure. 3. In database management, the retrieval of records by using a query. See *branch control structure*.

semaphore   A flag indicating the status of a hardware or software operation.

sequence control structure   A control structure that instructs the computer to execute program statements in the order in which the statements are written.

One of three fundamental control structures that govern the order in which program statements are executed; the sequence control structure is the default in all programming languages. Unless instructed otherwise, the computer carries out the tasks in the order in which they are written. The sequence can be altered by using the branch control structure and loop control structure. See *control structure*.

sequential access   An information storage and retrieval technique in which the computer must move through a sequence of stored data items to reach the desired one.

Sequential access media such as cassette tape recorders are much slower than random-access media. See *random access*.

serial   See *asynchronous communication, parallel port,* and *parallel processing.*

serial mouse   A mouse designed to be connected directly to one of the computers serial ports. See *bus mouse* and *mouse.*

serial port   A port that synchronizes and makes asynchronous communication between the computer and devices such as serial printers, modems, and other computers easier.

The function of the serial port is not only to transmit and receive asynchronous data in its one-bit-after-the-other stream; the serial port also negotiates with the receiving device to make sure that transmissions and receptions occur without the loss of data. The negotiation occurs through hardware or software handshaking.

→ **Tip:** To connect a serial printer to your IBM PC-compatible computer, you may need to use the DOS or OS/2 MODE command. See *asynchronous communication, modem, port, RS-232* and *Universal Asynchronous Receiver/Transmitter (UART).*

serial printer   A printer designed to be connected to the computer's serial port.

▲ **Caution:** If you are using a serial printer with an IBM PC-compatible system, you must give the correct MODE command to configure your system at the start of each operating session. Almost all users place the necessary command in the AUTOEXEC.BAT file (DOS users) or STARTUP.CMD file (OS/2 users), which the operating system consults when you start your computer. See your printer's manual for more details.

serif   The fine cross strokes across the ends of the main strokes of a character.

→ **Tip:** Serif fonts are easier to read for body type, but most designers prefer to use sans serif typefaces for display type. (The text in this book is serif text.) See *sans serif.*

server In a local area network, a computer that provides services for users of the network. The server receives requests for peripheral services and manages the requests so that they are answered in an orderly, sequential manner. Synonymous with network server. See *dedicated file server, file server, printer server,* and *workstation.*

server-based application A network version of an application program stored on the network's file server and available to more than one user at a time. See *client-based application* and *file server.*

service bureau A firm that provides a variety of publication services such as graphics file format conversion, optical scanning of graphics, and typesetting on high-resolution printers such as Linotronics and Varitypers.

setup string A series of characters that an application program conveys to the printer so that the printer operates in a specified mode. In Lotus 1-2-3, for example, the setup string \027G turns on an Epson printer's double-strike mode.

shadow RAM In '386 and '486 computers, a portion of the upper memory area between 640K and 1M set aside for programs ordinarily retrieved from read-only memory (ROM). Because RAM is faster than ROM, shadow RAM increases performance. See *random-access memory (RAM), read-only memory (ROM),* and *upper memory area.*

▲ **Caution:** Computer manufacturers like to equip their machines with shadow RAM because doing so improves the machines' performance on speed measurement tests. However, configuring part of the upper memory area as shadow RAM could cause problems with applications that try to use upper memory as extended memory. If you're running Microsoft Windows, or any other application that uses DOS 5.0 or requires extended memory, consult your computer's manual to determine how to disable shadow RAM.

shareware Copyrighted computer programs made available on a trial basis; if you like and decide to use the program, you are expected to pay a fee to the program's author. See *public domain software*.

sheet feeder See *cut-sheet feeder*.

shell A utility program designed to provide an improved (and often menu-driven) user interface for a program or operating system generally considered difficult to use. See *user interface* and *utility program*.

shift-click A mouse maneuver accomplished by holding down the Shift key when you click the mouse. Applications implement shift-clicking differently, but in most the action extends a selection.

Shift key A key pressed to enter uppercase letters or punctuation marks.

On early IBM keyboards, the Shift key is labeled with only a white arrow. Later IBM keyboards and most compatible keyboards label this key with the word shift. See *Caps Lock key*.

shortcut key A key combination that provides rapid access to a menu command or dialog box option. Using a shortcut key can save you time by removing the need to display two or more menus before reaching an option.

→ **Tip:** If you're using an application program interface such as Microsoft Windows or the Macintosh Finder, learn the shortcut keys for common tasks.

side-by-side columns The positioning of unequal blocks of text side-by-side on a page, so that a given paragraph is kept parallel with related paragraphs.

Side-by-side columns, often called parallel columns, include paragraphs meant to be positioned adjacent to one another. Newspaper column formats cannot handle this formatting task, because no relation exists between the paragraphs in one column and the paragraphs in another; on the contrary, they may move freely and independently of one another.

Because the paragraphs in a side-by-side format often are of unequal length, you cannot align them with tabs. The best word processing programs, such as WordPerfect and Microsoft Word, include commands that set up side-by-side columns and display the format on-screen as you type and edit. See *newspaper columns*.

SideKick   A popular desktop accessory for IBM Personal Computers and compatibles and the Macintosh developed by Borland International. The program includes an address book, an appointment calendar, a notepad, a calculator, and other utilities.

SIG   See *special interest group (SIG)*.

signal   The portion of a transmission that coherently represents information, unlike the random and meaningless noise that occurs in the transmission channel.

silicon chip   See *chip*.

Silicon Valley   An area in California's Santa Clara Valley with one of the largest concentrations of high-technology businesses in the world.

SIMM   See *single in-line memory module (SIMM)*.

simple list text chart   In presentation graphics, a text chart used to enumerate items in no particular order and with each item given equal emphasis. See *presentation graphics*.

simulation   An analytical technique used in computer applications, in which a phenomenon's properties are investigated by creating a model of the phenomenon and exploring the model's behavior.

One of the most important contributions the computer is making lies in its provision of new, useful tools for simulation. In aeronautical engineering, for example, the aerodynamic properties of a proposed aircraft could be simulated only through the time-consuming and expensive construction of a series of physical models, which were subjected to wind-tunnel tests.

Now, however, you can design and test thousands of alternative models in short order by using computer simulation techniques. The wind tunnel, therefore, is becoming an anachronism in modern aerospace firms.

In education, simulation techniques are enabling schools that cannot afford laboratory equipment to offer students a chance to engage in simulated, on-screen versions of classic laboratory experiments.

Simulation also is found in computer games, such as Microsoft Flight Simulator. This program is so realistic in its simulation of powered flight that it has been used as a prelude to professional flight instruction in many flight schools.

Users of spreadsheet programs frequently use simulation techniques to create a model of a business. Using simulation, a manager can ask what-if questions such as, "What is the effect on market share if we expend an additional 20 percent on advertising?"

As with any model, however, a simulation is only as good as its underlying assumptions. If these assumptions are not correct, the model does not accurately mimic the behavior of the real-world system being simulated.

single density   The earliest magnetic recording scheme for digital data used a technique called frequency modulation (FM) that resulted in low information densities (such as 90K per disk).

Disk drives designed for FM recording, therefore, could use disks (single-density disks) with relatively large-grained magnetic particles. Single-density recording disks have been superseded by double-density storage devices that use modified frequency modulation (MFM) storage techniques, double-density disks with finer grained partitions, and high-density disks with even finer partitions. See *double density, frequency modulation (FM) recording, Modified Frequency Modulation (MFM)*.

single in-line memory module (SIMM) A plug-in memory module containing all the chips needed to add 256K or 1M of random-access memory to your computer.

site license An agreement between a software publisher and an organization that enables the organization to make unlimited copies of the program for internal use. Often a company using a local area network purchases a site license for a program so that all the users on the LAN can access the program. Most site licenses stipulate a numeric limit on the number of copies that can be made. The cost per copy is much less than buying individual copies.

single-sided disk A floppy disk designed so that only one side of the disk can be used for read/write operations. Single-sided disks have low storage capacities and are used infrequently in today's personal computer systems.

sixteen-bit See *16-bit computer*.

skip factor In a graphics program, an increment that specifies how many data points the program should skip as it constructs a chart or graph.

Use a skip factor when a graph looks cluttered with too many thin, spindly columns or when the categories axis is too crowded with headings. A skip factor of 3, for example, displays every third data item, reducing the graph's complexity.

slide show In presentation graphics, a predetermined list of on-screen charts and graphs displayed one after the other.

Some programs can produce interesting effects, such as fading out one screen before displaying another and enabling you to choose your path through the charts available for display. See *presentation graphics*.

slot   See *expansion slot*.

slug   In word processing and desktop publishing, a code inserted in headers or footers that generates page numbers when the document is printed.

Small Computer System Interface (SCSI)   Pronounced "scuzzy." An interface standard for peripheral devices such as hard disk drives and laser printers.

   The most common SCSI device in use is the SCSI hard disk. Unlike ST506 and ESDI drives, the drive contains most of the controller circuitry, leaving the SCSI interface free to communicate with other peripherals. SCSI drivers generally are faster than ST506 drives. See *Enhanced System Device Interface (ESDI)* and *ST-506/ST-412*.

SMARTDRV.SYS   A DOS device driver that creates a disk cache in extended or expanded memory. See *device driver, disk cache, expanded memory,* and *extended memory*.

smart machine   Any device containing microprocessor-based electronics that enable the device to branch to alternative operating sequences depending on external conditions, to repeat operations until a condition is fulfilled, or to execute a series of instructions repetitively.

smart terminal   In a multiuser system, a terminal containing its own processing circuitry so that it not only retrieves data from the host computer but also carries out additional processing operations and runs host-delivered programs.

snaking columns   See *newspaper columns*.

snapshot See *screen dump*.

soft carriage return In a word processing program, a line break inserted by the program to maintain the margins; the location of the soft carriage return may change if the margins change or if text is inserted or deleted within the line. See *word wrap*.

soft cell boundaries In a spreadsheet program, a feature that enables you to enter labels longer than the cell's width (unless the adjacent cells are occupied).

soft font See *downloadable font*.

soft hyphen A hyphen formatted so that the program does not use it unless the hyphen is needed to improve the spacing on a line. Synonymous with *optional hyphen*.

soft page break In a word processing program, a page break inserted by the program based on the current state of the text; the page break may move up or down if insertions, deletions, margin changes, or page size changes occur. See *forced page break*.

soft return See *soft carriage return*.

soft-sectored disk A disk that, when new, contains no magnetic patterns of tracks or sectors. The patterns must be added in a process called formatting before the disk can be used. See *formatting*.

soft start See *warm boot*.

software System, utility, or application programs expressed in a computer-readable language. See *firmware*.

software command language A high-level programming language developed to work with an application, such as a spreadsheet or database management program.

Software command languages vary from the simple macro capabilities of word processing programs to full-fledged programming languages, such as the dBASE command language. The best software command languages enable users to create custom applications, complete with iteration, logical branching, and conditional execution of operations.

These languages give the programmer enormous leverage because the package already handles all details related to disk input/output, the user interface, data structures, error handling, and so on. A relatively simple program, therefore, can produce an extremely powerful custom application. See *control structure, dBASE,* and *HyperTalk.*

software compatibility The capability of a computer system to run a specific type of software. The Commodore 64, for example, is not software-compatible with software written for the Apple II, even though both computers use the MOS Technology 6502 microprocessor.

software engineering An applied science devoted to improving and optimizing the production of computer software.

software license A legal agreement included with commercial programs. The software license specifies the rights and obligations of the user who purchased the program and limits the liability of the software publisher.

software package An application program delivered to the user as a complete, ready-to-run system, including all necessary support and utility programs and documentation.

software piracy The unauthorized and illegal duplication of copyrighted software without the permission of the software publisher.

Software can be duplicated in a matter of seconds. To the consternation of software publishers, software piracy is extremely common and seems to be an endemic problem of personal computing.

As early as 1976, Bill Gates, a cofounder of Microsoft Corporation, complained that he could not remain in the business of selling a BASIC interpreter for the Altair computer if people kept on making illegal copies of his program. Worse, people who seldom break other moral or legal rules engage in software piracy without hesitation. The computer revolution appears to have happened so quickly that cultural norms and moral values have not had time to adjust accordingly.

Some argue that software piracy has a beneficial effect on the software industry; to motivate people to become registered users, software publishers are forced to make constant improvements to a program. There may be some truth to this claim, although many software revisions are motivated almost exclusively by competitive pressures.

Others argue that software piracy is a way of previewing a program—and a justifiable way, considering that most software retailers don't let you return a program after you have opened the package. If the pirate really likes the program, some argue that he will become a registered user, seeking the benefit of upgrades and documentation. Very few pirates, however, become registered users.

Attempts to stop software piracy through copy-protection schemes backfired on the companies that tried them. Such schemes prevent a casual, unsophisticated user from copying a disk, but they also imposed penalties on valid, registered users of the program, and the major software publishers gave them up.

Software piracy may be common and virtually undetectable when it occurs at home but can become a danger to a business or an organization. More than a few companies have been sued for damages attributable to unauthorized software duplication, and an industry consortium has established a toll-free hotline through which whistle blowers (or disgruntled employees) can report offenders. A wise manager establishes a policy that absolutely no unauthorized copies of software are to be kept near, or used with, company computers.

software protection See *copy protection*.

sort An operation that reorders data in alphabetical or numerical order.

Most application programs can perform sorts. Full-featured word processing programs, such as WordPerfect, provide commands that sort lists, and electronic spreadsheets provide commands that sort the cells in a range.

In database management programs, sorts are distinguished from index operations. A sort performs a physical rearrangement of the data records, resulting in a new, permanently sorted file—consuming much disk space in the process.

The permanently re-sorted records can be used later without repeating the sort operation, but you now have two copies of your database. If you forget to erase the first one, you can become confused about which copy you used to update the data.

An index operation, however, does not physically rearrange the records. Instead, an index operation creates an index to the records and orders the index rather than the records. The index consumes less disk space than a new copy of the whole database.

Even if you have a huge hard disk, however, indexing provides a much more important advantage; a good database management program (such as dBASE) preserves data integrity by updating all the indexes whenever you add records or update old ones. See *data integrity* and *sort order*.

sort key In database management, the data field used to determine the order in which data records are arranged.

In an employee database, for example, the LAST_NAME field or SOCSECNO (Social Security number) field can be used to arrange the records in alphabetical or numerical order. See *multilevel sort*.

sort order   The order in which a program arranges data when performing a sort. Most programs sort data in the standard order of ASCII characters. Synonymous with *collating sequence*. See *ASCII sort order, dictionary sort,* and *sort.*

source code   In a high-level programming language, the program as people write and read it, before the program has been compiled or interpreted into machine instructions that the computer can execute.

source file   In many DOS commands, the file from which data or program instructions is copied. See *destination file.*

spaghetti code   See *structured programming.*

special interest group (SIG)   A subgroup of an organization or a computer networking system consisting of members who share a common interest. See *user group.*

speech synthesis   The production by a computer of audio output that resembles human speech.

Computer voice recognition technology is still primitive. Even the best systems can recognize only a few hundred words, and they do so only after a lengthy training session in which the computer becomes familiar with an individual's specific voice patterns.

Speech synthesis technology, however, is quite well developed. Existing and inexpensive speech synthesis boards can do an impressive job of reading virtually any file containing English sentences in ASCII script—although, to some listeners, the English sounds as though it is being spoken with a Czech accent.

Speech synthesis is improving the lives of blind people by making written material more accessible to them; blind writers can proof and edit their own written work by having the computer read their work to them.

spell checker   A program often incorporated in word processing programs that checks for the correct spelling of words in a document. Each word is compared against a file of correctly spelled words.

A good spell checker displays the correct spelling of a misspelled word and enables you to replace that word. You usually can add words to the spell checker's dictionary.

spike   See *power surge*.

split screen   A display technique in which the screen is divided into two windows. In word processing programs that have split screen capabilities, independently displaying two parts of the same document is usually possible as is displaying two different documents.

spooler   A program, often included with an operating system's utility programs, that routes printer commands to a file on disk or in RAM instead of to the printer and then feeds the printer commands out of the file when the central processing unit (CPU) is idle.

A print spooler provides a variation on background printing; your program thinks that it is printing to a super-fast printer, but the printer output is being directed to RAM or a disk file. You can continue working with your program, and the spooler guides the printer data to the printer during those moments when the CPU is not busy handling your work.

spreadsheet   See *worksheet*.

spreadsheet program   A program that simulates an accountant's worksheet on-screen and enables you to embed hidden formulas that perform calculations on the visible data.

In 1978, a Harvard Business School student named Dan Bricklin got tired of adding up columns of numbers—and adding them up all over again after a few changes had been made, just to assess the effect of a merger. Bricklin, who knew a little about computers from summer jobs at Wang and other firms, came up with the idea of a spreadsheet program running on a personal computer.

Bricklin's teachers thought the idea was nonsense, but he and a programmer friend, Bob Frankston, produced a program they called VisiCalc for the Apple II computer, and an important new chapter in American enterprise was launched.

A spreadsheet program presents you with a matrix of rows (usually numbered) and columns (usually assigned alphabetical letters), that form individual cells. The on-screen display is called a spreadsheet. Each cell has a distinctive cell address, such as B4 or D19. Into each cell, you can place a value (a number), a hidden formula that performs a calculation, or a label (a heading or explanatory text).

The formulas make a spreadsheet powerful. A formula can contain constants, such as 2 + 2, but the most useful formulas contain cell references, such as D9 + D10. By placing formulas in a spreadsheet's cells, you can create a complex network of interlinkages among the parts of a spreadsheet. You don't see the formulas, which are hidden behind the cell, but you see the values they generate.

The point of creating a spreadsheet isn't just to find the answer to a problem. When completed, you can enter new values, and the spreadsheet is recalculated. In seconds, you can see how a change in one value ripples through the spreadsheet and affects the bottom line.

This form of sensitivity testing, the changing of values to see how they affect the outcome, is called *what-if analysis* and is one of the main reasons spreadsheet programs have sold so well. Using what-if analysis, you can examine the potential effect of a decision on your business bottom line.

VisiCalc was a huge success; more than 700,000 copies of the program eventually were sold, and VisiCalc was almost single-handedly responsible for the success of the Apple II personal computer. But VisiCalc met stiff competition from Lotus 1-2-3 in the IBM PC environment, and, by 1984, had disappeared from the market. VisiCalc may be gone, but its influence lives on in many ways; almost all spreadsheet programs use the famous slash key (/) command to bring up the command menu.

Spreadsheets have acquired many new features since VisiCalc's time. Lotus 1-2-3 is an integrated program that combines analytical graphics and database management with what is clearly a clone of VisiCalc's spreadsheet. Recent trends in spreadsheets include the three-dimensional spreadsheet programs, such as 1-2-3 Release 3.0, and graphics-based spreadsheets, such as Microsoft Excel, which bring some desktop publishing technology to spreadsheets.

As useful as spreadsheets are, remember that they are prone to error. Because you cannot see the formulas, you may not notice when one contains a serious error. You also may type a constant into a cell containing a formula while doing what-if analysis and destroy the interlinkages among cells without realizing what you have done. Both errors are very common, and occur even among people who should know better.

A spreadsheet is only a model of a business; any model includes only some of the significant determinants of a firm's behavior, and manipulating the model—as is commonly done in what-if analysis—may lead to serious errors in decision making even if all the formulas are correct. People may be tempted to tweak the assumptions so that they get the right answer.

David Stockman, the director of President Reagan's Office of Management and Budget, was instructed to produce a model of the American economy that would show the results of the President's tax cuts. According to William Greider's book *The Education of David Stockman,* Stockman found that the model suggested huge budget deficits. Because this answer was not the one he was looking for, he introduced a swift decline in prices and a rapid rise in productivity into the model, which then produced the "right" answer.

▲ **Caution:** Do not make business decisions based on a spreadsheet without carefully thinking through what you are doing. First, check all the formulas to see whether they are correct. Many programs include a command that displays the formulas on-screen. Third-party programs such as Spreadsheet Auditor (Cambridge Software) are available for the programs without this command.

Second, use cell protection on every cell containing a formula. Third, never place constants in a formula. Place all the constants in your spreadsheet in a special area at the top of the spreadsheet that contains the key variables. Fourth, bear in mind the limitations of a model; a model can never mimic reality, only part of it.

Fifth, remember that all good decisions aren't necessarily defensible on purely quantitative grounds. A model that suggests saving money may do so at the sacrifice of employee or community good will or of market share, and even though the results look good, they may wind up being catastrophic in the end.

SQL   See *Structured Query Language (SQL)*.

ST-506/ST-412   A hard disk interface standard that is widely used in IBM and IBM-compatible computers. ST-506 drives are slower and cheaper than drives using more recent interface standards. MFM and RLL encoding methods are used with the ST-506/412 interface. MFM has a 5 megabit per second transfer rate, and RLL has a 7.5 megabit per second rate.

ST-506/ST-412 is still the most common interface using the MFM encoding and is standard on AT-class computers. See *Enhanced System Device Interface (ESDI), interface standard,* and *Small Computer Systems Interface (SCSI)*.

stack   In programming, a stack is a data structure in which the first items inserted are the last ones removed. This data structure is used in programs that use branching or procedure/function structures; a stack enables the computer to track what it was doing when it branched or jumped to a procedure.

In HyperCard, stack refers to a file containing one or more cards that share a common background. See *Hypercard*.

stacked column chart   See *stacked column graph*.

stacked column graph   A column graph in which two or more data series are displayed, not adjacent to one another, but on top of one another. See *histogram*.

staggered windows   See *cascading windows*.

stand-alone computer   A computer system dedicated to meeting the computing needs of a person working in isolation.

A stand-alone system contains all the hardware and software a user requires. Links with other computers are incidental to the system's chief purpose. See *distributed processing system*, *multiuser system*, and *professional workstation*.

standard mode   In Microsoft Windows, an operating mode that takes advantage of extended memory in '286 and higher computers, but does not allow the use of the full technical capabilities of '386 and higher microprocessors. Standard mode runs Windows applications well, and is faster than the 386 Enhanced Mode. The disadvantages of standard mode are apparent only when you try to run DOS applications. In standard mode, DOS applications take over the screen, and virtual memory and multitasking are not available. In 386 Enhanced mode, you can run two or more DOS applications in their own windows, and each has 640K of clear, unobstructed memory. See *386 enhanced mode*, *extended memory*, *Microsoft Windows*, *multitasking*, *real mode*, and *virtual memory*.

➔ **Tip:** If you have a '386 or higher microprocessor and at least 2M of RAM, you can run Windows in the 386 enhanced mode, which makes true multitasking and virtual memory available.

star network   In local area networks, a centralized network topology with the physical layout of a star. At the center is a central network processor or wiring concentrator; the nodes are arranged around and connected directly to the central point.

Wiring costs are considerably higher because each workstation requires a cable linking the workstation directly to the central processor.

start bit In serial communications, a bit inserted into the data stream to inform the receiving computer that a byte of data is to follow.

startup disk The disk containing portions of the operating system that you normally use to start your computer. Synonymous with *boot disk* and *system disk*. See *hard disk*.

startup screen A Macintosh graphics file that, when placed in the System Folder, is displayed when the computer is turned on or restarted.

Most Macintosh users are content with the "Welcome to Macintosh" message, but you can see virtually anything you want to when you turn on your machine; you can save any bit-mapped graphic image as a startup screen. For example, you can display a bird, a volcano, or even a picture of yourself.

state-of-the-art An item that is technically sophisticated—containing the latest technology and representing the highest possible level of technical achievement.

statement In a high-level programming language, a command that trained programmers can read and understand. A statement successfully generates machine language instructions when the program is interpreted or compiled. See *instruction* and *high-level programming language*.

static random-access memory (RAM) A random-access memory (RAM) chip that holds its contents without constant refreshing from the CPU.

Although as volatile as DRAM chips, static RAM does not require the CPU to refresh its contents several hundred times per second. These chips, therefore, are substantially faster and preferable for high-speed computers based on microprocessors such as the Intel 80386.

They also are significantly more expensive than DRAM chips. See *dynamic random-access memory (DRAM)*, *random-access memory (RAM)*, and *volatility*.

station   See *workstation*.

statistical software   An application program that makes the application of statistical tests and measures to computer-readable data easier.

status line   A line of an application program's display screen that describes the state of the program.

Often included in status lines are the name of the file you currently are modifying and the names of the toggle keys you have pressed, such as Num Lock or Caps Lock.

stem   In typography, the main vertical stroke of a character.

stickup initial   An enlarged initial letter at the beginning of a paragraph that rises above the top of the first line.

▲ **Caution:** You can create initials with many word processing and page layout programs, but to avoid a common formatting error, make sure that the letter aligns precisely at the base of a line of text. See *drop cap*.

stop bit   In serial communications, a bit inserted into the data stream to inform the receiving computer that the transmission of a byte of data is complete.

storage   The retention of program instructions, initial data, and intermediate data within the computer so that this information is available for processing purposes. See *primary storage* and *secondary storage*.

storage device Any optical or magnetic device that is capable of secondary storage functions in a computer system. See *secondary storage*.

stored program concept The idea, which underlies the architecture of all modern computers, that the program should be stored in memory with the data.

An insight of the late physician and scientist John von Neumann as he beheld the hard-wired programs of the ENIAC (North America's first digital electronic computer), this concept showed how a program could jump back and forth through instructions instead of executing them sequentially. With this insight, virtually the entire world of modern computing was launched. See *von Neumann bottleneck*.

streaming tape drive A secondary storage device that uses continuous tape, contained in a cartridge, for backup purposes.

strikeout An attribute, such as type, struck through with a hyphen to mark text.

Strikeout often is used to mark text to be deleted from a coauthored document so that the other author can see changes easily. See *overstrike, Overtype mode,* and *redlining*.

string A series of alphanumeric characters.

string formula In a spreadsheet program, a formula that performs a string operation such as concatenation.

string operation A computation performed on alphanumeric characters.

Computers cannot understand the meaning of words, and they cannot, therefore, process them like people do. However, computers can perform simple processing operations on textual data, such as the following:

- Comparison. Comparing two strings to see whether they are the same.
- Concatenation. Joining two strings together.
- Length calculation. Calculating the number of characters a string occupies.
- Sorting. Arranging strings in ASCII order.

stroke font   See *outline font*.

Structured Query Language (SQL)   Pronounced "sequel." In database management systems, an IBM-developed query language widely used in mainframe and minicomputer systems. SQL increasingly is being implemented in client/server networks as a way of enabling personal computers to access the resources of corporate databases.

Originally developed by D. D. Chamberlin and other researchers at IBM Research Laboratories, SQL is the up-and-coming query language for microcomputers because the language can be used with a variety of database management packages.

SQL is data independent, because the user does not have to worry about the particulars of how data is accessed physically. At least in theory, SQL is device independent; the same query language can be used to access databases on mainframes, minicomputers, and personal computers. Currently, however, several versions of SQL are competing.

Because of its data and device independence, SQL is a fast-rising star on the personal computer scene. Many companies have purchased hundreds or even thousands of personal computers, which function well as stand-alone workstations, but the problem faced by many companies is how to enable users to access data on corporate minicomputers and mainframes.

SQL, therefore, rapidly is becoming a common language for computerized database management. A user who knows how to use a personal computer database that uses SQL already has learned the necessary commands and syntax, and the same query language is useful for accessing a database stored on a corporate mainframe.

SQL is an elegant and concise query language with only 30 commands. The four basic commands (SELECT, UPDATE, DELETE, and INSERT) correspond to the four basic functions of data manipulation (data retrieval, data modification, data deletion, and data insertion, respectively).

SQL queries also approximate the structure of an English natural language query. For example, the query, "Show me the TITLE and RATING of those videotapes in the inventory database in which the field CATEGORY contains 'Children' and order the result by TITLE," is represented by the following SQL query:

```
SELECT title, rating
FROM inventory
WHERE category = "children"
ORDER BY title
```

SQL is table-oriented; SQL queries do not display individual data records. Instead, the queries result in the on-screen display of a data table, consisting of columns (corresponding to data fields) and rows (corresponding to data records). See *data deletion, data insertion, data manipulation, data modification, data retrieval, natural language,* and *table-oriented database management program*.

style sheet In some word processing and page layout programs, a stored collection of user-created text-formatting definitions containing information such as type style, alignment, and line spacing specifications.

In the old days of professional typists, the typist interviewed the author and filled out a style sheet listing the author's preferences for all formats (such as titles, footnotes, body text paragraphs, and the like).

In word processing software, the term describes an on-disk collection of formatting definitions you create. For example, if you can have a style sheet entry for normal body text paragraphs that includes the following formats: Palatino, 10 point type size, ragged-left indentation, single line spacing, and 0.5-inch first line indentation.

stylus   A pen-shaped instrument used on a monitor's screen or on a graphics tablet for drawing or selecting menu options.

subdirectory   In DOS, OS/2, and UNIX, a directory listed within a directory that, when opened, reveals another directory containing files and additional subdirectories.

The directory you see when you use the DOS DIR command is an effective guide to a disk's contents until you create more files than one screen can display. With DOS, you operate under stringent limitations on the number of files you can place in one directory. You can place only 112 files in one directory on a 360K or 720K disk. You can place only 512 files in one directory on a hard disk. Subdirectories enable you to create a tree-like, hierarchical structure of nested directories in which you can store many more than 512 files.

To understand how subdirectories are linked, look at a typical root directory created when the disk is formatted—the one you see when you use the DIR command:

```
Volume in Drive A has no label
Directory of A:\
LETTER1   DOC      1651    3-24-89     12:01a
REPORT1   DOC      1102    3-24-89     12:01a
MEMO1     DOC      6462    3-24-89     12:00p
LETTER2   DOC      1651    5-24-89     12:01a
REPORT2   DOC      1102    5-24-89     12:01a
MEMO2     DOC      6462    5-24-89     12:00p
```

LETTER3	DOC	1651	7-24-89	12:01a
REPORT3	DOC	1102	7-24-89	12:01a
MEMO3	DOC	6462	7-24-89	12:00p

9 File(s) 280576 byes free

Like most of the directories DOS creates, this directory is organized haphazardly. (Imagine what the directory would look like if you had 350 files.) Grouping the LETTER files, REPORT files, and MEMO files would be better than mixing them. You can create three subdirectories—called LETTERS, REPORTS, and MEMOS—and place these files into them.

After you create the subdirectories and move the files, the directory looks different. The DIR command reveals the following directory:

Volume in Drive A has no label

Directory of A:\

LETTERS	<DIR>	9-24-89	1:14p
REPORTS	<DIR>	9-24-89	1:15p
MEMOS	<DIR>	9-24-89	1:16p

This directory now contains three subdirectories. Using the CHDIR command, you can open one of these subdirectories.

Directories are linked in a tree structure. Think of an upside-down tree. The main directory is like the trunk, and the subdirectories are like branches. The main directory created by DOS is called the root directory. The entire directory structure of the disk grows from this directory.

You also can create subdirectories within subdirectories. In this way, you can organize even a huge hard disk so that you never see more than a few files after typing DIR. See *root directory*.

submenu   A set of lower level commands available when you choose a top-level command.

subroutine A portion of a program that performs a specific function and is set aside so that it can be used by more than one section of the program.

　　A subroutine takes care of tasks needed frequently, such as writing a file to disk. In BASIC programs, subroutines are referenced by GOSUB statements.

subscript In text processing, a number or letter printed slightly below the typing line. See *superscript*.

suitcase In the Macintosh environment, an icon containing a screen font or desk accessory not yet installed in the System Folder.

superscript A number or letter printed slightly above the typing line.

Super VGA An enhancement of the Video Graphics Array (VGA) display standard for IBM Personal Computers; Super VGA boards and monitors can display at least 800 lines horizontally and 600 lines vertically, and up to 1,024 by 768 with 16 or 256 colors simultaneously displayed, although as much as 1M of video memory may be required for high performance.

support See *technical support*.

surge A momentary and sometimes destructive increase in the amount of voltage delivered through a power line.

surge protector An inexpensive electrical device that prevents high-voltage surges from reaching a computer and damaging its circuitry. See *power line filter*.

swap file A file used to store program instructions and data that will not fit in the computer's random-access memory (RAM). See *permanent swap file*, *temporary swap file*, and *virtual memory*.

swash   A type character that sweeps over or under adjacent characters with a curvilinear flourish.

switch   In DOS, an addition to a DOS command that affects the way the command performs its function. The switch symbol is a forward slash, which is followed by a letter (such as /s or /a).

synchronous communication   The transmission of data at very high speeds using circuits in which the transfer of data is synchronized by electronic clock signals. Synchronous communication is used within the computer and in high-speed mainframe computer networks. See *asynchronous communication*.

syntax   All the rules that specify precisely how a command, statement, or instruction must be given to the computer so that the machine can recognize and process the instruction correctly.

syntax error   An error resulting from the expression of a command in a way that violates a program's syntax rules.

SYSOP   Acronym for SYStem OPerator. Pronounced "siss'-op." A person who runs a bulletin board.

system   See *computer system*.

System   The operating system for Apple Macintosh computers contained in the Macintosh's read-only memory and the System File in the System Folder.

System 7   A 1991 version of the Macintosh operating system software that maintains Apple Computer's technological lead in graphical user interfaces.

  Among System 7's benefits are long-overdue improvements to Finder (the program and file-management system), true multitasking (rather than multiple program loading), program launching from menus, true virtual memory (with 68030 microprocessors), outline (scalable) fonts that work on the screen as well as the printer, peer-to-peer file sharing on networked Macs without the need of a file server, external database access, and hot links across applications that instantaneously update copied data. System 7 is a state-of-the-art operating system and the applications developed for it will redefine the way people work with application programs, especially when they are running more than one program.

→ **Tip:** Not all existing Mac applications are compatible with System 7. Apple dealers can run a diagnostic program that informs you whether any of your programs are incompatible with System 7. See *file server, Finder, hot link, Macintosh, multiple program loading, outline font, peer-to-peer network,* and *virtual memory.*

system date The calendar date maintained by the computer system and updated while the system is in operation.

Not all personal computers maintain the system date after the computer is switched off. To do so, the system must be equipped with a battery.

Computers without such batteries on their motherboards must be equipped with a clock-calendar board. If you are using an IBM PC-compatible computer that lacks battery-powered system date circuitry, you can set the system date manually by using the DATE command.

→ **Tip:** Be sure to set the system date. When you create and save files, the operating system records the date and time you saved the file. This information can be important when you are trying to determine which version of a file is the most recent.

system disk A disk containing the operating system and all files necessary to start the computer.

Hard disk users normally configure the hard disk to serve as the system disk.

system file   A program or data file that contains information needed by the operating system—distinguished from program or data files used by application programs.

System Folder   A folder in the Macintosh desktop environment that contains the System File and the Finder, the two components of the Mac's operating system.

In addition to the System and Finder files, the System Folder also contains all the desk accessories, INITs, CDEV, screen fonts, downloadable printer fonts, and printer drivers to be made available during an operating session.

Because the System Folder is the only folder that the Finder consults when searching for a file, many applications require that configuration files, dictionaries, and other necessary files be placed in this folder so that they can be accessed.

→ Tip: If you frequently see a message informing you that an application cannot find a needed file, place the file in the System Folder. See *blessed folder, control panel device (CDEV), desk accessory (DA), downloadable font, Finder, INIT, printer driver,* and *screen font*.

system prompt   In a command-line operating system, the prompt that indicates the operating system's availability for system maintenance tasks such as copying files, formatting disks, and loading programs. In DOS, the system prompt (a letter designating the disk drive, followed by a greater-than symbol) shows the current drive. When you see the prompt C >, for example, drive C is the current drive, and DOS is ready to accept instructions. You can customize the system prompt by using the PROMPT command. See *command-line operating system*.

systems analyst   A person who designs specifications, calculates feasibility and costs, and implements a business system.

Systems Application Architecture (SAA)   A set of standards for communication among various types of IBM computers, from personal computers to mainframes.

Announced in 1987, SAA was IBM's response to criticisms that its products did not work well together and to the competitive pressure exerted by Digital Electronic Corporation (DEC), which claimed that its products were optimized for easy interconnection.

Although SAA is little more than an evolving set of standards for future development, SAA calls for a consistent user interface and consistent system terminology across all environments. SAA influenced the design of Presentation Manager, the windowing environment jointly developed by Microsoft and IBM for the OS/2 operating system. See *Operating System/2 (OS/2), Presentation Manager,* and *windowing environment.*

system software   All the software used to operate and maintain a computer system, including the operating system and utility programs—distinguished from application programs.

system time   The time of day maintained by the computer system that is updated while the system is in operation.

Not all personal computers maintain the system time after the computer has been switched off. To do so, the system must be equipped with a battery. Computers without such batteries on their motherboards must be equipped with a clock-calendar board. If you are using an IBM PC-compatible personal computer that lacks battery-powered system date circuitry, you can set the system time manually by using the TIME command.

➔ **Tip:** Be sure to set the system time. When you create and save files, the operating system records the date and time you saved the file. This information can be important when you are trying to determine which version of a file is the most recent.

system unit   The case that houses the computer's internal processing circuitry, including the power supply, motherboard, disk drives, plug-in boards, and a speaker. Some personal computer system units also contain a monitor.

The system unit often is called the central processing unit (CPU), but this usage is inaccurate. Properly, the CPU consists of the computer's microprocessor and memory, usually housed on the motherboard, but not peripherals such as disk drives.

System V Interface Definition (SVID) A standard for UNIX operating systems, established by AT&T Bell Laboratories and demanded by corporate buyers, based on UNIX Version 5. See *UNIX*.

t

tab-delimited file A data file, usually in ASCII file format, in which the data items are separated by tab keystrokes. See *ASCII file* and *comma-delimited file*.

tab key A key used to enter a fixed number of blank characters in a document. The tab key often is used to guide the cursor in on-screen command menus.

table In a relational database management program, the fundamental structure of data storage and display in which data items are linked by the relations formed by placing them in rows and columns.

The rows correspond to the data records of record-oriented database management programs, and the columns correspond to data fields. See *table-oriented database management program*.

table of authorities A table of legal citations generated by a word processing program from in-text references.

table-oriented database management program   A database management program that displays data tables (rather than records) as the result of query operations. See *data retrieval, record-oriented database management program,* and *Structured Query Language (SQL).*

table utility   In a word processing program, a utility that makes the typing of tables easier by creating a spreadsheet-like matrix of rows and columns, into which text can be inserted without forcing word wrapping.

    When you create a table with tab stops, you must type the table line-by-line. If you later find that you have to add a few words to one of the items, the words may not fit, and you succeed only in forcing the rest of the line to wrap down to the next, ruining the column alignment. Table utilities solve this problem by making the cell, not the line, the unit of word wrapping.

Tagged Image File Format (TIFF)   Pronounced "tiff." A bit-mapped graphics format for scanned images with resolutions of up to 300 dpi. TIFF simulates gray-scale shading. See *bit-mapped graphic.*

tape backup unit   A secondary storage device designed to back up onto magnetic tape all the data on a hard disk at high speeds.

technical support   The provision of technical advice and problem-solving expertise to registered users of a hardware device or program.

telecommunications   The transmission of information, whether expressed by voice or computer signals, via the telephone system. See *asynchronous communication* and *modem.*

Telenet   A commercial wide-area network with thousands of local dial-up numbers. Telenet provides log-on services to a variety of commercial on-line computer services, such as Dialog Information Services and CompuServe.

teletype (TTY) display A method of displaying characters on a monitor in which characters are generated and sent, one by one, to the video display; as the characters are received, the screen fills, line by line. When full, the screen scrolls up to accommodate the new lines of characters appearing at the bottom of the screen.

The teletype display mode should be familiar to users of DOS. This mode uses a teletype display for accepting user commands and displaying messages to the user. See *character mapped display.*

template In an application program, a document or worksheet that includes the text or formulas needed for some generic applications and is available repeatedly for customization.

In word processing, templates frequently are used for letterheads; the on-screen version of the file contains the corporate logo, the company's address, and all the formats necessary to write the letter, but no text. You use the template by loading the file, adding the text, and printing.

In spreadsheet programs, templates are available for solving a number of common problems, such as calculating and printing a mortgage amortization schedule.

temporary swap file In Microsoft Windows, a disk file set aside for the storage and retrieval of program instructions or data in the program's 386 enhanced mode. This storage space is used in virtual memory operations, which use disk space as a seamless extension of random-access memory (RAM).

Windows creates a temporary swap file, if it cannot find a permanent one, to store program instructions or data that will not fit in RAM. A temporary swap file consumes less disk space than a permanent swap file, but storage and retrieval operations are slower. See *Microsoft Windows, random-access memory (RAM), swap file, temporary swap file,* and *virtual memory.*

tera Prefix indicating one trillion (10^{12}).

terabyte A unit of memory measure approximately equal to one trillion bytes (actually 1,099,511,627,776 bytes).

One terabyte equals 1,000 gigabytes, or one million megabytes. See *byte, gigabyte,* and *megabyte (M).*

terminal An input/output device, consisting of a keyboard and video display, commonly used with multiuser systems.

A terminal lacking its own central processing unit (CPU) and disk drives is called a dumb terminal; its use is restricted to interacting with a distant multiuser computer.

A smart terminal has some processing circuitry and, in some cases, a disk drive so that information can be downloaded and displayed later.

A personal computer is in many ways the opposite of a terminal. A terminal centralizes computing resources and denies autonomy to users. A personal computer distributes computing resources and enables users to make their own software choices.

Yet, a personal computer user can have many valid reasons for wanting to take advantage of centralized computer resources. To do so, the computer needs to be transformed into a smart terminal, which is the function of communications software.

Many different brands and models of terminals are in use and their electronic characteristics and capabilities differ. A given on-line service usually expects those contacting its computer to use a specific brand and model of terminal, such as the DEC VT100.

One important function of a communications program, therefore, is to configure the personal computer so that it communicates on-line as a specific terminal would. The better communications programs provide several terminal emulations including TTY (a plain vanilla teletype terminal), DEC VT52, DEC VT 100, and Lear-Siegler ADM/3A.

→ **Tip:** If you are contacting an on-line information service or a bulletin board for the first time, use TTY emulation. See *terminal emulation*.

terminal emulation   The use of a communications program to transform a personal computer into a terminal for the purpose of data communications.

terminate-and-stay-resident (TSR) program   An accessory or utility program designed to remain in the computer's random-access memory (RAM) at all times so that the user can activate it with a keystroke, even if another program also is in memory.

▲ **Caution:** If you are using DOS, use TSR programs with caution. Don't use TSR programs at all if you are working with valuable data or documents.

Using a TSR program all but guarantees a system crash sooner or later because DOS does not operate in protected mode. DOS has no provisions for keeping one program from invading the memory space of another, and such invasions cripple the invaded program or cause crashes.

With its protected mode processing, OS/2 enables the simultaneous execution of two or more programs without the peril of system crashes. See *multitasking, protected mode,* and *real mode*.

Texas Instruments Graphics Architecture (TIGA)   A high-resolution graphics standard for IBM and IBM-compatible personal computers. TIGA boards and monitors display 1,024 pixels horizontally by 786 pixels vertically with 256 simultaneous colors.

text chart   In presentation graphics, a text chart is designed for display to an audience using a slide or transparency. See *bulleted list chart, column text chart, free-form text chart, organization chart,* and *simple list text chart*.

text editor   In computer programming, a program designed for the creation, editing, and storage of object code.

A text editor resembles a word processing program in many respects; a text editor makes the entry and editing of words and numbers easier. Because a text editor is designed for writing computer programs, text editors generally contain only the most primitive facilities for text formatting and printing.

text file   A file consisting of nothing but the standard ASCII characters (with no control characters or higher order characters).

thermal printer   A nonimpact printer that forms an image by moving heated styluses over specially treated paper.

Quiet and fast, thermal printers have one disadvantage: most of them require specially treated paper, which has an unpleasant, waxy feel.

third-party vendor   A firm that markets an accessory hardware product for a given brand of computer equipment.

thirty-two bit computer   See *32-bit computer.*

three-dimensional spreadsheet   A spreadsheet program that can create a worksheet file made up of multiple stacked pages, each page resembling a separate worksheet.

In Lotus 1-2-3 Release 3, you can create one spreadsheet file that contains up to 256 worksheets.

Suppose that your organization has three divisions, each with their own income statements. You create three spreadsheets (called B, C, and D), one for each division. To sum the quarterly and total income amounts, you create a fourth spreadsheet, A. In this spreadsheet, you place formulas that use three-dimensional range statements. One statement may look like the following:

@SUM(B:B5..D:B5)

This statement says, "Sum the amounts shown in cell B5 of spreadsheets B, C, and D, and place the total here."

throughput   A computer's overall performance as measured by its capability to send data through all components of the system, including secondary storage devices, such as disk drives.

Throughput is a much more meaningful indication of system performance than some of the benchmark times commonly reported in computer advertising, which involve the execution of computation-intensive algorithms.

A computer equipped with an Intel 80386 microprocessor and running at 25 MHz, for example, has glowing benchmark speed but may have less-than-spectacular throughput if equipped with slow random-access memory (RAM) chips, lacking cache memory (or some other memory speed-up scheme), and using a slow hard disk.

→ **Tip:** Before you make a purchasing decision based on benchmarks, find out whether the benchmark includes a full range of computer tasks. *PC Magazine,* for example, tests CPU instruction mix, floating-point calculation, conventional memory, DOS file access (small and large records), and BIOS disk seek.

TIFF   See *Tagged Image File Format (TIFF).*

timed backup   A desirable application program feature that saves your work at a specified interval, such as every five minutes.

Power outages occur during storms, during periods of heavy demand, and when essential maintenance must be performed on a local circuit. If you don't have an uninterruptable power supply (UPS) or you haven't saved your work to disk, your work is gone forever. Your keyboard also can freeze if you are using a terminate-and-stay-resident (TSR) program that doesn't get along with the current application package.

Because power outages and system crashes can destroy many hours of work, good computer practice calls for saving your work at frequent intervals, but software can perform saves for you. The best word processing programs, such as Microsoft Word 5.0 (IBM

PC-compatible version) and WordPerfect, include timed backup features that enable you to specify the interval.

time division multiplexing   In local area networks, a technique for transmitting two or more signals over the same cable by interleaving them, one after the other. Time division multiplexing is used in baseband (digital) networks. See *baseband, frequency division multiplexing, local area network (LAN),* and *multiplexing.*

time-sharing   A technique for sharing a multiuser computer's resources in which each user has the illusion that he or she is the only person using the system.

In the largest mainframe systems, hundreds or even thousands of people can use the system simultaneously without realizing that others are doing so. At times of peak usage, however, system response time tends to decline noticeably.

toggle   To change a program mode by pressing a toggle key. See *toggle key.*

toggle key   A key that switches back and forth between two modes. See *Caps Lock key, Num Lock key,* and *Scroll Lock key.*

token passing   In local area networks, a network protocol in which a special bit configuration, called a token, is circulated among the workstations. A node gains access to the network only if the node can obtain a free token. The node that obtains the token retains control of the network until the message has been received and acknowledged.

The token can have two values: free or busy. Any workstation wanting to transmit captures a free token, changes the value to busy, and attaches to the token the address of the destination node and the data to be transmitted. Every workstation constantly monitors the network to catch a token addressed to that workstation.

When a workstation receives a token, it attaches an acknowledgment message to the token. When the token comes back to the source node, the token's value is set back to free.

Because token passing rules out the data collisions that occur when two devices begin transmitting at the same time, this channel access method is preferred for large networks that experience high volume. See *carrier sense multiple access with collision detect (CSMA/CD), contention, local area network (LAN),* and *polling.*

token-ring network In local area networks, a network architecture that combines token passing with a hybrid star/ring topology.

Developed by IBM and announced in 1986, the IBM Token-Ring Network uses a Multistation Access Unit at its hub. This unit is wired with twisted-pair cable in a star configuration with up to 255 workstations, but the resulting network is actually a decentralized, ring network. See *local area network (LAN),* and *token passing.*

toner The electrically charged ink used in laser printers.

toner cartridge In laser printers, a cartridge containing the electrically charged ink that the printer fuses to the page.

→ **Tip:** You can save up to 50 percent of the retail cost of new toner cartridges by using recharged toner cartridges.

toolbox A set of programs that helps programmers develop software without having to create individual routines from scratch.

topology See *network topology.*

TOPS A file-serving program for local area networks that enables IBM PC compatibles and Macintosh computers to be linked in one distributed processing system. TOPS is designed to work with AppleTalk and EtherNet networks.

File-serving software provides peer-to-peer file transfer in which each user has access to the public files located on the workstations of all other users in the network. (Each user determines which files, if any, are to be made public for network access.)

When a TOPS user decides to make a file public, he or she publishes the file on the network. Every node on the network, therefore, is potentially a file server.

A significant advantage of TOPS is that, when the user of an IBM PC-compatible computer accesses a file on a Macintosh, TOPS displays the file as if it were in a directory on a DOS disk. When the user of a Macintosh computer accesses a file on an IBM PC-compatible machine, the file appears as it normally would on the Finder's desktop display: as an on-screen icon.

Users of IBM PC-compatible computers, therefore, need not learn Macintosh skills, and Macintosh users need not learn IBM PC-compatible skills. See *file server*.

touch screen   See *touch-sensitive display*.

touch-sensitive display   A display technology designed with a pressure-sensitive panel mounted in front of the screen. The user can select options by pressing the screen at the appropriate place. Synonymous with *touch screen*.

track   In a floppy disk or hard disk, one of several concentric rings, encoded on the disk during the low-level format, that defines a distinct area of data storage on the disk. See *cluster* and *sector*.

trackball   An input device, designed to replace the mouse, that moves the mouse pointer on-screen as the user rotates a ball embedded in the keyboard or in a case adjacent to the keyboard.

tractor feed   A printer paper-feed mechanism in which continuous (fan-fold) paper is pulled (or pushed) into and through the printer using a sprocket wheel. The sprockets fit into prepunched holes on the left and right edges of the paper.

A disadvantage of tractor-feed mechanisms is that when printing is complete, you must tear off the sides of the paper and separate the sheets. For a long document, this job can become tedious, and

you can easily tear a page by accident. Dot-matrix printers normally
come with tractor-feed mechanisms.

traffic The volume of messages sent over a communications network.

transactional application In a local area network, a program that
creates and maintains one shared database that contains a master
record of all the transactions in which network participants engage,
such as filling out invoices or time-billing forms. See *nontransactional application*.

transfer rate The number of bits of data transferred per second between a disk and the computer after the drive head reaches the place
where the data is located.

The maximum transfer rate is controlled by input/output standards such as ESDI or SCSI. See *access time*.

transient See *power surge*.

transient command See *external command*.

translate To convert a program from one programming language or
operating system to another, or to convert a data file from one file
format to another. See *file format*.

transparent In computing, a hidden computer operation or entity
that is made invisible so that the user does not have to cope with it.
See *virtual*.

transpose To change the order in which characters, words, or sentences are displayed on-screen. Some word processing programs include commands that transpose text. These commands are useful
when characters, words, or sentences are in the wrong order.

trapping See *error trapping*.

tree structure A way of organizing information into a hierarchical structure with a root and branches. See *directory* and *subdirectory.*

troubleshooting The process of determining why a computer system or specific hardware device is malfunctioning.

→ **Tip:** When a computer fails, most people panic and assume that a huge bill is on the way. Most likely, however, the problem is a minor one, such as a loose connection. Turn off the power and carefully inspect all the cables and connections. Remove the computer's lid and press down on the adapter boards to make sure that they are well seated in the expansion slots. You also should check connections at peripheral devices.

True BASIC A modern, structured version of the BASIC programming language developed by its originators (John Kemeny and Thomas Kurtz) in response to criticism of earlier versions of BASIC.

With modern control structures and optional line numbers, True BASIC is a well-structured language used to teach the principles of structured programming. The language, which is interpreted rather than compiled, is not frequently used for professional programming purposes.

truncate To cut off part of a number or character string.

truncation error A rounding error that occurs when part of a number is omitted from storage because it exceeds the capacity of the memory set aside for number storage. See *floating-point calculation.*

TSR See *terminate-and-stay-resident program (TSR).*

TTY See *terminal emulation.*

turnkey system   A computer system developed for a specific application, such as a point-of-sale terminal, and delivered ready-to-run, with all necessary application programs and peripherals.

tutorial   A form of instruction in which the student is guided step-by-step through the application of a program to a specific task, such as developing a budget or writing a business letter. Some application programs come with on-screen tutorials that use computer-based training techniques.

twisted-pair cable   In local area networks, a low band width connecting cable used in telephone systems. The cable includes two insulated wires wrapped around each other to minimize interference from other wires.

typeface   The distinctive design of a set of type, distinguished from its weight (such as bold or italic) and size.

Today's typefaces stem from the columns of ancient Rome, the workshops of Gutenberg and Garamond, and the ultra-modern design philosophy of the Bauhaus school in twentieth-century Germany. Thanks to desktop publishing, personal computer users can lay claim to and use this heritage as another element in an overall communication strategy.

Many laser printers come with as many as a dozen or more typefaces available in the printer's ROM, and literally hundreds more can be downloaded. With this enhanced communicative power, however, comes the responsibility to use typefaces with good taste.

One of the best ways to get help in the selection of typefaces is to look at books, magazines, and brochures from a new viewpoint—the viewpoint of the publication designer. Notice which fonts are used for body type and display type, the message being conveyed by the typeface, the appropriateness of the type for the publication's message, the use of white space as a design element, and the overall color of each page. Books in which the design team takes pride often include a colophon, a brief note (often on the last page) that indi-

cates the typefaces chosen and the names of the principal designers.

Typefaces are grouped into two categories, serif and sans serif.
Serif typefaces frequently are chosen for body type because they are
more legible. Sans serif typefaces are preferred for display type.
This rule, however, often is broken by designers striving for unity
of design who prefer to use the same typeface (or closely related
typefaces) for display and body type.

typeover mode   See *Overtype mode*.

typeover   See *Overtype mode*.

typesetter   See *imagesetter*.

typesetting   The production of camera-ready copy on a high-end
typesetting machine such as a Linotronic or Varityper.

The current crop of office-quality PostScript laser printers can
produce 300 dots-per-inch (dpi) output, which is considered crude
by professional typesetting standards, but which may be acceptable
for many applications such as newsletters, textbooks, instructional
manuals, brochures, and proposals. See *resolution*.

type size   The size of a font, measured in points (approximately $\frac{1}{72}$
inch) from the top of the tallest ascender to the bottom of the lowest
descender. See *pitch*.

type style   The weight (such as bold) or posture (such as italic) of a
font—distinguished from a font's typeface design and type size. See
attribute and *emphasis*.

typography   The science and art of designing aesthetically pleasing
and readable typefaces.

u

undelete utility   A utility program that can restore a file accidentally erased from disk if no other data has been written to the disk since the erasure occurred.

  Available from commercial and shareware sources, undelete utilities work because disk drives do not actually erase the file; they delete the file's name from the file allocation table (FAT).

  The clusters used for the file, however, become available to the operating system for additional write operations, and if such operations occur, the file can be erased irretrievably.

  ▲ **Caution:** If you have just deleted a file by error, STOP! Perform no additional work with your computer that may result in write operations. Use the undelete utility immediately; if you don't have one, stop working and go buy one.

undo   A program command that restores the program and your data to the stage they were in just before the last command was given or the last action was initiated. Undo commands enable the user to cancel the often catastrophic effects of giving the wrong command.

unformat utility   A utility program can restore the data on a disk that has been inadvertently formatted. If the disk has been formatted using a safe format technique, the data is restored quickly. If the disk has been not been safe formatted, you still can recover the data if you have been using the MIRROR utility provided with DOS 5.0 or certain utility programs, such as PC Tools. See *safe format*.

unformatted text file   See *plain text document*.

uninterruptible power supply (UPS)   A battery capable of supplying continuous power to a computer system in the event of a power failure.

The battery, charged by line current, kicks in if the power fails and provides power for up to 10 minutes or more, during which time the computer can be shut down so that the integrity of crucial data is preserved.

Universal Asynchronous Receiver/Transmitter (UART) An integrated circuit that transforms the parallel data stream within the computer to the serial, one-after-the-other data stream used in asynchronous communications.

In early IBM Personal Computers, the UART was contained on the Asynchronous Communications Adapter, but the UART now is found on the motherboard in most designs. Serial communication requires, in addition to the UART, a serial port and modem. See *asynchronous communications, modem, motherboard,* and *serial port.*

UNIX Pronounced "yoo'-nicks." An operating system for a wide variety of computers, from mainframes to personal computers, that supports multitasking and is ideally suited to multiuser applications.

Written in the highly portable programming language C, UNIX is (like C) the product of work at AT&T Bell Laboratories during the early 1970s. Originally developed by highly advanced research scientists for sophisticated work in computer science, UNIX is a comprehensive programming environment that expresses a unique programming philosophy.

Creating software tools, each of which performs one (and only one) function, and making these tools part of the operating system is better than writing very large programs, each of which performs all functions. Application programs need not rely on their own features to accomplish functions, but can take advantage of the software tools in the programming environment. This philosophy helps programmers keep application programs in manageable bounds.

As appealing as this philosophy may be to programmers, it exacts a heavy toll on end users. The communication of data from one software tool to another is accomplished via a pipe, a user command that couples the output of one command to the input of another. Pipes are highly flexible and enable you to control virtually every aspect of the operating environment; you can extend the command set to create commands for situations not anticipated in the operating system's development.

With more than 200 commands, inadequate error messages, and a cryptic command syntax, however, UNIX imposes heavy burdens on people who do not use the system frequently and have little or no interest in gaining precise control over every conceivable operating system feature. The acceptance of UNIX as a system for end-user computing, therefore, has been prevented and remains restricted to technical and academic environments.

No reason exists why a UNIX operating system cannot be equipped with a shell that makes the system easy to use, and with the development of UNIX shells, the operating system may play a much wider role in computing.

NeXTStep, a shell for the NeXT workstation, is as easy to use and versatile as the Macintosh Finder. NeXTStep aids programmers because it includes an application program interface (API) that handles virtually all screen routines, freeing programmers from the tedious programming required to generate screen images from within an application program. IBM is expected to offer NeXTStep on its own UNIX workstations. NeXTStep is by no means tied to the NeXT workstation and can be made available for 80386 and 80486 computers.

When the user is insulated from the peculiarities of using UNIX at the system level, the operating system's other advantages quickly become apparent. Unlike most personal computer operating systems, UNIX was designed as a multiuser system. With its multitasking capabilities, UNIX can perform more than one function at a time.

In the past, these features have been in little demand by personal computer users, who use stand-alone machines to run one application at a time. UNIX, therefore, is seldom used on personal computers. If the future of personal computing lies in linking work-stations to corporate minicomputers and mainframes, however, UNIX operating systems—particularly when equipped with a shell such as NeXTStep—stand a chance of displacing DOS and even OS/2.

Because Bell Laboratories was prohibited from marketing UNIX by the antitrust regulations then governing AT&T, UNIX—the first version to gain significant distribution—was provided without charge to colleges and universities throughout North America, beginning in 1976.

In 1979, the University of California at Berkeley developed an enhanced and technically sophisticated version of UNIX for VAX computers. Much preferred in technical and engineering environments, Berkeley UNIX led to other versions made available commercially. In the early 1980s, AT&T gained the right to market the system and released System V in 1983.

As a result of these independent lines of UNIX development, many alternative and mutually incompatible versions of the system are in use. However, a standard UNIX version clearly is emerging. Although many thought that Berkeley UNIX would establish a standard, AT&T's System V caught up technically with Berkeley UNIX.

With the release of System V, AT&T established a set of UNIX standards called System V Interface Definition (SVID). SVID established a standard toward which most UNIX systems are migrating, especially now that major corporate purchasers are requiring this standard. IBM adopted the SVID standard for its own versions of UNIX. See *shell* and *System V Interface Definition (SVID)*.

update In database management, a fundamental data manipulation that involves adding, modifying, or deleting data records so that data is brought up to date.

upgrade To purchase a new release or version of a program, or a more recent or more powerful version of a computer or peripheral.

upload To transmit a file by telecommunications to another computer user or a bulletin board.

upper memory area In an IBM-compatible computer running DOS, the memory between the 640K limit of conventional memory and 1 megabyte. In the original PC system design, some of the memory in this area was reserved for system uses, but much is available. Memory management programs, as well as DOS 5.0, can configure the upper memory area so that it is available for system utilities and application programs. HIMEM.SYS comes with Microsoft Windows. See *conventional memory, HIMEM.SYS,* and *Microsoft Windows*.

UPS See *uninterruptible power supply (UPS)*.

upward compatibility Software that functions without modification on later or more powerful versions of a computer system.

USENET The news distribution and bulletin board channel of UUCP, an international wide-area network that links UNIX computers. See *UUCP*.

user See *end user*.

user default A user-defined program operating preference, such as the default margins to be used in every new document that a word processing program creates.

user-defined Selected or chosen by the user of the computer system.

user-friendly A program or computer system designed so that persons who lack extensive computer experience or training can use the system without becoming confused or frustrated.

A user-friendly program usually includes the following elements: menus are used instead of forcing the user to memorize commands; on-screen help is available at the touch of a key; program functions are mapped to the keyboard in a logical order and do not contradict established conventions; error messages contain an explanation of what went wrong and what to do to solve the problem; intermediate and advanced features are hidden from view so that they do not clutter the screen and confuse those who are learning the program; commands that could erase or destroy data display confirmation messages that warn the user of the command's drastic consequences and provide a way to escape without initiating the operation; and clear, concise documentation includes tutorials and reference information.

user group   A voluntary association of users of a specific computer or program who meet regularly to exchange tips and techniques, hear presentations by computer experts, and obtain public domain software and shareware.

user interface   All the features of a program or computer that govern the way people interact with the computer. See *command-driven program* and *graphical user interface (GUI)*.

utility program   A program that assists you in maintaining and improving the efficiency of a computer system.

In the best of all possible worlds, all the utility programs one needs would be provided with the operating system, but this scenario is rarely the case.

DOS, for example, provides many external commands, including utilities, such as backup programs, but many DOS users purchase additional utilities such as file compression utilities, defragmentation utilities, shells, undelete utilities, and vaccines, which DOS doesn't provide. Because DOS can be difficult to use, many users purchase utilities more user-friendly than existing DOS utilities, such as BACKUP and RESTORE.

UUCP   An international, cooperative wide-area network that links thousands of UNIX computers in the United States, Europe, and

Asia. UUCP has electronic mail gateways to BITNET. See
USENET.

V

vaccine   A computer program designed to detect the presence of a
computer virus in a system.

The vaccine detects the virus by checking for unusual attempts
to access vital disk areas and system files and by searching for specific viruses known to afflict many computer systems.

▲ **Caution:** The malevolent authors of computer viruses are
aware of vaccines and are busy creating new viruses to thwart them.
If your computer is to be used for vital business or professional applications, protect your data by using only fresh, previously un-
opened copies of software obtained directly from computer
software publishers. Synonymous with *antivirus program.*

value   In a spreadsheet program, a numeric cell entry.

Two kinds of values exist. The first kind, called constants, are
values you type directly into a cell. The second kind of value is produced by a formula placed into a cell.

▲ **Caution:** On-screen, the values you enter directly (constants)
and the values produced by formulas look alike. You easily can destroy a spreadsheet, therefore, by typing a constant on top of a formula. You see no apparent difference in the spreadsheet, probably,
but recalculation produces errors because you have removed a formula. Before changing a value you see on-screen, be sure to check
the entry line in the control panel to find out whether a formula is
in the cell. See *cell protection* and *label.*

variable   In computer programming, a named area in memory that stores a value or string assigned to that variable.

VDT   Acronym for video display terminal. Synonymous with *monitor.*

VDT radiation   The electromagnetic radiation emitted by a video display terminal.

Debate continues in the scientific community about whether VDTs are safe. Computer monitors produce X-rays, ultraviolet radiation, and electromagnetic fields. Studies show conflicting results. Most laboratory studies of these emissions show that they cannot be distinguished from the background radiation present in an average work environment.

Other studies, however, have demonstrated a correlation between VDT use and health problems, particularly miscarriage among pregnant users. Job-related stress, however, may be responsible for these problems. Labor unions continue to charge that the scientific research on VDT radiation is flawed and biased because the research has been conducted by the computer industry or on behalf of the computer industry.

Debate recently has come to focus on extremely low frequency electromagnetic radiation fields, created by strong electrical currents in power lines and electrical equipment. Correlations between the very strong fields emitted by high-voltage electrical power distribution lines and increased risk of cancer have been demonstrated by a number of studies, although other studies show no increased risk.

Some studies indicate that more risk may be involved for much more modest fields, such as those emitted by electric blankets and water bed heaters. A careful study conducted by *PC Magazine,* December 12, 1989, demonstrated that although computers and monitors emit such radiation, the level was below background radiation levels at a distance of 18 inches from the computer and display.

→ **Tip:** The evidence so far compiled does not suggest that prolonged use of computers and CRT displays is dangerous. To be on the safe side, however, keep your face and body at least 18 inches from the computer and display. If your computer displays varying font sizes, work with a large font such as 14 points while writing and reformat to a smaller font for printing purposes. To avoid repetitive strain injury (RSI), take frequent breaks. See *cathode ray tube (CRT)* and *repetitive strain injury (RSI)*.

VDU Acronym for video display unit. Synonymous with *monitor*.

vector font See *outline font*.

vector graphics A graphics display technology in which images are formed on-screen by directly controlling the motions of the electron gun to form a specific image, such as a line or a circle, rather than requiring the gun to travel across the whole screen line-by-line (as in raster displays). Vector graphics are not used for personal computer displays but are occasionally used for professional workstations in such fields as architectural or engineering design.

vector-to-raster conversion A utility available with many professional illustration programs (such as Corel Draw) that transforms object-oriented (vector) graphics into bit-mapped (raster) graphic images. See *bit-mapped graphic,* and *object-oriented graphic*.

Vectra A line of IBM PC-compatible computers developed and marketed by Hewlett-Packard, Inc., and featuring a windowing environment.

vendor A seller or supplier of computers, peripherals, or computer-related services.

Ventura Publisher A page layout program for IBM PC-compatible computers considered excellent for long documents.

version   A specific release of a software or hardware product.

A large version number indicates a later product release. For example, DOS 4.0 is a more recent product than DOS 3.3. In many cases, as in the DOS example, numbers (3.4–3.9) are skipped. Other products, such as FileMaker, have different versions, not necessarily in sequential order (FileMaker Plus, FileMaker 4, and FileMaker II).

Users are often wary of Version 1.0 products because such releases may lack extensive hands-on testing. Bug fixes often have even smaller intermediate numbers such as Version 1.02 or Version 1.2a.

vertical application   An application program created for a narrowly defined market, such as the members of a profession or a specific type of retail store.

vertical centering   The automatic centering of graphics or text vertically on the page. WordPerfect, for example, includes a Center Top to Bottom command that centers text vertically.

vertical justification   The alignment of newspaper columns by means of feathering (adding vertical space) so that all columns end evenly at the bottom margin.

A page layout program capable of vertical justification inserts white space between frame borders and text, between paragraphs, and between lines so that all columns end evenly on the bottom margin.

Vertical justification is by no means necessary. Vertical justification is common, but not universal, in newspapers and magazines, but many newsletter designers prefer to leave the bottom margin ragged.

very large scale integration (VLSI)   The fabrication on one semiconductor chip of more than 100,000 transistors.

VGA   See *Video Graphics Array (VGA)*.

video adapter   The adapter that generates the output required to display computer text (and, with some adapters, graphics) on a monitor. See *Color Graphics Adapter (CGA), Enhanced Graphics Adapter (EGA), Hercules Graphics Adapter, IBM 8514/A display adapter, monochrome display adapter (MDA), MultiColor Graphics Array (MCGA),* and *Video Graphics Array (VGA)*.

Video Graphics Array (VGA)   A color bit-mapped graphics display standard, introduced by IBM in 1987 with its PS/2 computers. VGA adapters and analog monitors display as many as 256 continuously variable colors simultaneously with a resolution of 640 pixels horizontally by 480 vertically.

Built into the motherboard of some PS/2 computers, VGA circuitry is downwardly compatible with all previous IBM display standards, including CGA, MDA, and EGA. VGA is superior to the EGA standard not only because of the apparently modest increase in resolution (the increase is perceptually much more significant than the numbers indicate): unlike EGA adapters, VGA technology preserves the aspect ratio of on-screen graphics images.

VGA's analog input technology also produces an unlimited number of continuously variable colors; the EGA is a digital monitor technology locked into a fixed number of color intensity levels.

The IBM VGA standard has been pushed to new heights by third-party vendors, who offer VGA adapters that can display two additional graphics modes—an enhanced resolution of 800 by 600 pixels and super VGA with a resolution of 1024 by 768 pixels—with up to 256 colors displayed simultaneously. Many of these adapters, however, are designed to work only with the 16-bit AT expansion bus of 80286 and 80386 computers and cannot be used in 8088- or 8086-based systems. See *analog monitor, aspect ratio, bit-mapped graphic, Color Graphics Adapter (CGA), digital monitor, Enhanced Graphics Adapter (EGA),* and *monochrome display adapter (MGA)*.

video monitor   See *monitor*.

video RAM   The random-access memory (RAM) needed by a video
adapter to construct and retain a full-screen image of a high-
resolution video display. As much as 512K of video RAM may be
needed by VGA video adapters.

videodisk   An optical disk used for the storage and retrieval of still
pictures or television pictures and sound. A videodisk player is required to play back the videodisk on a standard television monitor.
   Coupled with a computer that can control the videodisk player,
an application called interactive video becomes possible; the program enables the user to gain controlled access to the information
stored on the videodisk for instructional, presentation, or training
purposes. A standard videodisk can hold approximately 50,000 still
frames or up to two hours of television pictures.

videotext   The transmission of information, such as news headlines,
stock quotes, and current movie reviews, through a cable television
system. See *on-line information service*.

view   In database management programs, an on-screen display of
only part of the information in a database—the part that meets the
criteria specified in a query.
   Most programs enable you to save a view that can be useful for
certain purposes. Suppose that you have created a database of all
the videotapes available in your video store. The printout of all the
titles is long and expensive to duplicate. Rather than listing all the
tapes in every category, you decide to make seven different printouts, sorted by category. The SQL command that produces a view
of children's videotapes is as follows:

```
SELECT title, rating
FROM inventory
WHERE category = "children"
ORDER BY title
```

Most database management programs enable you to save views, and the best ones update each view every time you add or edit records.

virtual In computing, the on-screen representation of a computer entity or object (such as a disk drive) that does not exist. See *transparent*.

virtual device The on-screen simulation of a computer device or peripheral, such as a hard disk drive or port, that does not exist.

In a local area network, a two-drive computer might appear to have an enormous hard disk, which actually is made available to the workstation by means of the network links to the file server. See *file server, local area network (LAN),* and *workstation*.

virtual machine An on-screen simulation of a separate computer, as if the computer really existed and could run programs independently.

This simulation is made possible by a computer with the necessary processing circuitry and a large random-access memory (RAM). The Intel 80386 microprocessor, for example, can run two or more virtual DOS machines, each of which can run DOS programs concurrently in their own 640K memory space.

virtual memory A method of extending the apparent size of a computer's random-access memory (RAM) by using part of the hard disk as an extension of RAM.

Virtual memory has been around in personal computing for a long time; many application programs, such as Microsoft Word, routinely use the disk instead of memory to store data or program instructions. A true virtual memory system, however, is implemented at the operating system level, so that the memory is available to any and all programs. Under virtual memory, even a program such as WordPerfect, which insists that the entire document be placed in RAM, can work with documents of unlimited length (or length limited by the capacity of a hard disk rather than the capacity of RAM).

→ **Tip:** Virtual memory techniques currently are being implemented for most personal computers, but RAM is significantly faster than a hard disk. Virtual memory may result in delays of up to half a minute or more while the microprocessor waits to retrieve needed information from disk. With RAM chip prices at a reasonable level, equip a computer with additional RAM rather than relying on virtual memory techniques.

virtual memory management   The management of virtual memory operations at the operating system level rather than the application level.

Many personal computer programs use virtual memory. When there isn't enough memory to store all the program instructions and data, the program automatically creates a swap file (a temporary file) and stores the data or instructions on disk. However, a significant advantage to implementing virtual memory at the operating system level rather than the application level is that any program can take advantage of the virtual memory, with the result that memory extends seamlessly from RAM to the computer's secondary storage. To take advantage of virtual memory at the operating system level, however, the computer must be equipped with a microprocessor capable of extending memory addresses into secondary memory in this way. The Intel 8088, 8086, and 80286 microprocessors lack this capability; the 80386 and 80486 microprocessors are designed to enable it. Microsoft Windows, running it its 386 enhanced mode, can take full advantage of the virtual memory capabilities of these microprocessors. In the Macintosh world, Apple's System 7 makes virtual memory management available for users of 68030-based Macintoshes. See *386 enhanced mode, Intel 80386, Intel 80486, Microsoft Windows* and *swap file*.

virtual table   See *view*.

virus A computer program, designed as a prank or as sabotage, that replicates itself by attaching to other programs and carrying out unwanted and sometimes damaging operations.

When embedded in its host, the virus replicates itself by attaching to other programs in the system, including system software. Like a human virus, the effects of a computer virus may not be detectable for a period of days or weeks, during which time every disk inserted into the system comes away with a hidden copy of the virus.

Eventually, the effects manifest themselves. The consequences range from prank messages to erratic system software performance or catastrophic erasure of all the information on a hard disk.

→ Tip: To protect your system from computer viruses, observe the following rules:

- Do not download executable programs from public bulletin boards unless you are certain they are virus-free (you actually have seen someone else use the program without problems).

- Do not obtain executable programs from mail-order vendors of public domain or shareware programs unless they specifically promise to check each program they sell.

- Never download a recently uploaded program on a bulletin board until the SYSOP has checked it. When you do download the program, download it to a dual-floppy system so that the program cannot get near your hard disk.

- Don't copy pirated disks of commercial programs, because these disks may contain viruses.

- Purchase and use a vaccine.

See *vaccine*.

VLSI See *very large scale integration (VLSI)*.

voice mail In office automation, a communications system in which voice messages are transformed into digital form and stored on a computer network. When the person to whom the message is directed logs on to the system and discovers that a message is waiting, the system plays the message. Synonymous with *voice store and forward*.

voice recognition Computer recognition of human speech and the transformation of the recognized words into computer-readable, digitized text.

Computers share with people an unfortunate characteristic: they talk much better than they listen. In the most advanced research systems, computers can recognize only about one or two hundred words, and even this capability is achieved only after the speaker has trained the system to recognize his or her specific voice pattern.

Voice recognition involves some extremely complex pattern-recognition capabilities in the human brain that are not well understood. See *voice synthesis*.

voice store and forward See *voice mail*.

voice synthesis The audible output of computer-based text in the form of synthesized speech that people can recognize and understand.

Voice synthesis is much easier to achieve than voice recognition; virtually any personal computer can be equipped to read ASCII text with a minimum of errors. This capability has helped many blind people gain increased access to written works not recorded on cassette tape. However, voice synthesis is seldom used in computer user interfaces. See *voice recognition*.

volatility The susceptibility of a computer's random-access memory (RAM) to the complete loss of stored information if power is interrupted suddenly.

volume label In DOS and OS/2, the unique, identifying name assigned to a disk and displayed on the first line of a directory. The name must be no more than 11 characters. You assign the volume label when you format the disk.

→ **Tip:** To change or delete a volume label or to add one if you didn't do so when you formatted the disk, use the LABEL command.

W

wait state A null processing cycle in which nothing occurs. A wait state is programmed into a computer system to allow other components, such as random-access memory (RAM), to catch up with the central processing unit (CPU).

A microprocessor with a fast clock speed, such as 25 MHz, can outrace the main memory, particularly if the memory is composed of dynamic random-access memory (DRAM) chips. Wait states, therefore, are programmed into the machine to rule out the serious errors that can occur if DRAM does not respond to the microprocessor fast enough.

Wait states can be eliminated (resulting in a zero wait state machine) by using fast (but expensive) cache memory, interleaved memory, page-mode RAM, or static RAM chips. See *cache memory, central processing unit (CPU), interleaved memory,* and *random-access memory (RAM).*

warm boot A system restart performed after the system has been powered and operating; a restart is the electronic equivalent of turning on the system because it clears the memory and reloads the operating system.

A warm boot is preferable to a cold start after a system crash because it places less strain on your system's electrical and electronic components. With IBM PC-compatible computers, you restart the system by pressing Ctrl-Alt-Del, although sometimes this command will not unlock the system. You also can perform a warm boot by pressing the reset button (IBM computers or compatibles) or the programmer's switch (Macintosh computers).

Some IBM PC-compatible computers have buttons or switches that make a hardware restart possible; Macintosh users must install the programmer's switch before this maneuver is possible. See *cold boot*.

warm link   See *hot link*.

weight   The overall lightness or darkness of a typeface design, or the gradations of lightness to darkness within a font family.

A type style can be light or dark, and within a type style, you can see several gradations of weight (extra light, light, semilight, regular, medium, semibold, bold, extrabold, and ultrabold). See *typeface*.

Weitek coprocessor   A numeric coprocessor, created for computers that use the Intel 80286 and Intel 80386. This coprocessor offers significantly faster performance than the Intel 80287 and Intel 80387 and is widely used for professional computer-aided design (CAD) applications.

Unlike the Intel 80287 and 80387, however, programs cannot use the Weitek coprocessor unless they are modified to do so. See *computer-aided design (CAD)* and *numeric coprocessor*.

what-if analysis   In spreadsheet programs, an important form of data exploration in which key variables are changed to see the effect on the results of the computation.

What-if analysis provides businessmen and professionals with an effective vehicle for exploring the effect of alternative strategies, such as "What will my profits look like if I were to invest another $10,000 in advertising, assuming past trends hold true?"

what-you-see-is-what-you-get (WYSIWYG) Pronounced "wizzy wig." A design philosophy for word processing programs in which formatting commands directly affect the text displayed on-screen, so that the screen shows the appearance of the printed text. See *embedded formatting command*.

white space The portion of the page not printed. A good page design involves the use of white space to balance the areas that receive text and graphics.

wide-area network A computer network that uses high-speed, long-distance communications networks or satellites to connect computers over distances greater than the distances (one or two miles) traversed by local area networks.

widow A formatting flaw in which the last line of a paragraph appears alone at the top of a new column or page.

Most word processing and page layout programs suppress widows and orphans; better programs enable you to switch widow/orphan control on and off and to choose the number of lines. See *orphan*.

wild card Characters, such as asterisks and question marks, that stand for any other character that may appear in the same place.

In DOS, you have two wild cards: the asterisk (*), which stands for any character (and any number of characters), and the question mark (?), which stands for any one character.

Wild card	*Stands for*
REPORT1.*	REPORT1.DOC
	REPORT1.BAK
REPORT?.DOC	REPORT1.DOC
	REPORT2.DOC
	REPORT3.DOC

Winchester drive   See *hard disk*.

window   A rectangular, on-screen frame through which you can view a document, worksheet, database, or other application.

   In most programs, only one window is displayed. This window functions as a frame through which you can see your document, database, or worksheet. Some programs can display two or more parts of the same file, or even two or more different files, each in its own window.

   A windowing environment carries multiple windowing even further by enabling you to run two or more applications concurrently, each in its own window.

windowing environment   An applications program interface (API) that provides the features commonly associated with a graphical user interface (such as windows, pull-down menus, on-screen fonts, and scroll bars or scroll boxes), and makes these features available to programmers of application packages. See *application program interface (API)*, *DESQview*, *graphical user interface (GUI)*, and *Microsoft Windows*.

Windows   See *Microsoft Windows*.

Windows application   An application specifically designed to run in the Microsoft Windows windowing environment, taking full advantage of Window's application program interface (API), its ability to display fonts and graphics on-screen, and its ability to exchange data dynamically between applications. See *non-Windows application*.

Windows Metafile file format (WMF)   An object-oriented (vector) graphics file format for Microsoft Windows application. Graphics files with the .WMF format can be read by all Windows applications that support object-oriented graphics.

word   One unit of memory storage, measured in bits.

   The basic unit of memory storage for personal computers is the byte (8 bits). Longer words, however, may be used for number-crunching. See *floating-point calculation* and *numeric coprocessor*.

word processing program   An application program specifically designed to make the creation, editing, formatting, and printing of text easier.

The boundaries between page-layout programs (such as Page-Maker and Ventura Publisher) and word processing programs are narrowing as full-featured word processing programs, such as Microsoft Word and WordPerfect, increasingly include page layout features, such as the capability to position a text or graphic on the page so that text flows around it.

Word processing programs provide the tools a writer needs to create and edit the text (such as outlining, spelling checkers, replace commands, and fast-scrolling text displays); page-layout programs concentrate on providing all the features needed to handle page layout at a professional level.

word wrap   A feature or word processing programs (and other programs that include text-editing features) that wraps words down to the beginning of the next line if they go beyond the right margin.

workgroup   A small group of employees assigned to work together on a specific project.

Much of the work accomplished in contemporary corporations is done in workgroups, and if this work is to be done well and in a timely fashion, the workgroup needs to communicate effectively and share resources. Personal computer technology, especially when linked in a local area network (LAN), is thought to enhance workgroup productivity by giving the group additional communication channels (in the form of electronic mail), facilities for the group editing of technical documentation (see *redlining* and *strikeout*), and shared access to a common database.

worksheet In spreadsheet programs, the two-dimensional matrix of rows and columns within which you enter headings, numbers, and formulas. The worksheet resembles the ledger sheet used in accounting. Synonymous with *spreadsheet*.

worksheet window In spreadsheet programs, the portion of the worksheet visible on-screen.

With up to 8,192 rows and 256 columns, modern electronic spreadsheets are larger than a two-car garage in size. The worksheet window displays only a small portion of the total area potentially available.

workstation In a local area network, a desktop computer that runs application programs and serves as an access point to shared network resources. See *personal computer, professional workstation,* and *file server*.

WORM See *write-once, read many (WORM)*.

wrap-around type Type contoured so that it surrounds a graphic.
Because wrap-around type is harder to read than noncontoured type, use wrap-around type sparingly.

write A fundamental processing operation in which the central processing unit (CPU) records information in the computer's random-access memory (RAM) or the computer's secondary storage media, such as disk drives.

In personal computing, the term most often is used in the sense of storing information on disks.

write-black engine See *print engine*.

write head See *read/write head*.

write-once, read many (WORM) An optical disk drive with storage capacities of up to 1 terabyte. This disk becomes a read-only storage medium after data is written to the disk.

WORM drives can store huge amounts of information and have been touted as an excellent technology for organizations that need to publish large databases internally (such as collections of engineering drawings or technical documentation). The advent of fully read/write capable optical disk drives, however, has greatly diminished the appeal of WORM technology. See *CD-ROM* and *erasable optical disk drive*.

write-protect A prodecure for preventing a disk or tape from being written to.

write-protect notch On a 5¼-inch floppy disk, a small notch cut out of the disk's protective jacket that, when covered by a piece of tape, prevents the disk drive from performing erasures or write operations to the disk.

With 3½-inch disks, the same function is accomplished by moving a small tab toward the top of the disk's case.

WYSIWYG See *what-you-see-is-what-you-get (WYSIWYG)*.

X

x-axis In a business graph, the x-axis is the categories axis, which usually is the horizontal axis. See *bar graph*, *column graph*, *y-axis*, and *z-axis*.

AyAyAyAyAyAyAy

*Letters with the same nominal type size
may have different x-heights*

XENIX   An operating system developed by Microsoft Corporation that conforms to the UNIX System V Interface Definition (SVID) and runs on IBM PC-compatible computers. See *System V Interface Definition (SVID)* and *UNIX*.

x-height   In typography, the height of a font's lowercase letters that do not have ascenders or descenders (such as x, a, and c).

   Because many fonts have unusually long or short ascenders and descenders, the x-height is a better measurement of the actual size of a font than the type size measured in points.

XMODEM   An asynchronous file-transfer protocol for personal computers that makes the error-free transmission of computer files through the telephone system easier.

   Developed by Ward Christiansen for 8-bit CP/M computers and placed in the public domain, the XMODEM protocol is included in all personal computer communications programs and commonly is used to download files from computer bulletin boards.

XMS   See *eXtended Memory Specification (XMS)*.

XMS memory   In a '286, '386, or '486 computer, memory that has been configured as extended memory by a memory management program. Some DOS programs can use XMS memory to break the 640K RAM barrier.

XON/XOFF handshaking   See *handshaking*.

XT   See *IBM Personal Computer XT.*

X Windows   A network windowing environment commonly used on UNIX-based workstations.

   Originally developed at MIT and distributed freely to the academic community, X Windows is a device-independent API that can run under operating systems ranging from DOS to a mainframe OS. However, it is used most frequently on UNIX machines. Unlike

Microsoft Windows and other PC-based windowing environments, X Windows is designed for use on a minicomputer-based network.

The freeware version of X Windows has been adopted and separately developed in many different research labs and computer science departments, with the unfortunate result that there are many incompatible versions of X Windows in existence. As a result, a consortium of UNIX vendors joined with MIT to establish an X Windows standard in 1987. However, application development with X Windows is a formidable undertaking. For this reason, several vendors have developed proprietary toolkits for X Windows application development, with the inevitable compabitility problems. See *UNIX and* windowing environment.

x-y graph   See *scatter diagram*.

y

y-axis   In a business graph, the y-axis is the values (vertical) axis. See *bar graph, column graph, x-axis,* and *z-axis*.

YMCK   Acronym for yellow, magenta, cyan, and black. See *color separation*.

Z

zap Synonymous with erase and delete.

Zapf Dingbats Pronounced "zaff ding-bats." A set of decorative symbols developed by Herman Zapf, a German typeface designer.

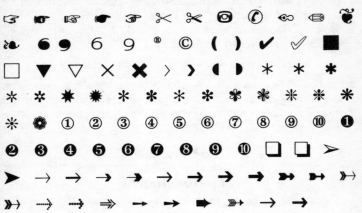

Zapf Dingbats

z-axis In a three-dimensional graphics image, the third dimension of depth. See *x-axis* and *y-axis*.

zero-slot LAN A local area network designed to use a computer's serial port instead of requiring the user to purchase a network interface card that occupies one of the computer's expansion slots. See *network interace card* and *serial port*.

   ▲ **Caution:** Zero-slot LANS are considerably slower than systems that use network interface cards which take advantage of the computer's high-speed internal bus. Therefore, they are best used for applications in which network applications are limited to occasional access to an infrequently used shared peripheral (such as a plotter) or electronic mail.

zero wait state computer   An IBM PC-compatible computer with memory optimized by using a scheme such as cache memory, interleaved memory, page-mode RAM, or static random-access memory (RAM) chips, so that the microprocessor does not have to wait for the memory to catch up with processing operations. See *cache memory, interleaved memory, page-mode RAM, static random-access memory (RAM)*, and *wait state*.

zoom   To enlarge a window so that it fills the screen.

zoom box   In a graphical user interface, a box (usually positioned on the window border) that you use to zoom the window to full size or restore the window to normal size by clicking the mouse. See *graphical user interface (GUI)*.

Add Terms to
*Que's Computer
User's Dictionary*

Que's Computer User's Dictionary defines and describes terms of interest to the typical user of personal computers. We have tried to include all terms appropriate to a general audience, but we know that we must have missed some that you think should be in this book. Please help us improve the next edition. Write down any terms you suggest we include, and send the list to

Que's Computer User's Dictionary
Que Corporation
c/o Karen Bluestein
11711 N. College Ave.
Carmel, IN 46032

Your feedback is important to us. Thanks for your help!